Networking the New Enterprise

The Proof Not the Hype

Harris Kern, Randy Johnson, Michael Hawkins, and Howie Lyke
with William Kennedy and Mark Cappel

Sun Microsystems Press
A Prentice Hall Title
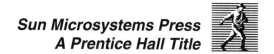

The publisher offers discounts on this book when ordered in bulk quantities. For more information, contact Corporate Sales Department, Prentice Hall PTR, One Lake Street, Upper Saddle River, NJ 07458.
Phone: 800-382-3419; FAX: 201-236-7141.
E-mail: corpsales@prenhall.com.

Editorial/production supervision: *Eileen Clark*
Cover designer: *M&K Design, Palo Alto, California*
Cover design director: *Jerry Votta*
Manufacturing manager: *Alexis R. Heydt*
Marketing manager: *Stephen Solomon*
Acquisitions editor: *Gregory G. Doench*
Sun Microsystems Press publisher: *Rachel Borden*

10 9 8 7 6 5 4 3 2

ISBN 0-13-263427-9

Sun Microsystems Press
A Prentice Hall Title

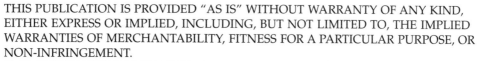

Sun Microsystems Press
A Prentice Hall Title

Contents

≡

10. Enhancing the Network   121

Dedication

This is our third book in the "New Enterprise" series. It has been a major undertaking for many people. We dedicate this book to our friends and family who stood by us during the stressful times.

Acknowledgments

Thanks to Dave Travis from Cisco Systems for his valuable comments.

Thanks to Kristle Hawkins, Michael's 10-year old daughter, for her help organizing files and diagrams.

Thanks to Richard Webster for his dedication and contribution.

A great deal of thanks to Rick Harder and John Reece for their contributions and support.

Thanks to Shannon Bushman for his vision and support.

Debt and servitude to Rich Reynolds for his knowledge, support, and patience.

Thanks to Kelly Johnson for always being there when we needed her.

Thanks to Shannon Kim for supporting our cause.

Finally, thanks to our friends in the Southwest for their help with Chapter 7.

Networking the New Enterprise

Foreword

First the mainframe, then the microprocessor (or the so-called *personal computer*), and at last, the network. Finally, we have a complete tool set with which to build truly effective user-based information technology solutions. For the first time we have at our disposal practical and affordable technology, which can be gauged to the specific needs of local business units but yet be delivered within the broader context of the information needs of the business as a whole, be it a local, national, or global in scope. Further, the increasing integration of processor and networking technologies promises even greater simplicity of use, ease of implementation, and business payoff.

To me, this phenomenal change in fundamental information technology summarizes the essence and vital importance of this new book by Harris and Randy. Its origins and the combined experience of its authors trace this evolution. Their first book together, *Rightsizing The New Enterprise*, published in 1994, was a journeyman's description of how to capitalize—on the power of client/server technology. Their book was a practical guide to realizing the power of locally focused, client/server applications. It made it possible for the reader to put client/server technology in context with legacy mainframe-based systems. It came at a time when many challenged the real value of the new technologies and afforded their readers both proof of the truth in the hype as well as a clear roadmap for implementation. In short, Harris and Randy retold their story of making this difficult, but hugely business-critical, transition at Sun Microsystems.

Earlier this year they followed with *Managing the New Enterprise*, a second book in which they, Michael Hawkins, Andrew Law, and William Kennedy reported their combined experience in managing the "after transition" results of an enterprise-wide move to client/server. Again, a clear guidebook for the IT professional on how to do it right, based on their own first-hand experience in doing it—at Sun and other organizations.

Now we have *Networking the New Enterprise*, a book focused on adding an enterprise-wide telecommunications backbone to interconnect local client/server installations to complete a migration to a full "New Enterprise" architecture. This book fulfills their vision of the technologies and management leadership necessary to enable the move by adding the integrating element, the dimension

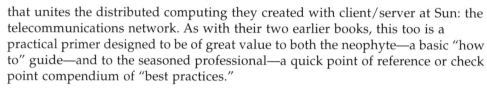

that unites the distributed computing they created with client/server at Sun: the telecommunications network. As with their two earlier books, this too is a practical primer designed to be of great value to both the neophyte—a basic "how to" guide—and to the seasoned professional—a quick point of reference or check point compendium of "best practices."

Having gone through the exercise of building a global telecommunications network myself once previously and being in the midst of beginning the process again, I only wish that I had had this book to draw on from the beginning. It would have saved me a great deal of time, money, and personal pain. It is clear from the first to last page that these guys have done it personally. From the basics of identifying the needs—determining the business case—to the details of network design, configuration and "in production" management, it's all here in clear understandable terms, with all the acronyms spelled out.

I urge you as you use this book—and once you've read it, I'm certain you will use it—to remember that it is a book of *proof*, a book whose content comes from the guys who have lived the experience and who have the gift of being able to document their experience in a way that is immensely beneficial to others. Experience I might add, that is pivotal to any enterprise wanting to remain viable and competitive in the new century. I too believe as do Harris, Randy, Michael, and Howie, that without these technologies effectively in place and functioning in harmony throughout the business organization as a whole, there will be no business. Customers and competitors alike will make the day-to-day presence of these capabilities a necessary condition for survival.

John C. Reece
Vice President, Information Technology
Time Warner, Inc.

BellSouth has long recognized communications and networking as key elements in the introduction of new information technology into our business environment, driven more perhaps by our size and scope than by our primary business function of providing communications services. As technology has driven more processing capability outside the traditional glass house, the issue becomes even more critical. This acceleration of truly distributed computing and data brings some very significant challenges, and the authors' view on the impact of those challenges on our Information Technology Organization's (ITO) structure, culture, and effectiveness are well worth reading.

Not being a career IT professional, but rather coming in and out of the organization every ten years or so, the impact of the shift of process and data ownership from the ITO to the user is probably more evident to me than to those residing in the technical forest. For example, it surprises me that many of our nontechnical clients are much more aware of the possibilities of the Internet than our experienced ITO staff. Perhaps we let our ITO staff focus so long on complex and elegant legacy problems that they cannot see a simple solution to anything. That issue alone makes this a useful read for IT professionals.

Complex problems generally demand simple approaches and that is what I find most appealing about *Networking the New Enterprise*. The authors break the complexity into fairly discrete process modules and then prescribe a fairly methodical approach to the resolution of that complexity. The search for the ultimate security blanket may continue, but there is a process for deciding which of the currently available (albeit faulty) solutions best meets your business needs. And that is ultimately what it's all about: solving business problems with the tools and methods you have available.

Rick Harder
Chief Information Officer
BellSouth Telecommunications

Networking the New Enterprise

Preface

You need a strong foundation to build anything of lasting value. We wrote *Networking The New Enterprise* for managers who need to understand both the fundamentals of today's networking technology and how to organize the people who create and maintain the enterprise network effectively. This is an unusual combination for one book. We are accustomed to seeing computer books tackling technology and management books handling people issues. From our perspective, the two have a yin-yang relationship—technology issues can't be addressed without organizing human resources properly.

Unless you are working at a startup, your predecessors started building the foundation to your enterprise network when they picked your organization's first mainframe or minicomputer. Not only did they influence the network-related decisions you need to make today and tomorrow, but they also started a culture in your Information Technology (IT) department. Technology issues are easy to understand, but analysis and implementation become difficult thanks to the cultural barriers separating legacy and client/server personnel.

We started this series with *Rightsizing the New Enterprise*, a practical guide for IT managers taking the plunge into modern client/server computer technology. We offered our real-world experiences in moving Sun Microsystems' corporate computing systems from a central mainframe to a distributed client/server environment. Our second book, *Managing the New Enterprise*, details the infrastructures, including networking, data centers, and system administration, needed to build and manage heterogeneous client/server computing systems. You don't need to read our other books to profit from *Networking The New Enterprise*. The management themes and approaches to organization we take here are built on lessons and real-world examples found in our earlier books.

Cultural barriers are the No. 1 client/server killer. The problem is to get the IT organization to work together as a team (legacy and client/server), then close the communication gap between IT and its customers. These barriers are permanent fixtures within many IT organizations and between IT and users. Even if you have reorganized and combined old and new IT, the cultural barriers still stand.

Meanwhile, the problems between IT and users of IT services represent the years of frustration users endured at the hands of legacy staffers. (We would rather not inherit this foundation, but there it is.)

The rest of the book focuses on the world's No. 2 problem, which is establishing the most critical part of the network infrastructure to support the new enterprise. What we are seeing is that client/server applications are being developed quickly without regard for implementing an infrastructure to support them. Everyone is saying how quickly you can develop an application these days (we don't disagree with that), but then there is this perception that you can just deploy it on a server, throw it on the network and, voila! high availability and reliability. We have a rude awakening for you. That is problem No. 2 in a nutshell!

Who Should Read This Book

Networking The New Enterprise should be read by IT executives, managers, and technicians who are either making a transition to network computing or are thinking about it. We wrote this book for business managers thinking about the issues they face while dealing with IT, and what IT should do to fix the communications gap, as well as for other professionals wondering how the new networked enterprise can improve business productivity while lowering costs. Some suggest network computing is a fad. To the contrary, it's the foundation for New IT in the 21st century.

It's Not All About Technology

Our meeting was not proceeding very well. In fact, it was a disaster. We had landed a consulting assignment—our first—to help fix the IT organization at a Fortune 100 company. "An easy job," we thought. "We'll just get the department heads from each IT section together for a one-day meeting to talk about technology issues, we'll collect our fee, and be on our merry way." Wrong!

We were trapped like rats in a room-sized cage with a dozen hotheads representing the company's help desk, data center, applications development, key client/server groups, networking, system administration, and several other vociferous factions. What was stunning wasn't the anger and bickering—we had expected some of that—it was the *source* of the friction: how to organize the *people resources*.

Session 2, Day 1: All Hell Breaks Loose

We may have been neophyte consultants, but we *did* have the presence of mind to schedule another, longer meeting. Our second session was at an off-site location, which we had reserved for a week. (We were loaded for bear!)

The first day started cordially, with a lengthy debriefing on their IT environment, their business, and how IT supported their enterprise's mission. After that we broke the ice by asking a set of questions related to network computing. See how you might fare with the questions we list in Appendix A.

By early afternoon all hell broke loose. Half of the group supported client/server while the rest argued in favor of the status quo—proprietary mainframes and minis, essentially.

We tried to break the logjam by asking if there was an overall IT strategic plan? "Yes," they admitted collectively, "we're moving towards client/server technology." Many in the group didn't know how or when to develop or deploy client/server technologies, and those that did had differing, often short-sighted, plans.

1

Session 2, Day 2: People, Please!

On the second day, we spent all our time focused on organization and people. We thought that this entire day would be spent on technology issues, but they never even came up. Establishing the proper organization, we discovered, was the critical path. The goal is not just distributed computing, but building a strong infrastructure out of a collection of hardware and software to support the entire enterprise. A tempting theme we discouraged was reorganizing IT to meet the requirements of technology. We encouraged the group to consider *managing* the entire enterprise *centrally with decentralized operations.*

Session 2, Days 3 and 4: Supporting the New Enterprise

On the third day we actually got down to working on the critical processes that are necessary for supporting their New Enterprise—disciplines like change management, problem management, disaster recovery, and so on.

On the fourth day we defined the roadmap to get us there and wrapped up our meeting with a day to spare. Our clients seemed happy in the end, and the experience turned out to be very enlightening for us.

While our early ending meant we'd earned a few hours less in consulting fees, we'd gained something far more valuable—the understanding that when it comes to establishing the New Enterprise, there are issues that supersede and precede the technology. To implement an effective, mission-critical, distributed-computing environment in the New Enterprise, you must first break down barriers between disparate organizations within IT and design a high-level business plan for implementing the proper *people-oriented* infrastructure.

The New IT

An opportunity has arisen as IT organizations move forward with client/server computing. It paves the way for us to make a change in how IT provides services to its users.

In the 1970s, the mavens of mainframe-based, corporate IT, hoarded computing resources and dictated computing practices and disciplines to customers. Even the computing architecture of host-terminal technologies showed an ambivalence, if not downright disdain toward anyone outside the glass walls of the data center.

In the 1980s, users got their revenge. By hook or by crook and rarely under the auspices of corporate IT, they sneaked in PCs with an assortment of personal-productivity applications and joined the power-on-the-desktop revolution. "Who needs IT?" they shouted! Those renegade PCs revolutionized business but made a mess of corporate computing, which IT is called on to clean up.

In the 1990s, the opportunity is there for IT to again be the defining, guiding light in corporate computing, not the dictator of bureaucratic policies. IT needs to win its customers back. As companies shift paradigms from host/slave to client/server distributed computing, it will be the perfect time to dramatically improve customer satisfaction.

Regaining customer approval will not be an easy thing to do because of the damage done over the past few decades from behind the glass walls. To borrow a phrase or two from the self-help industry, IT needs a six-step program to help bring itself and its enterprise not only to health, but in fighting trim to compete in the modern global economy.

Six Steps to a Successful IT

There are six critical steps we advise IT organizations to follow as they transition to the New Enterprise:

1. IT needs a clear understanding of how to organize and better support the New Enterprise. It needs a relevant mission, a roadmap to a more efficient enterprise.

2. IT needs unity to fulfill its mission statement. All IT people (mainframe, UNIX, and PC) must work together as one team.

3. Before it can change other parts of the organization, IT itself must change the way it works. It must demonstrate the return-on-investment of client/server distributed computing, reengineering, or whatever catchphrase you choose, with real-life, undeniable evidence.

4. The IT staff needs to learn and use techniques found in sales and marketing. IT needs to market and sell its services.

5. IT needs to develop skills in identifying processes and bureaucratic procedures ripe for streamlining.

6. Hardest of all, IT needs backing from an organization's highest levels to help when encountering sticky political or bureaucratic resistance to change.

The introduction of client/server means an opportunity for change. By following this six-step program, that change means breaking down the walls between IT and its users, between mainframe and UNIX and PC people.

1

Issue One: People

Building and supporting an efficient, cost-effective, enterprise-wide distributed-computing environment is not just a matter of implementing a new technology. It's a lot about people dealing with change. How else can one explain why the worldwide banking system, stock exchanges, airline reservation systems, newspaper paginators, telephone switches, air-traffic controllers, and voice-mail boxes (which are all computer-dependent operations) are stone-ax reliable, while some computer-related efforts fail spectacularly? We all have access to the same hardware, software, and methodologies. We do not have access to the same coaches and players.

The *biggest* challenge in the 1990s and beyond is in the process of understanding and working with a diversity of mentalities and cultures; it is *not* in the "understanding" of the technology.

Now more than ever, technology users in the enterprise need a new IT, a strong IT, a centralized, authoritative, but user-responsive IT. In honest moments, users admit they are tiring of supporting their own computers and systems. The department manager knows all too well that supporting this stuff is difficult and costly. Still, users remember that they had to install their own local area networks (LANs) to collaborate in their work and share resources. Central IT refused to assist and often stood in the way of progress in distributed technologies. IT needs to win back the trust of the user.

However, for many IT organizations the first order of business is to become "user friendly." Analysts estimate that more than half of the client/server initiatives fail. We think they fail because of people issues.

Coordinate IT

It sure was easier in the olden days to clearly identify and understand who did what and when in your legacy computing infrastructure. We're talking about supporting the mainframe-based production environment with groups like Networking, Applications, Systems Programming, Data Center Operations, and so on. We had clearly defined and written job descriptions. Everyone in management information systems (MIS) knew what their job responsibilities were and, more importantly, knew when and how to get involved to support production problems. We not only knew exactly what our responsibilities were, but we also knew how to interact with other departments within MIS to get the job done.

That was then, when almost everything computing-wise was in one place. Now everything is distributed over the entire network. Desktops here, databases there; one for Sales, one for Marketing. Even the Loading Dock has a shipment tracking system. What was once focused support of a centralized system is now often a cloud of uncertain responsibilities. Stormy weather expected. With applications running wild all over the enterprise, there is often no clear understanding of where a problem occurs and which group is responsible for resolving it. The tools may be there to notify IT when a problem occurs (that's easy), but it's also when the fun just begins. Today, because services have become distributed and decentralized, even the help center person has a difficult time finding the right group or groups in IT for guidance and quick resolution to problems.

If you know about us at all, you know about our ministry. We preach the same organizational methodology of centralized control of systems as had worked so well in the mainframe-based world of centralized computing. The only real difference is that today IT personnel are scattered throughout the enterprise to provide local support of distributed systems, and the need for a process to bind these IT groups together has become more important. The need for coordination of resources and support is less obvious, of course, until a problem occurs and various IT groups either deny responsibility or lack a mechanism for cooperative action.

Remember the Service Level Agreement (SLA)? (Mainframers do; UNIX gurus who brought us distributed computing usually do not.) An SLA is a signed agreement between IT and its customer that clearly defines what computing services and support are provided. You need to use the SLA process to best serve IT customers. More on this later, but it brings up a related idea: For distributed-computing systems, let us introduce the concept of the Internal Support Agreement (ISA).

Like an SLA, the ISA is a guide for support and problem resolution. The difference is that while the SLA is between IT and the customer/user, the ISA is an understanding and agreement among the different IT groups. Its primary purpose is to clearly define support roles, responsibilities, and the set of expectations. It tells everyone in IT when and how production support is responsible for performing system administration functions such as special restores, backups, OS patches, and so on. A good, well-thought-out ISA clearly defines all these expectations.

Get Your People Together

The other people issue besides intra-IT cooperation is the people themselves. With the introduction of distributed systems and the infusion of heterogeneity into that mainframe "glass-house," friction and skepticism between the old and new staff can run rampant. The legacy system counterrevolutionaries do not believe that with UNIX, NT, and NetWare you can maintain the same levels of RAS (short for reliability, availability, and serviceability—the three golden rules of

1

a disciplined computing system) as they do with their big iron boxes. The angry young men decry legacy practices as too disciplined, bureaucratic, reactionary, and (the unkindest cut of all) tired.

When left to their own devices, legacy systems groups and client/server groups—even when pressed into service within the same centralized IT organization—simply will not work together. There will be more finger pointing and bickering than there ever has been in the history of data processing. Confusion reigns if roles and responsibilities are not defined clearly.

In the New Enterprise, IT needs to develop and implement better-streamlined, more flexible, and cost-effective RAS processes. We call them "modified disciplines," but modified or not, you cannot manage high RAS without disciplines!

On the other hand, IT personnel must learn how to deal with users in the trenches effectively, not hide behind the glass-house walls as had become the practice in unnecessarily disciplined mainframe bastions. We need to modify or change our old *reactive* ways, exemplified by the help desk. IT personnel need to become *active*, to create a process that will bond users with IT.

Tear Down the Walls

In our experience, the first reaction IT has when contemplating a client/server installation is to isolate it from the legacy stuff. Put it in a cocoon. Keep it out of harm's way. To salvage morale, IT management might let some of the legacy gang work on the new fun stuff. A nice gesture—appease the troops? Oh, what a mistake that is!

You need to mesh your entire organization. Never, ever separate legacy systems (usually mainframe) and client/server. Don't even refer to them as separate parts of your organization. When you start referring to your "mainframe" group versus your "client/server" group, that's when a barrier, thicker than the Great Wall of China, starts to rise. We see it in just about every company around the world.

Surprisingly, the CIO usually has no idea it's there and that the organization has contracted a virus that is slowing their progress to client/server implementation. No one will talk about it, because they are afraid it will jeopardize their careers. But how can you successfully implement such a huge undertaking without everyone moving in the same direction, working as a single unit?

In our first book, *Rightsizing the New Enterprise,* we discussed how to integrate training for mainframe and UNIX people. But technical training is only a small part of the people issues. We visited companies who claimed they did not have these walls to break down, that all was organized properly to get the utmost communication between the different groups. These words usually come from upper management. We begged to differ after getting down and dirty in the trenches with the troops where the walls separating legacy and client/server computing stood ten feet high and ten feet wide.

Get the entire organization working together on projects to manage the enterprise. Start them with useful tools and utilities. The lingua franca in UNIX today is Perl. Ask your *whole team* to develop Perl scripts to address, automate, and/or enhance operations processes. An example of this is a process called shift turnover.

Shift turnover is well known in mainframe shops. It was usually a piece of paper on a clipboard that listed the late shift's special requests. When all requests had been completed, the turnover report would be placed in a file cabinet for future auditing if required. Task your team (yes, a team) to automate the shift-turnover process with Perl or UNIX shell scripts. Have them strip away antiquated procedures and automate the entire process so that it can be accessed online anytime. Instead of having a piece of paper on a clipboard being passed around to the different staff, wouldn't it be nice to type in on your desktop a command like "shiftT" and have a schedule appear? It could even retain each night's special requests in a database for future auditing. Now, depending on your current environment, this process can easily be integrated into HTML (hypertext markup language) and loaded onto a Web server for true Intraneting. If your enterprise doesn't yet have a Web server, what better time and project to start with? What will we do with all those empty file cabinets?!

This project brings your mainframers up to speed on the latest script language fad and teaches your UNIX propeller-heads a thing or two about 24 x 7, industrial-strength, computing-support practices. There are dozens of such legacy processes that could be streamlined. Mainframers write *clists* to automate wherever possible, so what is the difference? You can't just talk about teamwork, demonstrate action behind your words!

Involve management with these projects. Make sure each project is documented in monthly status reports. Mix senior personnel with junior staff (computer operations with systems programming, for example) from both legacy and client/server groups. Show them that you care about everyone contributing to client/server computing. It sounds corny but it works.

A message to those who divided their IT organizations....

You made a grievous mistake. Reverse course. If you separate the distributed systems (typically UNIX) people from the legacy people, you invite chaos and class warfare. Mix the staff. Do not put one team on one side of the hall and

1

another team on the other. You may think you are being efficient or pragmatic, but creating even subtle boundaries now will only delay integration of the new technologies and team-building later.

Believe us. We have been down that rocky road. Divide and be conquered. The sooner you can get the mainframers to teach the UNIX guys some discipline while the UNIX guys teach the mainframers about the New Enterprise of distributed computing, the sooner you can start enjoying peace and the enterprise can achieve new heights of prosperity. Otherwise, your successor (yes, you will fail) will curse you for many years to come.

Issue Two: The Right Infrastructure

Infrastructure means technology, doesn't it? After all, we are doing what we do because we want to transition to the New Enterprise and take full advantage of the new distributed-computing technologies. So, if the number one issue is people, technology must be the second issue?

Sorry, no. When we talk about infrastructure, we mean support—the disciplined practices, processes and procedures that ensure the highest levels of RAS for the enterprise-wide distributed-computing environment. The single most difficult problem in this regard is deploying the proper infrastructure. It took the IT industry three decades to establish the mainframe infrastructure. How quickly we all forget it was the disciplines (standards, processes, and procedures; see Appendix B) that provided high RAS. It wasn't that iron box!

Problem #1

In many organizations the legacy disciplines that were held so dear in the glass house are being pushed aside to expedite the deployment of the new wave of distributed applications. The new technologists don't know any better, and the old ones aren't cooperating (see Issue One earlier in this chapter). Most resources are being spent on the development of new applications with very little, if any, on deploying standards, policies, and procedures from the desktop to the server.

Don't fool yourself. Technology does not support itself. IT still needs to be disciplined so it can deliver highly efficient and reliable applications for the New Enterprise.

Problem #2

Software-development groups all around the enterprise are deploying client/server applications at an accelerated pace. Development groups now boast how quickly they can launch a new application to meet the escalating demands of their users. That's good. The practice responds to the needs of the user.

Unfortunately, those software developers typically wait until the very last moment to involve IT for support. So now everyone is wondering why these hotshot applications do not have the same RAS as legacy systems. Where is the stress testing? Where is the operations support documentation that we called Runbook[1] for mainframe technology? Runbooks were the bible for operational support. Each application had Runbooks associated with it spelling out the support requirements for that application e.g., scheduling dependencies with other applications, special backups, and print handling.

We are not suggesting that we need to preserve the legacy bureaucracy. We don't and we shouldn't—it is too slow and does not respond to the needs of our users. Nonetheless, we do need a single process that will initiate and expedite the deployment process for any application from development to production. That way, we know it will have been tested before we put it into use, and once deployed, we can support and maintain it.

To do that, the deployment process must encompass:

- Communication within the IT organization
- Communication between IT and its users
- Runbooks
- Testing
- Compliance with guidelines and standards
- Defining everyone's roles and responsibilities
- Service Level Agreements

A substantial portion of our second book, *Managing the New Enterprise*, is devoted to an application deployment/ support process that we know works: We refer to it as Client/Server Production Acceptance (CSPA). Chapter 9 of that book contains the details.

Problem #3

Companies are buying system management tools at a rate that suggests desperation. Unfortunately, and all too often, these "quick fixes" are selected without regard for defining functional requirements or process. Always select tools based on functional requirements and defined processes' needs and options that are well documented before beginning product selection and purchase. Remember, tools are only as good as the processes behind them. On the

---

1.   A Runbook outlines the support requirements for a particular batch process on the mainframe, including scheduling dependencies, special tape handling, and so on.

mainframe, we took extra time to properly select the best security product or the best storage management solution based on functional requirements. So why should we treat the system management requirements any differently for client/server?

New IT Standards

What must the New IT do to support the New Enterprise? Develop standards and provide services for those technologies across the enterprise network, applications platform, and user desktops. The types of standards and guidelines are based on corporate culture. This allows for some diversity, which is good, but diversity is not free. How much diversity is allowed should be based on how much the corporation can afford. Minimize the number of supported standards for the three areas identified in Table 1-1. Those listed are what most corporations currently have installed. And when we present this to most corporate IT staffs, they ask; what about the database? In most cases in a distributed-computing environment, the database is supported on any of the application platforms.

Desktop	Applications	Network
DOS	MVS	SNA
Windows 3.1	VM	IPX
Windows 95	VMS	DECnet
OS/2	UNIX	IP
NT	NT	Ethernet
	UNIX	Token Ring

Table 1-1   Standard New IT Areas of Support

It's tough to create and support network-based applications without standards. When you implement an application (and make it reliable), you must know which operating environments will require integration and support. For example, you implement a client/server-based set of financial applications that lives on a server somewhere in the network, and it's going to be accessible by many clients over the wide area network (WAN). The challenge will be on the client side given a variety of desktop operating environments. If your clients include Microsoft Windows, DOS, and NT, then a GUI (graphical user interface) front end (or some kind of access) to the application would be required for each. This involves much extra work and testing to provide the high RAS users expect.

We think operating environments should be as standardized as possible. In this heterogeneous world, you may not be able to standardize on one, but you can, at least, keep it to a minimum. Just think how much easier it would be if all three were UNIX! If the desktop environment is Windows, then it should be documented as the supported environment. The same goes for UNIX and MVS as the application platform. The network can be all TCP/IP (Transmission Control Protocol/Internet Protocol) and Ethernet. Users should not have to worry about the technology, just the applications they need to run their business. Remember, the more standardized you become, the easier it is to provide effective service and lower the cost of support.

Other areas you should consider standardizing are third-party software and electronic mail (e-mail). IT should provide standard suites of third-party software and a corporate e-mail standard. We prefer IT be responsible for licensing third-party software and implementing new version/releases. This goes for e-mail too.

Here are two examples of what we call "low-hanging fruit" for cost reduction. Think of the cost savings from having corporate-wide licenses for software tools like spreadsheets, publishing, and even Windows rather than having each department/business unit negotiate their own. There is also the cost savings of providing one e-mail environment versus each business unit implementing its own. Guess who will be asked to provide gateways and support between the many e-mail environments for "corporate e-mail." You got it! And that just adds to the total cost of IT, when you are being challenged to reduce cost constantly.

Users should concentrate on applications to run their business. They should not deal with third-party tools, e-mail, or the operating environments that support their applications. As part of the marketing and sales function, IT must meet with users on an ongoing basis to get input and inform them of standards. The dictate could be: "As long as the application runs within our operating environment, IT will support it." This allows some diversity, makes end users feel as if they have some control, and helps define standards, procedures, and guidelines. And if it is well communicated and documented, everyone will know the costs associated with diversity. Also, remember to inform an organization of additional cost burdens. We never say we cannot support more requirements; we only want executives to understand (and agree to) any added IT costs.

	Nice to have	Reality
Change Management for online applications	•Receives requests for change •Determines potential impacts •Tracks down and verifies approvals •Publishes change control notification •Verifies status of changes and publishes	•Routes request to approver •Receives manual input for approval notification •Publishes change control notification •Prompts personnel responsible for making the change for status—once manual input is received, tool publishes changes.

Table 1-2   Crucial elements in today's "light's out" environment (table 1 of 7)

1

The Network

The network is the key infrastructure to support our model of network-based computing and applications. In our vision, you must first implement the enterprise-wide network and design it for high availability. Keep the user's perspective in mind: Applications are located on the network; users shouldn't care where the server or application actually resides. Think in terms of an investment where you are spending money to save money. Investing in a standardized, world-class network will help reduce overall support costs.

We have seen the proof: One organization built an enterprise-wide network that grew from eight locations to more than 100 without increasing network support staff. If you use a metric of number of network hubs per network support engineer, you can see the drastic productivity improvement for this company.

Many vendors, suppliers, and partners that make your business a success need access to your critical applications and data. We think an appropriate solution is the Internet. Just imagine having one of your major business systems connected to the Internet (highly secure, of course) accessible by your suppliers, vendors, partners, and even customers while keeping your organization's internal operations private. Providing this kind of functionality will attract the best in the business and improve your competitive advantage. Now that's service and partnership!

Applications Platform

The next key piece, the applications platform, is critical for effective service in the New Enterprise IT. Application platforms must be flexible enough to provide an environment that will support business requirements when implementing a

	Nice to have	Reality
Configuration Management/ Release Distribution	•Automated system detection on network to: •Detect configuration of new system and/or device •Log and report changes •Globally change to accept system from all monitoring processes on the network. •Grant appropriate authority to new system •Back out from a change if deemed unsuccessful	•Track the configuration and "package" of objects to be changed •Back out from a release or change

Table 1-3   Crucial elements in today's "light's out" environment (table 2 of 7)

network computing model. Flexibility gives customers control over their applications. The platform must support applications (bought or built) that the department needs to support its business model. Otherwise, customers will feel that IT is not providing the right services, and they will want to "do their own thing" once again. There must be standards, however. The standards must be aligned with your company's culture and diversity model, and support business requirements cost effectively.

Since you already have existing platforms that have new or legacy applications on them, like MVS, VM, VMS, and others, the next step is to define the applications platform architecture for the future. Again, we feel standards are required.

If you pick a network applications platform like UNIX, then most of the department diversity issues can be addressed. Studies have indicated that up to 40 percent of all new business applications are being developed for UNIX. If your strategy is to buy versus build and your platform is UNIX, most of the business problems can be solved.

You may, on the other hand, end up with a hodgepodge if you let the departments pick the platform. And big problems will consequently arise in the network computing model. Complications will come when you are asked to manage, support, and integrate the environment. How will you support operational policies like backup and recovery, job scheduling, change control, disaster/recovery, and operating system maintenance? Just wait until one department needs to integrate applications and/or data with another. You will be spending much time and money on the middleware to support this integration.

If you have the ability to define this standard architecture up front, you will keep IT costs in line and support the new IT services model. If required, market and sell the ideas to your users. It does work...eventually.

	Nice to have	Reality
Event Management	•Actively monitor the system (network, database, application, etc.) •Automatically react and resolve problem using an information database.	•Monitor the system (network, database, application, etc.) •Automatically react to problem by notifying the proper support person without human intervention •Human intervention to resolve problems

Table 1-4   *Crucial elements in today's "light's out" environment (table 3 of 7)*

1

The Desktop

Standard desktop environments are tough to implement, especially with users in control. This is probably going to be the toughest sell you will have in implementing your New Enterprise network computing model. Remember, the desktop should be seen as a corporate asset and must be treated as such. Desktops are for business productivity improvements, not games!

Start by using IT as the test environment. Use a model that defines the desktop configurations by job function. Define the standard desktop and desktop operating environment, whether it be Windows, NT, DOS, or UNIX. Build a software server environment that provides standard versions of supported desktop software and then put in the processes to support them. This involves change control, automated software distribution, and help desk support. Once you have built this environment and learn how to support it, it becomes easier to sell to others.

Why do you need standard desktops? Again, it goes back to our network computing model. If you are deploying client/server-based applications in the network, concentrate on the interface between the client and the server. Each different operating environment at the desktop will require a separate interface to the application server (one for Windows, one for NT, and one for UNIX, for example). Testing, deployment, and support become more difficult. If this kind of interface is required, you will also need to set up what we call "a one-of-a-kind network." This network should be installed in an IT lab that includes one of every operating environment deployed in your company. This is required to effectively test, quality-assure, and deploy new or revised applications. If this testing effort delays the deployment life cycle, then IT gets the blame for "not providing effective service." They will say the same thing if you deploy an application in "production" and it breaks because you have not tested that particular desktop environment.

	Nice to have	Reality
Network Management	•Capture resource utilization (system, disk, network, bandwidth CPU, I/O, database transaction) real time •Locate the bottleneck or problems •Automatically resolve or tune with no human intervention	•Capture resource utilization •Notify support when threshold exceeds predefined limit, by way of the event monitoring system •Provide information or hints for further analysis •Have procedures to address global performance troubleshooting

Table 1-5   Crucial elements in today's "light's out" environment (table 4 of 7)

The Network Is the Data Center

Computing and information flow in the client/server-based New Enterprise is decentralized, with mission-critical applications running on distributed systems all throughout the organization. Yet, we have found that the only way to ensure the success of the distributed-computing applications and services critical to your enterprise (at reasonable cost) is to employ a centralized IT. That presents a bit of a conundrum, does it not?

The solution actually is simple: Use the network. For years, Sun Microsystems' marketing has promoted the idea that, "The network is the computer." It is now a phrase no pundit, Web surfer, or any other sane person aware of the Internet would argue with today. In that vein, we argue and firmly believe that, in the New Enterprise, The Network is the Data Center, a point we make in detail in our second book, *Managing the New Enterprise*.

	Nice to have	Reality
Problem management	•Automatically detect problems anywhere on the system •React and resolve with no human intervention	•Log, track, escalate (auto-paging, etc.) and report problems and their resolution •Information support database
Scheduling	•Detect new application batch processes and schedule •Schedule jobs to run at the "best" time •Check for dependencies •Restart if failed processes	•Schedule jobs •Check for dependencies •Restart if processes fail
Security	•Handle request, approval, technical administration, and auditing for user access processing to the network database application and transaction levels. •Detect, configure, and authorize access privileges for new users •Introduce applications introduced to the network, system, and database •Automatic detection and reporting for security breach of •Network, system, database, and transaction levels	•Have an on-line application to process request, and approval routing, providing auditing, for user access to the system, database, and transaction levels •Tools and streamlined process to administer access •Individual tool to audit and secure network, system and database •Interface event monitoring process when there is intrusion

Table 1-6   *Crucial elements in today's "light's out" environment (table 5 of 7)*

1

The New IT can use the enterprise network to provide services over the wide-area, metropolitan-area, campus-area, and local-area network, right down to the desktop. There, users should be able to readily access an important application and critical information and not care where the application resides. The application could be on the LAN, somewhere over the WAN, or even across the global Internet. Mainframe applications included, too.

To support this kind of service at a reasonable cost, the enterprise must establish some networking and computing standards. Who understands standards, guidelines, and processes better than IT? We've been doing it for 30 years!

Reorganizing IT to Meet the Challenge of New Technology

Must be time to reorganize. Right? Wrong! It is wrong to reorganize purely for technical reasons. Only rarely does a technology come along that changes, in a profound way, the way people work or the way an organization fulfills its mission. Remember when client/server hit the front pages? Decentralization of IT services was the common theme. How many millions (dollars, lost hours, torn hair follicles, antacid tablets, you name it!) have organizations wasted due to the effects of wanton decentralization? It is not only nearly impossible, but it is, as many organizations have found, extraordinarily expensive to decentralize mission-critical computing services. You cannot hope to establish full-service computing centers in each department worldwide and provide local computing services with on-site personnel. Indeed, we strenuously argue that a decentralized IT is IT in chaos.

What is the answer? We have found only one answer: centralized control with a twist of decentralized operations. To control costs by deploying standards and disciplines throughout your enterprise, you must maintain centralized control. No ifs, ands, or buts about it. Over the past half-dozen years, we have seen hundreds of organizations founder in computer anarchy because no one was willing or able to control the organization's computer environment.

	Nice to have	Reality
Software Distribution	•Automatically distribute software products from the server to the desktop, automating license requirements, software releases, and client architecture	•Standardize on 3-tiered architecture to ensure: •Centralized administration for bug fixes, patches, upgrades •Reduced requirements for system administration •Consistency of software •Reliable backup processes

Table 1-7   Crucial elements in today's "light's out" environment (table 6 of 7)

The model we know works reengineers business processes and deploys new client/server applications to support them. The need of the user wags the IT dog's tail, not the other way around.

The Organization

The organizational chart we show in Figure 1-1 presents our organizational model for the New IT. It may not be exactly right for your organization, but it is a model that we know works. It empowers the right people with the right responsibilities in the right place in the enterprise.

The CIO

There needs to be one person responsible for IT. The title and reporting relationships make a difference—we can usually understand how important IT is to the success of the enterprise by where the head of IT fits in the overall organization and the respective title. To have a successful IT within your organization, the enterprise should have a chief of the New IT, the chief information officer (CIO), who must be empowered and committed to make dictates, understand technology, and enforce the new service model throughout the enterprise.

Architects

Although the CIO must be conversant with the new technologies, it is next to impossible that one person can and will understand innovations and the details sufficiently to implement them in the New IT. That's why we recommend a small group of technology architects.

	Nice to have	Reality
Storage Management	•Backups start at scheduled time on system-labeled tapes •Robotic tape loading and archiving with built in cataloging •Physically organize tapes for third party vendor pick up and delivery •Restore data files for users automatically •For user requests for restoration, system automatically contacts third-party vendor for return of tapes	•Reliable back ups start at scheduled time •Robotic tape loading and auto cataloging systems •Automatic completion status sent to control and display layer

Table 1-8   Crucial elements in today's "light's out" environment (table 7 of 7)

Architects are full-time technologists who critically examine new technologies, interface with business units to introduce those new technologies to discover how they might meet their computing needs, and define the three- to five-year strategic plans for IT to meet those critical business needs.

We should note that the plans are really targets. If you think of a real target with a bulls-eye and the center of the bulls-eye represents time, like 6 to 12 months, you can publish your architecture as a target. IT understands what the architecture will be in the next 6 to 12 months, but after that, it is only a target. Technology changes so fast that the architectures must be flexible.

The Architects cannot be prima donnas or be perceived as being "in the ivory tower." They must work effectively as a team with the development organization(s) and the infrastructure operational units (networking, data center, and desktop support). They must produce a "minimum and sufficient" architecture that has the support of the rest of IT and the CIO.

Another function Architects perform in the New IT organization is one of checks and balances. In the old IT, when a "customer" came to us with a need for something different or new, we simply said, "No, you must follow the standards

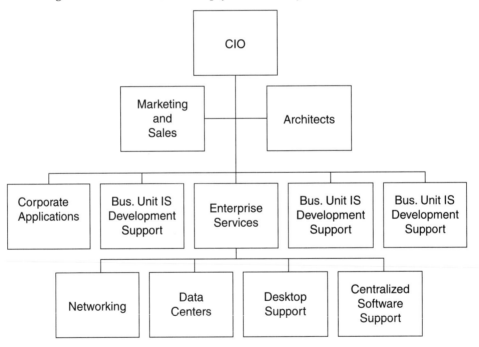

Figure 1-1   The New IT Organizational Chart

that we support," or, as in the case of LANs, "No, we don't support that, but you can do it yourself."

In the New Enterprise, we still must define and publish standards. The difference in the New IT, however, is that if a customer comes to us with a new technology that is not part of our supported standards, the Architects get involved and see if it should be considered part of IT's arsenal. The Architects determine whether it should be part of the service model and determine the additional costs and training for IT to support it.

Yes, being an Architect is a full-time job, and we recommend it be staffed from the current operations organization. Why? Because they understand the business!

Marketing and Sales

This job title within IT may surprise you, but it is one of the most important New IT functions. As we argue throughout this book and elsewhere, the New IT must become a truly customer-driven organization for the good of the entire enterprise, lest computing services become dictatorial again. IT must sell its information services. That means developing a marketing plan, meeting with users, departments, and business units, competing with outside vendors for contracts.

New IT Sales and Marketing may not be supported by head-count, but it is a function. All IT organizations must include Marketing and Sales responsibilities.

Corporate Applications

There have always been enterprise-wide business applications, such as for human resources, finance, and payroll. In the New IT, there should be a small, centralized group of developers for these systems.

The New IT must have a focus on these applications for architecture and overall cost. Think of those instances when each department or business unit tries to solve its own issues related to these types of applications. Think of the cost of trying to integrate them from a corporate perspective!

For smaller organizations with an IT staff of 50 or fewer, the Corporate Applications group has responsibility for all applications. As always, do not separate development of new applications on new technology, such as going from mainframe to client/server, into a new group. Keep the groups the same, especially to keep up staff morale.

Business Unit IT

Business Unit (a.k.a. department, agency, and so on) IT is responsible for business unit applications. In large corporations, each business unit/department has different systems requirements to meet their business needs. Groups should be defined to meet those specific needs. Defining an IT function for each allows them to focus on those particular needs. In the New IT, this allows each business unit to have control of systems and application requirements. Each is responsible for maintaining its own set of priorities and backlogs and can make changes accordingly based on the budget. They can change the priorities and reduce or increase the backlog without negotiating with some large, centralized bureaucracy that never satisfies anyone. This fixes that!

The Business Unit IT Manager or Director must report directly to the CIO and have a direct relationship with the business unit's General Manager. While serving more than one master is not recommended for most positions, it is necessary in this case to seal a high-level relationship between the New IT and its customer.

The Business Unit group within IT should include both applications development and applications support and maintenance. We recommend the support and maintenance function be aligned with the business unit, not a large, centralized function, so each can determine its maintenance and support priorities and backlog. The development and support organizations should be separate but report to the same business unit IT manager. Again, business unit applications development must be owned by IT so that the CIO can understand and own the total cost of IT and implement standards where possible, such as enterprise-wide, applications development methodologies and tools (a dictate). Also, by reporting to the CIO, they can be charged to focus on business systems, not technology. (The Architects handle the technology.)

Enterprise Services

Enterprise Services is the infrastructure implementation and operational support function for the New IT. Infrastructure includes "utility" services for Networking, Data Center(s), desktop (user) support, and centralized third-party software. The infrastructure is where most of the total cost of IT resides and should be centrally controlled and managed. In the new distributed enterprise, there need to be controls and standards down to, and including, the desktop.

The desktop is becoming mission critical and must be managed by IT. In the Old Enterprise, desktop support reported to business units. In the New Enterprise, we want business units to focus on business requirements, not technology.

Centralized Software Services

In the New IT, there should be a centralized function, as part of Enterprise Services, that is responsible for all third-party software for the entire organization. We define third-party software as desktop tools and applications like spreadsheets, desktop publishing, middleware, and so on. We also recommend a standard menu of tools that provide more than one solution for each of the functions required, because different people like different tools. There should be no dictates in this area.

However, we can help reduce the cost of this suite of tools by providing corporate licenses through Centralized Software Services. The group should work closely with a purchasing function to negotiate corporate licensing agreements. This goes a long way in helping reduce the total cost of IT. Any new version of the third-party software is delivered to the group from the vendor. They are then charted to test and quality-assure the new version before it goes on the network file server or desktop. This is yet another example of IT dealing with the technology issues rather than having the user or business unit license, install, and qualify the software. We think this model can help the New IT become a true service organization (and, oh, by the way, the marketing document should include competitive pricing) that is adaptable to change and supports the New Enterprise's business requirements more effectively.

It's the Big Guy's Fault

Most CIOs understand the difficulties in adopting distributed network-based computing systems. Corporate headquarters wants to know why it is such a big deal. How come these "off-the-shelf" computers cost so much? How come you're not downsizing faster? How come these new systems seem unreliable, even sometimes unusable? It must be the CIO's fault.

Upper management isn't stupid. Most just don't have a clue what it takes to implement this crazy New Enterprise. Without their support, you will fail. You need to talk smart and get the support you need.

Led by the CIO, the IT team must first refresh the corporate memory. Remind the powers-that-be how difficult it was in years past to exchange one mainframe operating system for another. Remind them of the months of planning and testing to move the organization from, essentially, one railroad track to another. Then remind them that going from the mainframe to a distributed-computing system is like having a fleet of trucks replace the old iron horse. (How quickly people forget the three decades it took to establish the procedures that form the foundation for a secure and reliable data center.)

Executives and users are demanding and impatient, spurred on by competition and oftentimes glowing accounts in trade magazines of client/server bliss. They often fail to recognize that not only is a small system change tough under ideal conditions, establishing the New Enterprise means making many large changes and adopting a computing system with double or perhaps triple the number of variables.

1

Both executives and users need to understand that today's network-based computing paradigm implies wide-ranging organizational changes far beyond Microsoft's plan for selling Windows 95 to the hoi polloi and Windows NT to the more-demanding user. By change, we mean establishing a new, fast-moving, flexible organization where information is available promptly to those who need to make decisions rapidly.

The Network in the New Enterprise 2

The New Enterprise depends on a well-built IT infrastructure to promote communications and coordination among groups inside and outside the organization. It is obvious you need some sort of network. It is the essential element of the IT infrastructure in the New Enterprise. The enterprise network is the conduit through which clients and servers communicate queries and exchange data. Integrating applications, computers, data, and communications, the enterprise network is a strategic asset vital to the New Enterprise's viability

Our view of the network transcends the common and simplistic pipeline metaphor; for us, "The network *is* the data center." A distributed network for your New Enterprise is more than just the sum of its wires, interfaces, and protocols. We elevate the collection of simple networks with desktops encircling departmental servers up to a unified system of many servers that provides users with global access to information, communications, and a variety of client/server (often mission-critical) resources. To do this, we build a world-class network infrastructure and manage that enterprise network with world-class processes and tools. In other words, we build what we call a "production-quality" enterprise network.

Characteristics of the New Enterprise Network

The new enterprise network differs significantly from other networks. Where common networks support local requirements, such as departmental file- and print-sharing, the enterprise network spans all organizational boundaries. The enterprise network affects the whole organization. It supports diverse requirements of the entire enterprise, and, in doing so, the enterprise network allows groups throughout the organization to share files, applications, and computing resources. It also lets users access key sources of information and business-critical applications on mainframes and client/server systems. The enterprise network raises workgroups to a level where they can span the entire organization.

2

The new enterprise network is integrated, global, dynamic, and has production-quality levels. Using common facilities, it provides a way to access different types of applications, services, and information like data, images, voice, and video. Some networks give users access only to specific applications. For example, some companies have two networks: one for access to legacy mainframe applications and another for access to client/server applications, desktop productivity tools, and shared services. What good are those client/server apps and productivity tools when all the important corporate information is buried in the mainframe data warehouse? By definition, the enterprise network gives users reasonable access to all data and applications.

Being global, the scope of the new enterprise network extends beyond the organizational boundaries. Far more information is available on global systems than can be contrained or managed by your internal network. Users in the New Enterprise can access important sources of information and other key resources anywhere in the world, independent of time and space.

For the New Enterprise to adapt and survive in a fast-paced international and competitive environment, it depends on an enterprise network that is also adaptable. The network in the New Enterprise is dynamic, flexible, and extensible, so it changes as the New Enterprise changes in its environment. The New Enterprise network can support current requirements as well as future enhancements without major modifications. It can change as user requirements and technology change. For example, we expect future enterprise networks to support more than simple data and to include multimedia applications without major remodeling. Conversely, we also expect the enterprise network to be a catalyst and facilitator of change in the New Enterprise.

Since the New Enterprise network is a strategic asset, it must have production qualities. A production-quality network has the levels of reliability, availability, and serviceability that the New Enterprise requires to achieve its strategic objectives. This simply means it is manageable and supports your mission-critical applications and other production systems. This remains one of our overriding objectives: how we implement enterprise networks with production qualities.

Minimizing the Cost of Ownership

One of the principal components in our equation for networking the New Enterprise is minimizing the cost of ownership. Planning, building, and managing an enterprise network is not about technology; it is about minimizing the cost of ownership and maximizing its value.

Although your enterprise network has many components—cables, connectors, hubs, routers, switches, servers, and so on—the capital costs for network devices are only a small portion of the total cost of network ownership. More than 80 percent of the network costs are related directly to the cost for operations and management. Installing network hardware and software, moving desktops to different locations on the network, solving problems, installing upgrades, performing backups, adding and modifying user profiles are all time-consuming and costly activities.

Another high-priced item is downtime. Depending on the nature of the business, network downtime can cost your organization thousands to millions of dollars per hour in lost business activity. So the underlying objective for planning, designing, implementing, and managing your enterprise network is to minimize the cost of downtime. The only way to do this is to ensure your network has high levels of RAS, so every authorized user in your organization has uninterrupted access to business-critical information and efficient communications.

Guidelines for Success

The enterprise network is an intricate and complicated web of technology. It only makes sense that you should plan carefully and put the kinds of controls in place that will ensure its success from the outset. In our experience, there are four main areas that need equal attention when implementing and managing an enterprise network. Unless you deal with network complexity and change properly, invest in personnel, keep a broad scope, and plan to manage your enterprise network carefully, all will surely transform into an affliction that affects the health of the enterprise.

There are an infinite number of ways to connect the hardware and software in a network. In practice, only a few work. To add insult to injury, enterprise networks are highly integrated, so modifying one component often will affect the operation of others, no matter how apparently isolated they may be. That can lead to disaster in an undisciplined network. After all, change is the way of business in the New Enterprise. New technologies, new software releases, hardware upgrades, and new user requirements are the norm in today's distributed-computing environments. You can't avoid the problems and constraints that complexity and change bring to your enterprise network. You can, however, facilitate and manage them through a structured, standardized network architecture.

You also need a well-trained staff capable of implementing and managing your enterprise network. Sure, training is time consuming, and it places an extra burden on limited resources, but that's penny-wise and pound-foolish thinking. We plan for adequate personnel training from the very beginning and use a variety of alternative curricula, such as computer-based training and online information services.

Make sure the plan and design of your enterprise network has a broad scope. Although typically departmentalized for efficiency, organizations don't exist for long if parts of the business starve. Don't balkanize the network design, or it will surely become an impediment to change, and, worse, it can cost you plenty for interconnectivity and interoperability after the fact.

Last, but most important, plan to manage your network well. Put in place the applications, tools, and practices that will help manage your network. Don't wait for a disaster to happen before you plan for a cure. Invest in forethought and planning. Preventive medicine is less difficult and less expensive, plus the patient usually lives.

Formal Network Methodologies

Network management can be a complex and costly undertaking. With network operations and management contributing to more than 80 percent of network costs, you must design a network management infrastructure to ensure your enterprise network is a strategic asset that meets expected service levels. Comprising technology, people, processes and tools, the network management infrastructure must be well planned from the start.

If you have little experience planning, designing, and implementing an enterprise network, we recommend using a formal methodology. Even if you do have experience, you will benefit from a methodology that brings discipline and structure to a large network project. Most of the leading consultants use comprehensive methodologies for designing networks and managing network projects. Methodologies will take you through a step-by-step checklist to help you define your project.

Before selecting a particular methodology, there are several strategic issues to consider. One is cost. Most methodologies come with a high price. Another is flexibility. No methodology matches the organization's unique requirements. Unforeseen events will occur, so the methodology should be flexible to fit the culture.

A last issue concerns creativity. Because many methodologies are essentially checklists, simply following a strict methodology will not lead to a world-class enterprise network. To engineer the enterprise network, you need a structured and disciplined approach, but, just as importantly, you need an approach that allows you a measure of creativity.

PRINCE

One formal network methodology we like is PRINCE (PRojects IN Controlled Environments). The United Kingdom's government developed it for large IT projects. We have used variations of PRINCE to develop network project plans, to manage network implementations, and to develop organizational structures for network management. It is an effective methodology that focuses on integrating technologies, people, and processes. Planning, monitoring, and change controls are some of the key areas covered by the methodology. The PRINCE methodology is in the public domain, so information, books, and training are available at a low cost.

You can acquire the PRINCE Handbook (around US$25) and course notes (around US$10) from:

> SPOCE Project Management Ltd.,
>
> Homelife House,
>
> Bournemouth,
>
> Dorset,BH8 8EZ
>
> England
>
> Tel: +44 (0) 1202 780 740

While we recommend some training, the PRINCE methodology is relatively easy to use. This is important because complex methodologies require extensive training before you can begin to be use them effectively. With a complex methodology that is difficult to learn, you will find yourself spending more time learning the intricacies of the methodology instead of rethinking your network. Besides cost and ease of use, the PRINCE methodology meets our other essential requirements by addressing the five key areas for managing a large project:

- Planning: Identification and scheduling of project tasks
- Authorization: Formal review and authorization of project plans
- Monitoring: The actual project measured against the plan
- Replanning: Minimizing the effects of any unforeseen events (you can be sure there will be many)
- Change control: Maintaining a database of alterations to the network

Network project management is the art and science of managing change, and change control is one of the most important elements of successful project management. Without effective control over change, you cannot manage a large network project. The methodology you adopt for your enterprise network should addresses the five areas listed above.

Organized Lines of Responsibility

Make sure the network methodology provides an outline for critical project processes and an organizational structure. These are essential elements of a methodology because they identify areas of responsibility and facilitate communications among various project team members. The essential project implementation processes—change management, inventory management, configuration testing, documentation, deployment, operations, problem, capacity and new requirements processes—are the same processes we depend on for operating a distributed enterprise network. We describe the processes in more detail in Chapter 12.

A network organizational structure as part of Enterprise Services and based on the methodology (Figure 2-1) provides a foundation on which you define the lines of responsibility and communications. Without these, it is impossible to coordinate and monitor the activities of different project team members, particularly when they may work in different divisions in your organization. Keep in mind that any methodology you evaluate should provide these mechanisms to integrate people, technology, and processes. The organizational structure for your network project is also important to quality assurance.

The PRINCE methodology depends on control mechanisms to provide structure to a large and often chaotic network project. These control mechanisms revolve around a project board, the members of which formally review the quality of the project (how well the network project conforms to the requirements) in both regularly scheduled and ad hoc meetings. Regarding tools, the PRINCE

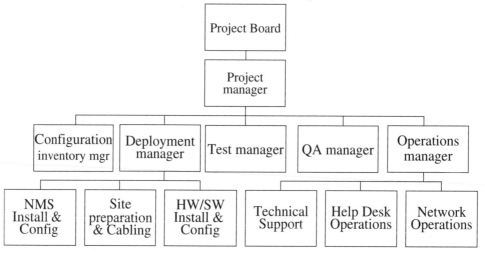

Table 2-1   *Figure 2-1: A Network Project Management Organizational Chart*

methodology is flexible, so you have choices.

Our favorite project management tool is Microsoft Project. It is an inexpensive, comprehensive application that runs on notebook computers. Microsoft Project easily develops schedules, monitors costs and time, and organizes information for presentations.

You can also use other automated tools, such as Computer Associates' SuperProject, which is very good.

As with other methodologies, PRINCE focuses mainly on project management: flow diagrams, scheduling, functional areas of responsibility, organizational structure, and monitoring resources. Unfortunately, few methodologies address the network design process. Most provide simple checklists without discussing the relative advantages and disadvantages of alternative approaches. We describe our network design methodology in the remaining chapters of this book. We divide the network design process into the essential areas—network architecture, facilities, cables, backbone network, concentrators, internetworking, wide area networking, server and desktop connectivity, protocols, Systems Network Architecture (SNA) integration, high-speed technologies, security, and network management—where we outline the important techniques and guidelines for planning, designing, implementing, and managing your enterprise network.

2

Networking the New Enterprise

Developing a Network Architecture 3≡

Network design never stops. After an initial requirements analysis, which leads to a basic design, you buy and deploy equipment. After the network is up and running, the organization discovers unforeseen uses for the network, which leads to design changes, new networking equipment, and new discoveries. The cycle goes on and on. The network architecture provides a framework for this continuing cycle of analysis, design, and implementation. Like the blueprints for a large building, the network architecture gives managers an overall view of how all the components of the network infrastructure—technologies, people, processes and tools—fit together. And it is a map of how to get where you want to go. An effective network architecture should define key strategies and objectives, network structure, standards, and methods.

Objectives for Network Design

Before designing the network, you need to establish objectives from two perspectives: designers' and users'. To the user a network should be just like plumbing—reliable, efficient, safe, and invisible. It should perform well enough that when users are surveyed about your network, they should be unaware. People don't notice things that operate reliably. They expect devices or services to complete their tasks in about the same amount of time each time. If a replacement device operates twice as quickly, great! On the other hand, don't expect users to sing you high praises. If something suddenly takes twice as long to complete its appointed rounds, whether it be a computer, train, or coffee maker, users will complain.

Aside from the plumbing qualities, users also want:

- To work with other users regardless of the computers used
- The network to expand as they find other uses for it
- The ability to add and move users without bureaucracy
- To keep outsiders from reading their files
- The ability to manage their networked devices from one place

3

Service Level Objectives

To satisfy strategic business objectives and user requirements, you need to break these ambiguous notions into concrete service objectives. A service agreement, which you negotiate with users, is the criterion for quantifying how the enterprise network is satisfying key business requirements.

For example, you might measure functionality by the types of services that can be accessed across the network; performance by response times, or better yet, transactions in a period of time; and availability in mean time between failure (MTBF), hours of downtime, and time to restore. We list some service level benchmarks in Table 3-1.

Network Availability	99.8—100 percent
Mean Time to a Hardware Failure	1 Month
Mean Time to a Software Failure	1 Month
Mean Time to Respond	10 Minutes
Mean Time to Repair	1 Hour
Maximum Time to Repair	24 Hours
Network Performance	95% responses in <2 seconds
Mean Throughput	64 Kbps
Mean Time to Restore Disk	4 Hours
Mean Time to Restore Single File	1 Hour

Table 3-1   Service Level Benchmarks

Availability service levels, uptime, and mean time between failure are relatively straightforward analyses and can be evaluated quantitatively. However, performance-related service requires special consideration: you must define different types of service-level measurements for different applications. For example, response time is an effective way to measure simple transaction-processing applications. But you need to define exactly what "response time" means. A customary definition is the time it takes to start receiving a response after submitting input, such as pressing the Enter key on a keyboard. You call; I answer.

Today's client/server applications complicate the definition of response time, to say the least. One input stream from a client may set off a chain reaction of activity between several local and distant servers. In the real world, you need to think of measuring performance in terms of transactions per time, where each transaction may comprise several data exchanges between a client and servers. Depending on the nature of the applications, you might even need to measure transactions per minute or per hour. An example might be an insurance claims application where you may measure a series of complex tasks to process claims by the number of claims completed per hour.

For large data transfers, response time and the number of transactions per unit time aren't very useful. For example, when you execute a large file transfer, you are concerned mainly about throughput or the amount of data transferred per second.

Analyzing Network Requirements

After analyzing service level objectives, you next decide how to design a network that meets those service needs. The first step is to identify your organization's business requirements.

Where are you now? Where do you want to go? What are the available solutions and technologies? What can you afford? You need a network that will meet your organization's objectives—strategic, operational, and business. When you decide what you can afford, it becomes a business decision to determine if your proposal offers more value than it costs. If so and if it satisfies your business needs, then your network becomes an asset rather than a cost center.

Unfortunately, because every enterprise network is unique and dynamic, there are no well-defined methodologies to help you identify and evaluate all requirements. Rather than focusing on details, take a big-picture approach. That way, you can refine your requirements iteratively and add more detail as you learn.

Partition your network requirements by broad categories, such as applications and services, facilities and cables, desktops, LANs, WANs, protocols, servers, and network management software. This is a simple guideline we will use to define requirements. Feel free to use another way to segregate your own business requirements.

Requirements for Applications and Services

Identify the applications, services, and information sources users need to access across the enterprise. These might include old mainframe and new groupware and client/server applications. You also need to consider other types of network-based services, such as e-mail, facsimile, and Internet and Intranet access. And don't forget multimedia—many organizations want to eventually combine voice and video conferencing with their data networks, if they are not already doing so.

3

After you identify your applications and services, you will have a better idea of the types of information that will flow across your network. This is important because data, images, voice, and video require different levels of network performance, availability, and security.

Requirements for Facilities and Cables

In our experience, cabling accounts for many network problems. It is not unusual for organizations to install critical network components in exposed areas with poor power and ventilation. If you don't already have wiring closets and equipment rooms for your important network devices, you need to build them. If you use a mainframe, plan to use your data center for critical network components.

Desktop Systems Requirements

Most large organizations suffer from an incompatible jumble of desktop hardware and software. You need to decide which desktops you will connect to your network, which ones you'll discard, and which you'd best leave to a reclusive lifestyle.

Local Network Requirements

Where are your legacy LANs? Do they fit into your enterprise network plans? Evaluate the various types of networks such as Ethernet, Token Ring, Fiber Distributed-Data Interface (FDDI), and Fast Ethernet, and decide which standards are best for your organization.

Wide Area Network Requirements

As with LANs, review your WANs and evaluate your options. WANs require special attention because of their staggering cost. WAN network components, in particular, probably account for the biggest chunk of your capital equipment budget. Also, various carriers and local telephone companies (called "telcos" in the trade), offer a variety of services at corresponding prices. Study your data traffic and predict its growth so you can evaluate your options intelligently. Another important consideration is Internet connectivity. What type of Internet access do you need? Is e-mail access adequate or do you need full access to the World Wide Web?

Protocol Requirements

Pick a standard protocol for your network. If you have networks in place already, you will likely want to retain these protocols for some time. However, you might save money in the long run if you switch to a single protocol. Many organizations plan to migrate to TCP/IP, while predominately SNA installations often expect to migrate all systems to Advanced Peer-to-Peer Networking (APPN).

If you plan to use multiple protocols, you need to decide how you will distribute the protocol stacks and if you need gateways. Will you use nonroutable protocols? If so, will you allow them across the backbone, or will you imprison them in specific subnets?

You also need to evaluate routing protocols, such as Routing Information Protocol (RIP) and Open Shortest Path First (OSPF), and find out how they might affect your network design.

Server Requirements

Novell and UNIX administrators commonly deploy desktop computers as file, e-mail, and printer servers. As these functions become more mission critical, you should upgrade the hardware to make them more fault resilient.

Do your servers offer the performance and reliability you need? The operating systems you choose will depend, to some degree, on your applications requirements. Your server hardware requirements, such as type of processor, memory, disk space, and fault tolerance will depend on their applications and operating systems.

Requirements for Network Management

Network management is the final and most important requirement. You cannot build a network with production qualities without well-defined requirements for network management. What network and systems management tools do you use today? What mainframe-based tools are you using that also would be useful for your distributed-computing environment? It is common for enterprises with mainframes to manage their SNA networks with NetView. If your enterprise is one of these, you will want to consider NetView for your distributed network. Many organizations will find SunNet Manager and OpenView meet their network management requirements.

We will discuss network management and security strategies later. For now, identify the key important network management requirements.

And don't forget about your support organization. What kind of processes and structure do you need? What kind of training is required to provide high levels of support for your network?

3

Sources for Technology Information

To plan, design, build, and manage an enterprise network, you need access to accurate and timely information. You need information about your needs, and information about the available software and hardware that may meet your requirements. Fortunately, we enjoy a variety of information resources, including text books, training courses, computer-based training, trade magazines, e-mail lists, and the World Wide Web.

If you haven't already done so, we recommend that you get personal access to the Internet now. Most of the popular network suppliers maintain Web pages and CompuServe forums. Users of popular products often start Usenet discussion groups and e-mail lists. Table 3-2 lists several Web sites with links to useful references for a broad range of network technologies.

Many Network Links	http://web.syr.edu/~jmwobus/lans
Internet and TCP/IP	http://www.cis.ohio-state.edu/hypertext/information/rfc.html
Network Links	http://www.connectworld.net/c6.html
Network Links	http://www.msic.com/technical_info.html
LAN Magazine	http://www.lanmag.com
Ethernet Links	http://wwwhost.ots.utexas.edu/ethernet/ethernet-home.html
Keyword Search	http://www.infoseek.com
Directory and Search	http://www.yahoo.com/Computers_and_Internet
SNA Integration	http://www.raleigh.ibm.com/app/aiwinfo/aiwsites.htm

Table 3-2   Web Sites about Network Technologies

Another enlightening source of technical information are Requests for Information (RFI). RFIs present, in a formal and consistent way, your requirements to different suppliers, which, in turn, respond with sales pitches for their products and services.

Standards for Networks

Before you start building your enterprise network, you should evaluate and select your network standards. There are many to choose from. We recommend you select as few as necessary but adhere to them devoutly. You can't evaluate components if you haven't picked your standards.

We also recommend a conservative approach. Pick the popular, proven standards for no other reason than finding compatible equipment and management tools. If you are considering an emerging standard or one not popular, make sure it will satisfy a key business requirement in your organization today and in the future. You don't want to throw away an expensive new technology that works now but offers a short life.

Today's predominant network standards are summarized in Table 3-3. The Institute of Electrical and Electronics Engineering (IEEE) Society's 802.3 and 802.5 standards for Ethernet and Token Ring are two of the proven standards for networks. 10Base5, 10Base2, and 10BaseT are all widely used versions of IEEE 802.3. Another noteworthy standard is the American National Standards Institute (ANSI) X3T9.5 for FDDI. More recently, 100BaseT (Fast Ethernet), Asynchronous Transfer Mode (ATM), and 100VG-AnyLAN are rapidly becoming important standards for enterprise networks. Fast Ethernet is similar to your existing 10BaseT networks (just 10 times faster), whereas ATM and 100VG-AnyLAN are completely new technologies.

For many of the emerging technologies, standards are either nonexistent or incomplete, which means products from different suppliers may not interoperate. As we write this in 1996, products following the ATM "standard" are essentially proprietary. If you decide to use proprietary products, make sure they will satisfy your longer-term business requirements. If not, you may find yourself with an expensive short-term solution. For more information about the key network standards, browse the Web sites listed in Table 3-4.

Technology	Standards	Other Names
Ethernet	IEEE 802.3	10Base5 (ThickNet), 10Base2 (ThinNet), and 10BaseT
Token Ring	IEEE 802.5	
FDDI	ANSI X3T9.5	
100BaseT	IEEE 802.3	Fast Ethernet
100VG-AnyLAN	IEEE 802.12	
Frame Relay	Frame Relay Forum	
ATM	ATM Forum and International Telecommunications Union	Broadband ISDN (B-ISDN) Cell relay

Table 3-3   Key Network Standards

Develop a Logical Topology

After you identify your network requirements and technologies and select your key network standards, you're ready to jump into the physical design, right? Wrong! Remember, network design is complex. The essence of a good design is to keep a broad view of the big picture and take a top-down approach. We find excellent staffs possessing outstanding technical skills with a keen knowledge of different technologies at many organizations. Alas, we rarely find visionaries with a broad view of the big picture.

Key Methods

Although we focus on centralization as one of the key methods to maintain control over your network, there are other methods that are just as essential. In addition to centralization, you also need to distribute, consolidate, separate, and duplicate network components and processes to ensure that your enterprise network meets business requirements. At first these methods may appear contradictory. However, they are actually complementary. The essence of designing an enterprise network is finding the optimum mixture, which is an never-ending process. For example, you may build an enterprise network with a variety of components, such as routers and hubs, that are distributed across different locations. Some may find homes in secure wiring closets throughout a large complex, while others are left out in the open at branch offices. Hopefully, your critical devices, such as servers and backbone routers, will hum along undisturbed in your controlled data center.

For your network management systems, you need to centralize the applications in your data center where they collect information from management agents distributed everywhere your network reaches.

http://www.itu.ch	International Telecommunication Union
http://www.ieee.org	Institute for Electrical and Electronic Engineers
http://www.iso.ch	International Organization for Standardization
http://www.ansi.org	American National Standards Institute
http://frame-relay.indiana.edu	Frame Relay Forum
http://www.atmforum.com	ATM Forum

Table 3-4   Network Standards

With your building backbone routers centralized in a data center, you can consolidate several small routers into one large multiport router to enhance manageability and performance. Then, you can duplicate this single backbone router to make your backbone network more reliable. You may also duplicate vital communications links in your wide-area network for better reliability and performance. For systems that are security sensitive, you can use separate servers on separate networks isolated by firewalls to ensure less secure systems and networks do not impose risks.

We discuss these concepts and the process of centralizing, distributing, consolidating, separating, and duplicating throughout the book.

Logical Design

Start with a simple logical design. Figure 3-1 is a simple, high-level diagram of an enterprise network. Taking a top-down approach, you can iteratively refine higher-level diagrams with more details, as shown in Figure 3-2. Successive iterations will eventually lead to a detailed physical design.

Strategy for Network Management

Network management and control loom as important concerns. While many organizations build comprehensive network management technologies, the underlying processes for managing the distributed-network environment are usually insufficient. Processes, people, and technology combine under the distributed management and control umbrella. Any solution failing to meld all three will founder.

Network management introduces infrastructure that allows you to anticipate problems, identify their source, and start corrective action before the afflicted user starts to dial your help desk. Only a comprehensive management system that combines processes, people, and technologies provides an effective solution for active management.

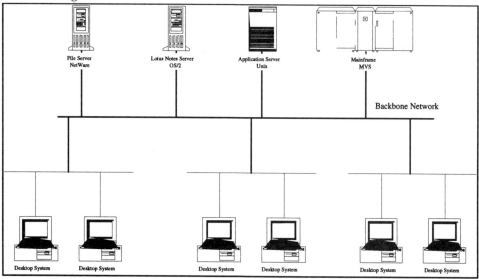

Figure 3-1   *Figure 3-1: Simple High-Level Diagram of an Enterprise Network*

■ 3
═

Centralized Control

We recommend a central point of control, a headquarters if you will, for your network management. But do not centralize all network management processes. Any process may be distributed to any point on the network, but all processes should be controlled from one place. Centralization maximizes the skills and knowledge of one of your most expensive resources—your staff.

Network Management Hierarchy

For networks that span geographical regions, you need to organize your network management domains in a hierarchy. We recommend that you define your network management domains "in the largest possible sizes, but no larger" to maximize the skills of your network management staff.

You face a number of network management domain issues, including how the domains are defined, who is responsible for each domain, what information should be available to each domain, and who has overall responsibilities for the network. For example, a logical way to divide responsibility is to define each country as a separate domain. Each of these logical sites is responsible for performance monitoring, and each forwards information to network headquarters only when there is a problem.

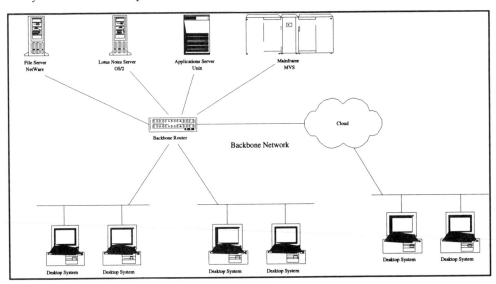

Figure 3-2   Refined High-Level Diagram of an Enterprise Network

Network Control Centers

Create primary and secondary network control centers. The secondary network control center backs up the primary center. For example, the secondary center would take over if the primary center was disabled by an earthquake, flood, hurricane (typhoon), or power blackout. Since each country is an autonomous region, you might establish a primary network control center at each local headquarters. Each needs a backup. A control center in Hong Kong, for example, may serve as the secondary control center for the Asian region.

How you organize primary and secondary control centers will affect your network management platform and the way you configure your management database. Your network management system and its configuration database should support a distributed view of the network. The network management systems in different primary control centers need to share a common database that contains information about the entire network. Not all network management products do this today, but all are expected to do so soon.

Network Security Policies and Strategies

Security is essential for business-critical systems handling sensitive transactions and confidential data. An effective network security strategy revolves around *layered* security countermeasures based on a well-defined security policy. Military planners call this layering *defense in depth.*

Develop a security policy that includes policies for network security Before you write this policy, study and revise (or perhaps create) an overall IT security policy. A security policy identifies sensitive information and its value to your organization (and competitors), potential risks and their probabilities of occurrence, and the required countermeasures and controls.

No matter how many controls and safeguards are in place, total security is impossible. (Just ask Aldrich Ames, formerly of the CIA.) However, risks can be minimized to an acceptable level.

Security policies can affect your capacity to manage a network. For example, your policies will dictate the schedule for full and partial server backups, loading shareware on PCs, copying copyrighted software from application servers, and editing configuration files like CONFIG.SYS, AUTOEXEC.BAT, and Windows INI files.

You need other security-related policies for

- Taking hardware and software inventories
- Prohibiting shared passwords

- Expiration of passwords

You need to evaluate security policies in many areas. Start this evaluation in the beginning, as you will uncover key policy decisions that will affect your design and the products you buy. This is particularly important for network management, where you will want to identify management applications and tools that bring your policies to fruition.

Implementing the Network
Management System   4≡

Before building your enterprise network, you must first establish the vital components of your management infrastructure. Start with a network control center and test lab at the outset. Unfortunately, this is often not the case in many organizations. In fact, most organizations do not have any network management strategy at all. It just "happens"—usually after the network is installed, which is too late. Save your organization time and money (and perhaps your job) by installing the management functions first so that you can provide first-class network service from day one.

Don't be fooled by the flashy brochures and pretty graphics: network management systems are serious business. Installing and configuring a network management system is complex and requires planning and training.

The Network Management Platform

A network management platform is software that provides a set of functions to collect and display information about the devices connected to a distributed network. These functions can manage the network directly, or they can be used indirectly by applications that run on top of the management platform.

Be conservative and buy a standard, well-known network manager, such as SunNet Manager, HP's OpenView, or IBM's NetView. Then, base all of your network management applications on that one management platform. While this might seem obvious to someone who has managed a network before, we have seen too many big sites violate this common sense with expensive consequences. Most third-party applications run on two or more of these platforms.

Selecting a network management platform is only part of the solution. The major platforms continue to evolve. They still lack key features needed to manage large networks effectively. Without a distributed-network management system that gives you a central view of the entire network, you will never gain all the benefits of centralized network management. As your network grows you will be forced to add management stations, each with its own isolated network view. Extra management stations require more staff. Also, information from independent management stations must be correlated manually—not nice when you need to resolve a problem quickly.

Sun, HP, and IBM have all promised to deliver distributed versions of their management platforms—someday; real soon now. With Sun's Solstice Enterprise Management and HP's Tornado, you should be able to configure your different domains to have a common distributed view of the whole network. In the meantime, several companies have developed management systems to process and correlate management information from disparate management systems for large networks: Alcatel's NM-Expert, Objective Systems Integrators' Net Expert, and Command Post from Boole & Babbage, for example. The downside is that these tools use complex expert systems that require extensive customization and programming.

Install your network management software on a hale and hearty workstation running UNIX. Some organizations install their network management software, such as HP OpenView, on a Microsoft Windows-based computer. They usually end up regretting the choice, since the Windows versions usually are not comprehensive. More importantly, Windows itself is not up to the task of handling heavyweight, busy software that runs 24 hours a day, seven days a week.

PCs with Windows may be inexpensive, but they are also cheap. Spend the money on a UNIX workstation. They are built to collect and process large volumes of data, not play games, recalculate spreadsheets, or reboot when one application goes astray.

Network Management Standards

Although it suffers a number of limitations, Simple Network Management Protocol (SNMP) is the protocol of choice in modern network management. SNMP was initially intended as a elementary Band-Aid until the more comprehensive Open Systems Interconnection (OSI) solution could be defined by the International Organization for Standardization (ISO). The TCP/IP-based SNMP, however, became more popular than expected, while OSI failed to gain market share.

SNMP polls network devices directly, which consumes bandwidth. Also, SNMP lacks security, does not support non-TCP/IP protocols, and does not allow network manager-to-manager communications for effective distributed management. Standards committees are looking at enhancements to SNMP. In the meantime, we recommend you use SNMP-based standards and keep a weather eye open for upcoming enhancements. And beware, there are nonstandard versions of SNMP out there.

Look for products that understand the latest version of SNMP, SNMPv2, and take advantage of its special features. It has more information about error and better performance than the original SNMP. For example, with SNMPv2's GetBulk command, you can retrieve more network management information to your network management station with fewer requests and replies, which allows your management station to process the information faster while conserving network bandwidth. However, security is still an issue, but it is being addressed, slowly, by the standards committees.

While this should go without saying, make certain all network hardware communicates with the network management system using SNMP.

Network Management Database

Network management software depends on a database for storing historic information. Until recently, most management platforms offered two unsavory choices: buy their proprietary database or use their favorite commercial database. Today you can buy the database you want: Sybase, Ingress, or Oracle.

Network Management Applications

The network management applications you need depend on the types of network devices you use. Organizations normally acquire their network hardware and management applications from the same supplier For example, many organizations use CiscoWorks and Optivity to manage devices from Cisco Systems and Bay Networks, respectively.

Often, organizations do not configure their network management software to take advantage of its full capabilities. System administrators presiding over these network managers do not realize they are sitting on applications that can automate key configuration, performance, and problem management tasks for almost every network device. The SNMP-collected information includes network utilization by segment, router utilization, number of bad frames by type and network segment, distribution of frame sizes, traffic loads between pairs of nodes, and traffic loads by source or destination. Threshold conditions can also be set to activate warning alarms automatically when problems arise. The management system can display information about the performance and errors in the various devices in both tabular and graphical formats.

We recommend that you implement trend analysis applications for capacity planning. Because the volume of information coming in to a centralized management platform from a large network can get overwhelming, we recommend you invest in other, specialized applications that automate and consolidate statistics collection and analyses. For example, Trendman from Bay Networks collects statistics over time and displays trends for capacity planning. CiscoWorks also offers trend analysis applications.

Other network management applications will depend on your management strategies and policies. The network management platform will support a variety of other applications such as accounting/billing, asset management, and help desk systems.

Network Management Tools

It's a good idea to buy a few protocol analyzers and cable testers while you are out shopping. Although a centralized network management system can diagnose and fix common problems, sometimes the failure is so severe you must access the device or cable directly.

A protocol analyzer decodes data packets so you can analyze them in more detail. The data packets often contain information that helps identify the source of a problem. The important features to look for in a protocol analyzer are:

- Support for the protocols and access methods of your network
- Support for your WAN technologies
- Operates at network speeds so it doesn't drop data packets
- Has a graphical-user interface so it is easy to learn and use
- Easy to program so special test conditions can be set up to isolate difficult problems

(The ability to analyze protocols on multiple ports is also useful, but not a requirement.)

We use the DA-30 protocol analyzer from Wandel & Goltermann extensively because it meets these requirements. We also recommend the Internet Adviser Series from Hewlett-Packard, the LANalyzer Network Analyzer from Network Communications, and Network General's Network Sniffer.

A cable tester is another good diagnostic tool. We recommend the hand-held cable testers from MicroTest and Fluke. Cable testers for Category 5 unshielded twisted-pair (UTP) cables should measure a variety of cable performance characteristics at frequencies up to 100 MHz. Key measurements you should look for in a cable tester are:

- Near-end crosstalk (NEXT)
- Cable length
- Wire mapping (continuity, open circuits and shorts)
- Attenuation
- Impedance
- Capacitance
- Electrical noise

For complex networks with an extensive array of WAN technologies, another useful tool is a network simulator, which can model the performance of your network for different scenarios and costs. Although somewhat expensive, organizations with large networks will find that a simulator is a cost-effective way to test proposed changes. By testing the effects of changes before making them to your network, you can save time and the cost of downtime. For example, you can simulate a new network topology and test new router tables before you actually make the changes in your production network routers. With a network simulator, you also can compare the effects of several changes so you can select the best solution. Being able to perform a what-if analysis, you avoid making multiple changes to your network to test each scenario.

Optimal Performance from Optimal Networks is a Windows-based network simulation package that gets input data from Network General's Network Sniffer. CACI Products' COMNET III is another Windows-based simulation package. We prefer NETSYS from NETSYS Technologies. It is a UNIX-based package that supports a wide variety of network technologies and protocols, including IP, IPX (Internetwork Packet Exchange), and SNA. With NETSYS we can detect a variety of common problems that can arise when configuring large internetworks. It also enables us to identify potential connectivity and performance problems and to simulate link failures.

Test Network

Start your own test lab, consisting of an isolated network where you can experiment with new hardware and software on a collection of your existing network devices. Why? Controlling change in a distributed environment is difficult, since you need to account for so many variables. How will modifications to one part, a new software release or hardware upgrade, for instance, affect others? Run every new networking device and every line of software through your lab before unleashing them on your unsuspecting network.

4

Centralized Network Management System

By consolidating management activities that were once sprinkled across the network, the central network management system supports our successful strategy for centralized control of distributed systems to contain costs while delivering high RAS services.

There is more to building a comprehensive network management system than simply installing a few applications, though. Network management software, such as SunNet Manager, OpenView, CiscoWorks and Optivity, must be configured properly to have full utility. To minimize network operational costs and maximize productivity of the network operating staff, the centralized network management system should deliver management data to mission control, present only relevant information, and automate configuration, performance, and problem management tasks from mission control.

It is surprising how many companies with state-of-the-art network management systems fail to configure and use them properly. In one large insurance company—one that depends on a large network to access mission-critical information —we were requested to review their network design and make recommendations to improve the architecture to run upcoming client/server applications. They had a network management system, so naturally we wanted to see the latest copies of their performance and reliability reports. They couldn't do it. There were none! All they could do was produce a diskette with some ASCII data they collected during some recent tests of their application. Before designing a new one, they better get their current network under control, and fast.

We recommend you develop network management policies and, of course, set your software to enforce these policies. This means configuring your network management system to monitor the key network variables and display important information based on your thresholds and priorities. This will also involve defining responses and resolving unusual information.

Implement your network management domain strategy by configuring your management system to support the different management domains. Ensure that the system displays only relevant network information for each domain and that network administrators can access only the commands they need and no more.

In large networks, filtering out irrelevant management information lifts administrators above the flood of picayune data. Cautiously at first, but aggressively over time, configure the network management system to initiate corrective actions automatically when it detects critical network events. For problems that require human intervention, configure the system to display step-by-step instructions to complete corrective actions. Configure your system to record all corrective actions. This information forms the cornerstone of your private support database.

Ensure that each network administrator understands his or her responsibilities. This means you should define user profiles in the network management system so administrators are only allowed to manage and receive messages for the portions of the network for which they are responsible.

Configure your network management system to log all messages so that you can analyze network traffic patterns and other trends. It also helps if you assign each message a severity code, which indicates the relative importance of events.

A weak area in most network management systems is alarm correlation. It is common for a single incident to set off more than one alarm. With multiple alarms blaring and blinking, it is difficult to isolate an incident's root cause. Suppliers claim they are beefing-up their wares in this area.

Remote Network Management

Remote site management is difficult. Remote sites usually do not have dedicated staffs to install, configure, and monitor equipment, to make upgrades, and to solve problems. You need to compensate by planning carefully how you can provide the same RAS at your far-flung offices as you offer at headquarters.

First, keep your remote networks simple. Easy manageability flows from simplicity. Second, deploy standard configurations, just as you should throughout the organization. Third, build, configure, and test all network equipment at the central site before shipping it for installation at the remote office. And, finally, build and use tools, such as installation scripts, to automate configuration.

Just as NASA has various backups at mission control for space flights, the mission control for your network requires failovers too. What happens if the main link between headquarters and a remote office fails? With some planning, you can be ready to establish "out-of-band" connections to your remote site using modems and ordinary dial-up telephone lines. Most critical network devices, such as servers, routers, hubs, and switches, offer an RS-232 serial port, allowing remote management by way of modem. An alternative is to use an RS-232 port switch, which allows you to use a single remote modem device that can be switched between different devices with RS-232 port connections. However, these switches become a critical point of failure. In our experience, we find they complicate small, simple remote networks. For most sites it is not difficult or expensive to install a few extra modems and telephone lines.

4

Don't forget security for the remote network. You do not want hackers accessing your critical network devices. Ensure any remote management solution has strong security countermeasures built in. We discuss security in greater detail in Chapter 11.

Remote control power switches reset a device, such as a server, PC, or printer. We have used, with good luck, Server Technologies' Sentry and InControl from ARvee Systems.

Flash EPROM (Erasable Programmable Read Only Memory) is another important remote management feature in some internetwork devices that can greatly reduce the time and trouble expended to update and upgrade the network configuration. Because many internetwork devices depend on software, you will need a way to load software updates on remote devices. You may also need to reload the software in remote components if there are problems. With Flash EPROM technology, you have a convenient way to load software to remote devices' memory over the network.

Facilities and Cabling Infrastructure 5≡

Without secure facilities and dependable cabling, your collection of state-of the-art distributed hardware—servers, routers, hubs, switches, and desktop computers—is a waste of money. To build an enterprise network with high RAS, you must find or build spaces for your equipment that are secure, clean, and have sufficient elbowroom, power, ventilation, and lighting.

Wiring Closets and Equipment Rooms

While wiring closets and equipment rooms contain many of the same devices and components, they differ slightly (Figure 5-1). Wiring closets sequester network hubs and distribution panels for the cabling system. Equipment rooms house those devices tended by administrators, such as servers, printers, and test instruments. The distinction between wiring closets and equipment rooms is important because each offers different power, air conditioning, ventilation, security, space, racks, lighting, and other environmental items. Because wiring closets and equipment rooms contain equipment crucial to network RAS, we treat both as miniature data centers.

Layout

Organizations spent fortunes building clean, controlled, and secure data centers to serve their royal mainframes. This was essential since mainframes ran business-critical applications and held precious data. Today, with business-critical applications running over your network, you must also ensure that your equipment rooms and wiring closets, like your data center, are designed properly.

A well-planned layout will, of course, leave plenty of room for devices, but also gives plenty of room for personnel to move around to install equipment and perform routine maintenance and troubleshooting. Important tip: ask your electrician to install twice as many electrical outlets as you think you will need. Double-check the ambient lighting and ventilation, too.

Racks

Racks are essential to ensure that network equipment is installed properly and remains orderly. Don't plop critical components on the floor (we see it happen more often than not.) Most internetworking devices, such as routers, switches, and hubs, fit nicely in standard 19-inch racks. Modular server racks allow you to easily access the console screens and keyboards.

Power Protection

Power problems cause many network ailments. Electrical maladies include voltage drops and surges, complete or partial power loss, and noise. Our recommended tonics include installing voltage regulators, surge suppressors, and uninterruptable power supplies (UPS). The more critical (or expensive) the component, the more you should spend on safeguarding the device. Backbone routers, for example, need UPS's.

A common cause of electrical problems for many large networks is damage from lightning strikes. There are two critical areas to consider to minimize this problem. One is the building's grounding system, which must comply with building codes to ensure that differences in the building ground potential are minimized. Bad ground is common in older buildings. The other critical area of protection involves the use of surge protectors. With single- and multiport surge protectors connected to network equipment, you can divert any electrical surges to ground before they cause any damage.

Structured Cabling System

A number of wireless network products seem to be quite promising technologies.[1] Nonetheless, the vast majority of networks still use physical wires to connect network devices.

Wires, connectors, distribution panels, patch cables, modular outlets, cause half to three-quarters of all network problems. You can make your job much easier by ensuring that your cabling system is installed and functioning properly before you start to install your network devices.

---

1. Robert Metcalfe, inventor of Ethernet, predicted in a recent *Infoworld* column that we'll see ubiquitous wireless computer networks about the same time we see pipeless bathrooms.

Structured cabling systems offer several features that distinguish them from unstructured systems. An ordered system simplifies cable installation and management. Second, the structured cabling system comprises well-defined cable segments, which include the vertical segments that form the backbone network and the horizontal segments that connect desktops. And third, the structured cabling system is configured in point-to-point, or star design.

An unstructured cabling system has no underlying order or well-defined segments. It simply runs from one computer or device to the next in a bus or ring configuration. The cable end depends on the location of the device or computer. If you insert a new computer into the network, or move one, you face some rewiring, which is difficult and expensive.

In structured cabling, each cable connecting a desktop computer to the network has well-defined ends. You can connect and reconnect the segments to construct different cable configurations and make modifications easily without difficult and expensive rewiring. When adding a new desktop or relocating an existing desktop, normally you only need to change the connections at the distribution panels in the wiring closets by using patch cables. This means that your structured cabling system will support your network requirements and technologies today and tomorrow without major (read "expensive") changes.

Cabling

The main components of the structured cabling system are the vertical and horizontal cable segments and the main and intermediate distribution panels (Figure 5-2). The vertical cable segments typically connect a centralized main distribution panel in a building complex to the intermediate distribution panels in the wiring closets on each floor.

The horizontal cable segments connect the desktop computer to the wiring closets in star configurations. Patch cables make cross-connections between the vertical and horizontal cable segments on the distribution panels. This allows you to make changes easily to support different cabling configurations without major rewiring.

Because the vertical cable segments normally connect the wiring closets on different floors in a backbone network, we recommend that you use fiber-optic cables. Fiber-optic cables will support the high-bandwidth technologies you will need for your backbone.

5

Cabling Standards

The industry-leading EIA/TIA (Electronic Industries Association and Telecommunications Industry Association)[2] publishes cabling standards. The standards also give guidelines for building structured cabling systems, including cabling topologies, cable types for different network speeds, and the performance specifications for cables and connectors. Before you start a major cabling project you should be familiar with the four significant EIA/TIA standards.

The first standard is EIA/TIA-568A, which guides the building of cabling systems for different types of networks. EIA/TIA-568A is mainly concerned with the performance characteristics for twisted-pair and fiber-optic cables.

EIA/TIA-569 defines guidelines for construction within and between buildings to support the cabling system. It describes wiring closet layouts and space in wiring conduits.

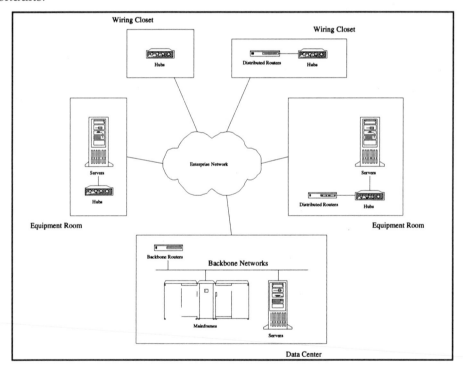

Table 5-1   Data Center, Equipment Rooms, and Wiring Closets

---

2.   To get more information about the EIA/TIA standards, access the EIA Web site at http://www.eia.org

EIA/TIA-606 outlines guidelines for managing a building's network cable infrastructure. It specifies how to label and color-code cable components.

EIA/TIA-607 describes a building's electrical ground requirements.

There are variations of the EIA/TIA 568 standard. We generally recommend 568B. Although the EIA/TIA recommends 568A, most cabling system products conform to 568B. The primary difference is the connector pinout configuration, which is the way the pairs of wire in a UTP cable are connected to the pins in an RJ-45 connector. The 568B standard is sometimes referred to as the AT&T specification because AT&T has been using the same pinout configuration—called 258A—in its cabling system for many years. 568B is used more widely for this reason. It doesn't make much difference whether you use 568A or 568B, as long as you select one and stick with it.

Types of Cables

We subscribe to the tenets of the Commercial Building Wiring Standard—a.k.a. the EIA/TIA-568 standard for structured cabling. The EIA/TIA-568 standard specifies a variety of cable types, including UTP, fiber-optic, shielded twisted-pair (STP), and coaxial cables. Data-grade UTP and fiber-optic cables are the threads of choice to spin reliable and inexpensive enterprise webs. The 100-ohm UTP cables, each with four cable pairs, are lightweight, easy to work with, and relatively inexpensive.

Several categories of data-grade UTP cable are defined for different network requirements. With a smaller number of twists per foot, Category 3 UTP works best on slower networks like standard 10 megabits-per-second (Mbps) Ethernet. Category 4 and 5 UTP cables have more twists per foot, so they are designed for networks that operate at 16 and 100 megabits per second, respectively. For production-quality enterprise networks today, we recommend that you install Category 5 UTP cables that will support the 100 megabits-per-second networking technologies. If you do not need the high bandwidth now, you will soon.

EIA/TIA-568 is the official specification for 62.5/125-micron fiber-optic cable. Although it is more expensive than twisted pair, fiber-optic cable has distinct advantages. Using light pulses rather than electrical signals, fiber-optic cable is immune to most types of electrical and radio interference. It does not broadcast radiation, either, and is nearly tamper-proof. (Taps, legal or not, are not accomplished with simple alligator clips.) This makes fiber-optic cabling the ideal choice for high-speed, long-spanning networks.

Fiber-optic cables aren't perfect, though. Fiber requires skill and expensive tools to splice. And, as you might expect from a thin, glass-like plastic filament, fiber is susceptible to stress and breakage if you give it a sharp bend.

5

The EIA/TIA-568 standard specifies 150-ohm STP cable. Unlike common coaxial cable, STP cable has an additional shield to protect the network data from electrical interference. That makes STP cables heavy, stiff to work with, and more expensive than Category 5 UTP. STP's half-inch diameter occupies much limited space in wiring conduits and is difficult to bend around tight corners. STP cables have been used mostly in Token Ring and SNA networks. Unless STP is already installed, we prefer Category 5 UTP and fiber.

The EIA/TIA-568 standard also specifies 50-ohm coaxial cable, commonly used in 10Base-2 Ethernet networks. Coax and STP share many of the same advantages and disadvantages. Being heavier and more rigid, coax is more difficult to install and maintain than UTP.

Pre-engineered Cable Systems

With EIA/TIA-compliant cable and connectors, you can roll your own structured cabling system. Or, you can buy pre-built systems from a cable supplier. In the past, pre-engineered structured systems from the major suppliers worked with their equipment only. (Can you say "proprietary?")

Today, most structured cabling systems from the major suppliers, such as AT&T, Northern Telecom, Digital Equipment, and IBM, comply with EIA/TIA-568 standards and work with the variety of open systems networking equipment. For a large enterprise, we recommend you use a pre-engineered system to ensure that high quality components are used everywhere. *Caveat emptor*: Suppliers claiming to comply with EIA/TIA-568 may not meet the entire standard. Review a vendor's specifications closely, and look for a certification from the Underwriters Laboratories (UL).

Cable Installation Guidelines

Unless you are thoroughly familiar with the EIA/TIA standards and have extensive experience in installing and maintaining cabling systems, we recommend that you enlist the services of a professional cabling contractor. Because your cable system can be a source of costly, difficult-to-solve problems, spend the extra money to make sure your system is installed properly the first time. It will be well worth it. Your first job, then, is to find an experienced cabling contractor. Once contracted, you need to work closely with the contractor to ensure the cabling system complies with the specifications outlined in the EIA/TIA standards.

As mentioned earlier in this chapter, electromagnetic interference presents a vexing problem. The EIA/TIA standards define a minimum distance between cables and other electronic devices (power cables, motors, elevators, fluorescent lighting, electronic switches, motors, generators, copy machines, and so on.) for various levels of electromagnetic radiation. You should also ensure that cable segment lengths are within the maximum limitations specified in the EIA/TIA standards. The horizontal Category 5 cable segments between the wiring closets and modular outlets near the desktop should not exceed 90 meters in length. Patch cables that connect your desktops to the modular outlet should not exceed 3 meters.

Another potential problem arises from improperly attached connectors. It is very important that UTP cables are not untwisted when you attach connectors. You may not notice the problem until you try to transmit data at 100 megabits per second.

Use your high-quality, hand-held cable tester (Chapter 4) to test all cables as they are installed. In addition to each cable segment, each channel should be tested end-to-end to ensure that the connectors, patch cables, and distribution panels are all functioning properly. Important twisted-pair cable operating characteristics you need to consider are attenuation, near-end crosstalk, and electrical noise.

Take the time to label each cable properly during construction, since it will be almost impossible to do it accurately later on.

Install more cable segments than you think you need. We often find that these extra cables are lifesavers when one cable segment fails. It is not uncommon for Category 5 cables to fail due to the pressure exerted by the connector termination.

We recommend that you install at least two Category 5 UTP cables between every desktop and a wiring closet. In many installations, we recommend three, so there are connections for other devices like printers, telephones, and fax machines. For the vertical cable segments that form the backbone, we recommend that you install about 20 percent extra fiber-optic cables.

5

Backbones and subnets 6

With your facilities, cables, and network management systems in place (many places, actually) you now can start building a backbone network and connecting your client and server subnets to the enterprise network.

Topologies

One of three topologies defines the physical layout of one or more portions of your network: bus, ring, and star (Figure 6-1). Ethernet uses a bus topology where each node is a link in a chain. A bus topology is comparably economical, since it requires less cable and fewer devices. Though, like a chain, a problem at any link breaks the whole network.

Figure 6-1   Common Network Topologies

It also is difficult to add nodes and make modifications to a bus network. To insert a new node, for instance, you must either bore a hole through the cable with 10Base5 (a.k.a. thick Ethernet) or cut the cable and insert a T-connector with 10Base2 (a.k.a. thin Ethernet). Adding or moving devices in a bus network often requires recabling to ensure the wires run near each network node.

Although bus-style 10Base2 and 10Base5 networks don't work nicely as a structured cabling system, there are some cases where they are the right choice. For example, if you have a working 10Base5 network in place and you don't expect to make any modifications soon, it is probably okay, and certainly less expensive, to leave well enough alone.

Token Ring- and FDDI-based networks use a ring topology in which the node connections form a closed loop. As with a bus topology, ring reliability is limited because a failure at any point affects the entire network. It is also difficult to add and move ring-connected nodes.

We prefer a star network topology. It is also the basis for structured cabling systems. Although it requires more cable and a special, central hub (which we discuss later), a star makes it easy to change and manage nodes, which will probably save you money in the long run. A failure at any segment of the star (except the hub, of course) is isolated, so other portions of the network continue unabated. Also, you can easily add and move nodes without affecting the others.

10BaseT Ethernet uses the star topology, as do most Token Rings. For 10BaseT, the hub that forms the center of the star sends the data transmitted on one segment to all segments, so all nodes see the data as if they were on a bus. For Token Ring networks, the hub emulates a ring passing data from one node to the next.

Access Methods

One of the main functions of the data link layer, the second layer in the OSI model[1] (Table 6-1), is access control. Media access control (MAC) ensures all nodes share the network cable in an orderly manner. The differences between Ethernet, Token Ring, and FDDI are their topologies and access control methods. Carrier Sense Multiple Access/Collision Detect (CSMA/CD) is the access method for Ethernet, and Token Ring and FDDI use variations on token passing.

Layer Number	Layer Name	Main Functions
7	Application	Network applications such as remote login, file transfer, or World Wide Web
6	Presentation	Translates between different data formats
5	Session	Manages sessions between applications
4	Transport	Provides reliable end-to-end transport, using sequence numbers and acknowledgments
3	Network	Uses network addresses to select network routes between two systems
2	Data Link	Builds data packets and uses physical addresses to transfer the packets across a network segment
1	Physical	Defines the characteristics of the physical medium to transfer binary signals

Table 6-1   The OSI Model for Networking

---

1. The popular seven-layer OSI model describes a common framework for network devices to communicate. More information about the OSI model and related standards is available from ISO's Web site at http://www.iso.ch.

CSMA/CD

Except for minor differences in frame structures, Ethernet and IEEE 802.3 are identical. Both use CSMA/CD, in which each node listens to the data traffic on the network. If there is none, any node is free to send its own data. While sending its data, a node also listens to the network. If it detects a collision (more than one node attempting to send data at the same time), the nodes will pause before attempting to send data again.

Token Passing

Token passing sends a special packet, called a token, around the ring like a hot potato. The token asks each node if it has data to share. If so, the node inserts its data into a frame that contains the addresses of the sender and receiver nodes. The frame is attached to the token, which proceeds to the next node in the ring until it arrives at the destination.

A receiving node, upon recognizing its address within the frame, copies the data and sends the frame back to the original sender. The sending node is responsible for stripping received data from the frame and releasing the token for use by others.

Note that a problem at any node can waylay or damage the frame, which afflicts the entire network. Token Ring and FDDI employ different methods to handle wayward nodes and other societal problems.

Internetworking 101

Enterprise networks comprise local area networks connected to each other and to a backbone with ties to the entire organization. To accomplish the configuration means dividing the network into logical, manageable segments, which restricts local network traffic to local nodes, and avoids the bandwidth-debilitating effects of redundant network traffic. (Imagine creating one big ring from east to west coast, not to mention the light-years response times if you had to pass a token to each of thousands of nodes across the globe!) To segment the network yet at the same time tie all those segments together into an enterprise platform, you need to employ a number of specialized devices, some "intelligent," some not. Repeaters, hubs, bridges, routers, and switches not only link computers, they also make the so-called internetwork possible.

Repeaters and Hubs

A repeater, the simplest interconnecting device, works to extend the size of a network by mindlessly amplifying all data packets whose electrical signals may have become attenuated by a long cable segment. Because data packets must travel from one end of an Ethernet network to the other within a certain time, the

Ethernet standard limits the network's length and the number of repeaters. Since each repeater introduces delay, you can have only four per Ethernet network before exceeding the time limit.

Hubs are fancy repeaters. The terms *structured cabling*, *star topology*, and *network hub* are almost synonymous. Like the hub of a wheel, a network hub is the central device to which all nodes connect, forming the shape of a star. The hub consists of a box of electronics to transform the star-wired network into a bus-like Ethernet segment or a ring-like Token Ring or FDDI. Because all network data traffic passes through the hub, it is also a key point for network management.

Hubs can be chassis based or stackable and are classified as managed or unmanaged. Most enterprise networks mix all four types.

Chassis-based Hubs

Chassis-based hubs let you build complex networks by inserting Ethernet, Token Ring, and FDDI modules in a single chassis with a fixed number of slots. Each module also can have connections for different types of cables. If you need more ports to connect network devices, you simply insert additional modules. Various modules often can be mixed and matched within the same chassis to build different configurations. And you can add management modules that collect and process information about the data traffic flowing through the hub. Some chassis-based hubs boast fault tolerance with redundant power supplies and fans. While chassis-based hubs are flexible, they are also expensive.

Another issue is wire management. Some chassis can accommodate modules that support hundreds of connections. Terminating that many cables at a single device in wiring closet gets messy fast. If you make dozens of connections to a chassis-based hub, we recommend that you use telephone-style connectors. One telco connector supports a dozen connections to a punchdown block, a small distribution box where you make cross-connections between the wires going to the hub and the wires going to the larger distribution panel in the wiring closet.

Stackable Hubs

A stackable hub is an inexpensive alternative to a chassis-based hub. Like a modular stereo unit to which you may later add a turntable, CD drive, tuner, and so on, you add network hubs to a collection of stackable hubs as needed. That way, you build the network in smaller increments with a correspondingly incremental capital investment. Stackable hubs offer a lower price per port than chassis-based hubs, yet provide the same or better levels of fault tolerance because each stackable module sports its own power supply.

Hub modules are interconnected through their backplanes so they operate as one repeater unit. This enhances manageability because one stackable management module manages the entire stack. An alternative would be to daisy-chain the hubs together through their network ports, but this has some disadvantages. First, it uses limited network ports, which you want to use to connect your computers. Also, each hub would be a separate repeater, which introduces network delay. CSMA/CD limits the number of daisy-chained hubs to four. This is not a constraint in a stacked configuration.

Integrated Hubs

Hubs can do more than act as intelligent repeaters and collect network traffic information. You can add a variety of other modules into a chassis-based hub so that all network functions are integrated in one device. You have a choice of adding Ethernet, Token Ring, and FDDI switching to the hub, as well as routing and remote access capabilities. Before buying a hub that does everything, you should decide if the extra functions are worth the money.

For a remote office with no support staff, integrated hubs are a smart buy. One hub combining different functions is easier to manage than the inverse. You simply identify the failing module and replace it, or you send someone to replace the entire hub.

Integrated hubs save you money and space, since all components share the same chassis and power supplies. On the other hand, integrated hubs are less flexible and usually aren't appropriate for large networks with on-site network administrators and analysts. Big sites may find that purchasing hubs, routers, and switches separately offers more bang for the buck.

Spanning Networks

Bridges and routers control the flow of data and let you divide a large network into smaller, less traffic-congested segments. The network in Figure 6-2 is divided into three segments interconnected by two bridges (or routers). It is theoretically possible to build an enterprise-wide network that connects all computers and devices to one LAN. This, of course, would make network administration easy and inexpensive. But as we mentioned earlier, network traffic would quickly slow to an electronic rendition of "molasses in January." Bridges break big networks into smaller, interconnected network segments. Routers do the same thing, but are smarter. They divide a network into what are called subnets, each with its own network-layer address. Routers let you interconnect subnets to build larger internetworks, segment a large network into smaller, interconnected subnets, and control the flow of data across the backbone.

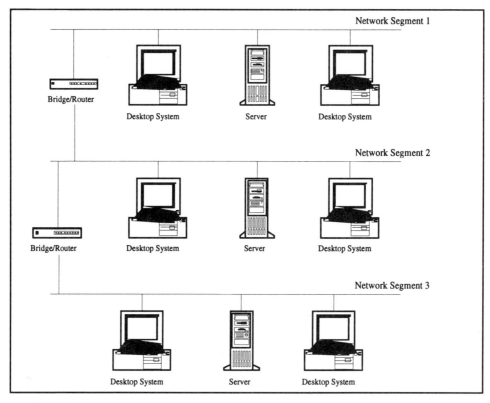

Figure 6-2   Interconnected Network Segments

To achieve reasonable network performance, you need to confine routine local traffic and broadcasts made by devices seeking network resources and services to their logical network neighbors.

For example, TCP/IP nodes commonly use Address Resolution Protocol (ARP) broadcasts to learn the MAC address of a node with a known IP address. Nodes use MAC addresses to send data packets to another node in the same Ethernet or Token Ring segment. To determine a destination node's MAC address, the sending node sends a broadcast packet, called an ARP request, to all the nodes on the subnet. Every node on the subnet will process the ARP request, but only the node with the given IP address will respond with its MAC address. If you don't limit the number of nodes on a segment, the din of ARP and other broadcasts will clearly become a preoccupation for all nodes, so much so that they'll be able to do little else.

Bridges and routers differ in the way they control data flow. You may or may not care what distinguishes a bridge from a router. If you don't, all you need to know is that routers are more flexible (and expensive) and work better for large networks. The Internet, for example, is the world's largest collection of routers.

While there are well-defined differences in the classical definitions of bridges and routers, in actual practice it is difficult to define the boundary between many of the internetworking products on the market. This is made more complicated with the emergence of another interconnecting device—the switch (Chapter 10). Bridges and switches typically operate at layer 2 of the OSI Network Model, while routers operate at layer 3. Some bridges and switches, however, perform some layer 3 functions.

Bridges

The main difference between bridges and routers is the way they forward data packets from one network to another. Bridges use MAC addressees, which are physical addresses assigned to each network device. The MAC address is hardwired into each device's network adapter. A bridge does not examine the content of the data packet, so it is not aware of layer 3 (IP) network addresses.

Generally, a bridge is a node on each of two network segments, acting as a relatively dumb access gate. It works by examining every data packet that travels on the network on either side of the bridge. In each data packet is the MAC address of the destination, which the bridge compares with an internal table of addresses for the incoming side. (Bridges automatically build tables of network device addresses on each segment by examining the source addresses of the data packets.) If a match occurs, the bridge ignores the packet. Otherwise, the bridge forwards the packet, presuming it was destined for the opposite side.

As with repeaters, we recommend you avoid building a big network with bridges and restrict their use to the workgroup level of your network architecture hierarchy. Bridges lack the ability to handle IP addresses, so they must examine every packet on each network, rather than just those data packets addressed to the opposite side. It is easy for bridges to overload and collapse unless restricted to very local use.

While many bridges now employ filters to minimize network broadcasts, they still pass certain unwanted broadcasts across the network, which affects the overall performance of the network. For example, TCP/IP depends on broadcast

6

messages to locate network nodes before transmitting data. NetWare servers use broadcasts to announce their presence to the network. Bridges propagate these messages throughout the network creating broadcast storms.

In addition to consuming network bandwidth, broadcasts also affect the performance of clients and servers. Every time a node broadcasts a message, most computers must interrupt whatever they are doing to assess whether they should process the message.

Moreover, bridges are ignorant of the network layout, so they can't make efficient routing decisions, which limits your potential network configurations. For example, you cannot construct networks with loops, so say goodbye to multiple paths between two locations. Bridges ignore redundant links in your network and can't use them for extra capacity or reliability.

Bridges come in four flavors. The most common is the transparent bridge, which connects two or more networks using the same technology. For example, a transparent bridge connects two Ethernet networks. By contrast, a translational bridge connects two incompatible networks, such as an Ethernet to Token Ring.

Source route bridges connect Token Ring networks using source routing protocols. Source route bridges process explorer packets that are broadcast by nodes waiting to send data. Each bridge and Token Ring is assigned a unique number. As explorer packets travel though the network, they update the Routing Information Field (RIF) in the packet headers with the number of the Token Ring networks and bridges they traverse. When the destination node receives the explorer packet it returns the packet to the sending node with the correct route in the RIF.

The encapsulation bridge connects two network of the same technology using an intermediate network based on a different technology. For example, you can use encapsulation bridges to connect two Ethernet networks across an FDDI backbone.

You should also ensure that the bridges you use in your enterprise network comply with the spanning tree algorithm (STA). As described in the IEEE 802.1d standard, STA defines how bridges communicate so they can detect and logically eliminate any loops in your networks. With STA you can build reliability and availability into your bridged enterprise network. Without loops it would be impossible to build redundancy between the bridges. Sending special packets between bridges, STA can determine if a connection between two bridges fails. Using redundant connections that were logically eliminated in the original spanning tree, STA reconfigures a new spanning tree to bypass the problem.

Routers

As you might expect, routers allow you to build networks using a larger variety of configurations. You can build fully meshed networks so you can take advantage of multiple links between locations. Utilizing several links as one logical link, you can enhance performance and reliability. They do so by acting as an intelligent gatekeeper for one or more discrete subnetworks.

Unlike bridges, routers examine the data packets' contents. Routers use the ISO Model's layer 3 network addresses in the packet headers to determine the best way to route the data through the network. Each router interface has its own network address, so routers examine only the data packets that are addressed to them. Because routers are protocol dependent, they must understand the protocols on your network. Some routers understand only one or two protocols such as TCP/IP and IPX, whereas others understand ten or more.

Upon receiving a packet to forward to another network, the router must decide which interface to use. Many routers will have tens of interfaces or more. If there

Multiple network segments (high densities)
Multiple network topologies (Ethernet, Token Ring, FDDI, etc.)
Multiple serial ports
IP and IPX routing
Transparent, translational, and source-route bridging
Distance vector (RIP and IPX RIP) and link state and enhanced (OSPF, NLSP, and EIGRP) routing support
WAN protocols (SLIP, PPP, HDLC, X.25, Frame Relay)
Access control lists
Load balancing
Custom queuing
Priority queuing
Dial-on-demand routing
Compression
Encryption
Hot-standby routing protocol
Telnet access
SNMP MIB II support
Flash EPROM for software updates
Network management applications

Table 6-2   Essential Router Features

are several possible interfaces, the router must select the best one by using some combination of metrics, including cost, speed, and availability.

If a link is unavailable due to an outage or congestion, the router can determine the next best alternate path. The router uses a routing table that holds a map of the network containing links between different locations. Routers also provide a variety of ways to manage traffic and control its flow. Because routers understand the upper-layer network protocols and examine the contents of data packets, they can filter data packets according to protocols and fields within the protocols. This is why routers are often used as parts of security firewalls (Chapter 11), which restrict network traffic to authorized users.

While many large networks combine bridges and routers, we recommend that you use routers for their flexibility and manageability. All router makers claim to follow standards. None guarantee complete interoperability between routers from different suppliers. Avoid building large heterogeneous router networks, and limit the number of router suppliers.

Some internetworking products are designed for large enterprise networks, whereas other routers are intended for branch office or departmental networks. When you evaluate internetwork devices, such as routers for your network, keep your organization's needs paramount. Important criteria you should consider include performance, reliability, fault tolerance, network protocols, routing protocols, the ability to select the best network path efficiently, expansion, migration strategies to faster bandwidths and emerging technologies, manageability, ease of use, and security.

We summarize these networking features in Table 6-2.

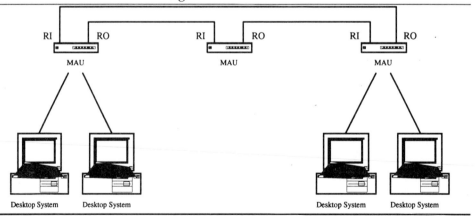

Figure 6-3   Interconnected Token Ring MAUs

General Network Design Rules

You've got all the parts. Now what? How do you decide the overall length of cable, the number of repeaters, and so forth? The authority for designing Ethernet and Token Ring networks are the IEEE 802.3 and 802.5 standards, respectively. Design rules for Fast Ethernet networks are also defined by the IEEE. For FDDI, the design rules are described in the ANSI X3T9.5 standards. You should also consult your suppliers' documentation when designing networks, as many standards-compliant products may suffer peculiarities or nonstandard features.

To ensure that all your network devices detect collisions properly, Ethernet networks must conform with certain design rules, such as the maximum network diameter (length) and the number of delay-causing repeaters. The maximum lengths for 10Base5 and 10Base2 segments are 500 and 185 meters, respectively. Using four repeaters, you can extend a 10Base5 and 10Base2 network to 2,500 and 2,000 meters, respectively. For 10BaseT, it is important that the cable between the hub and a node totals less than 100 meters. As with 10Base2 and 10Base5, you cannot connect more than four 10BaseT hubs in series. If you need to extend an Ethernet network over a greater distance, use fiber-optics instead of wire.

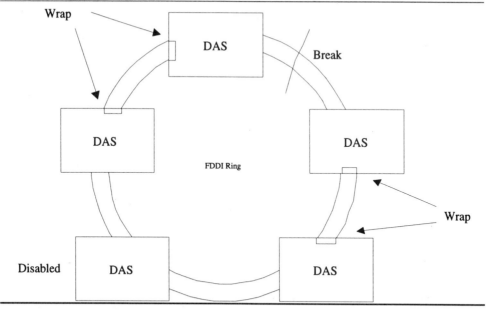

Figure 6-4   Wrap Around on an FDDI Network

Token Ring vendors heeded the clarion call to innovate. As a result, products from different suppliers sport different electrical characteristics, which affect the maximum length of the cables you can install. Consult vendor documentation for additional guidance.

Although Token Ring operates like a ring using token passing, physically it is a star; a Multistation Access Unit (MAU) forms the center. It provides point-to-point connections to servers and desktops. Each MAU also has special ports—ring-in (RI) and ring-out (RO)—that connect to other MAUs (Figure 6-3).

Operating at 100 megabits per second, FDDI uses two fiber-optic cables in a ring. As with Ethernet, modern, multimode, fiber-optic cables let you stretch an FDDI network to several kilometers. Data normally traverses the primary ring, while the secondary ring waits in the wings. Some hubs use the primary and secondary rings to attain an aggregate data rate of 200 megabits per second.

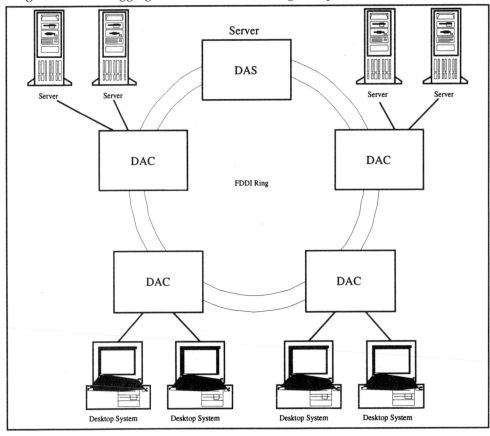

Figure 6-5   FDDI Network with Dual-Attached Concentrators

Dual Attached Stations (DAS) take advantage of FDDI's wraparound capability. A DAS could be a router, server. or desktop system, that connects both to the primary and secondary rings. In the normal operating mode, when there is a break in the primary ring (Figure 6-4), data will automatically wrap around to the secondary cable to bypass the break and maintain connectivity to the other nodes. If you increase the number of nodes on the FDDI rings, it is more likely that a break will occur at more than one place. This causes the FDDI ring to be segmented.

Avoid connecting desktops and servers directly to the FDDI ring. Desktops and some servers are shut down frequently, causing breaks in the ring. A better solution is to include FDDI hubs. As illustrated in Figure 6-5, four Dual-Attached Concentrators (DAC), or FDDI hubs, connect to both FDDI rings. A DAC

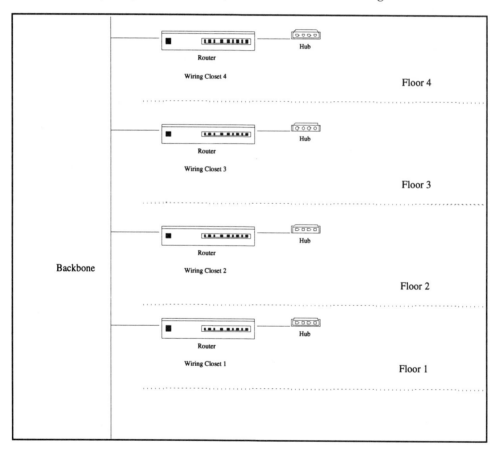

Figure 6-6   Distributed Backbone Network

6

provides backup, using FDDI's wraparound capability, in case a cable breaks. Other nodes are added to the hubs using a single cable, so they are called Single Attached Stations (SAS).

Designing the Backbone Network

Because the backbone network consolidates the data traffic from many subnets, you must ensure your backbone network is reliable and scalable and, most importantly, offers sufficient capacity. Rather than lashing together the networks in your enterprise in a tangled web, use a backbone to provide structure. While we distinguish distributed, centralized, segmented, hierarchical, and meshed backbones, the enterprise backbone network will most likely offer elements of each.

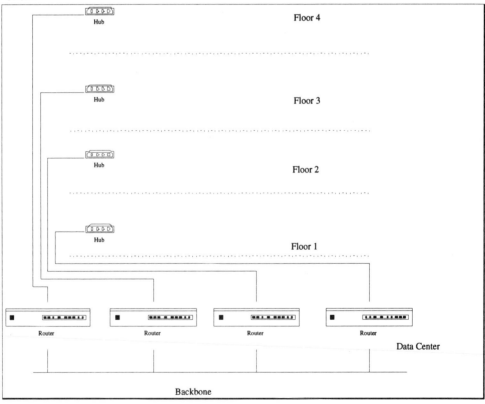

Figure 6-7   Centralized Backbone Network

Distributing the Backbone

The backbone in Figure 6-6 interconnects all the networks in a building complex. Using small routers on each floor, you can construct a backbone network that connects the networks throughout the building. From one perspective, this distributed backbone configuration is highly reliable. If one backbone router fails, only a small portion of the backbone network goes dark. However, it is difficult to manage complex internetwork devices when they are spread throughout a large building.

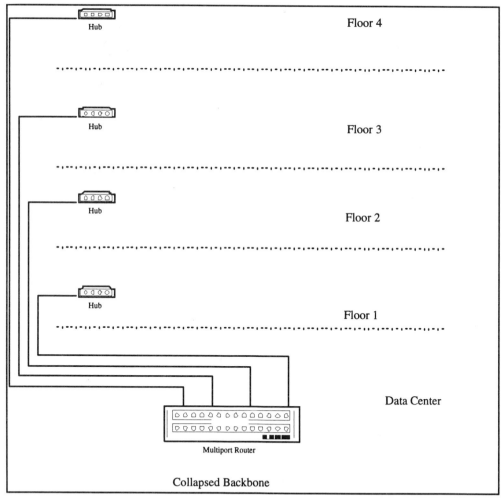

Figure 6-8   Centralized Collapsed Backbone Network

6

Centralizing the Backbone

Leverage the skills of your centralized network staff and improve network manageability by centralizing all backbone routers in your data center (Figure 6-7). You can even extend the concept of centralized routers a bit further.

By collapsing the smaller, centralized routers into a single, multiport router (Figure 6-8), you build a backbone that's easier to manage. While two heads are better than one, two (or more) routers can be a headache to maintain. A collapsed backbone also offers better performance. In effect, the backbone network is the router's backplane, which can operate at gigabits per second (Gbps). The disadvantage of this collapsed configuration is the single point of failure. If your backbone router fails, you lose your entire network.

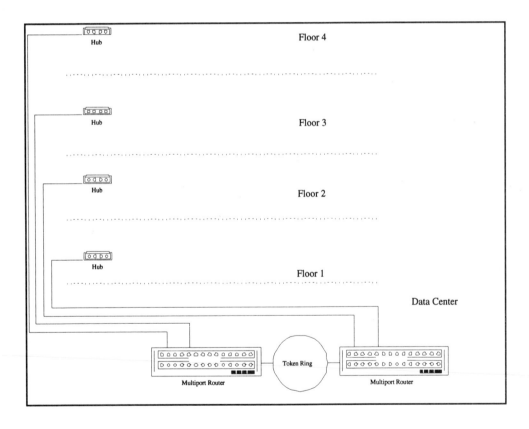

Figure 6-9   Segmented Backbone Network with a Single Token Ring

Segmented Backbone

We don't recommend the polar extremes of either anarchic dispersal or fascist centralization of backbone networks. The essence of design is to strike a creative balance, building on the strengths of each element. We recommend you use the segmented backbone configuration in Figure 6-9, where two collapsed backbone routers are connected through a Token Ring backbone segment. In this configuration, the Token Ring segment is a critical point of failure, but you can simply add more Token Ring segments to improve reliability.

The backbone network in Figure 6-10 comprises three router segments, three Token Ring segments and a wide area network. Using a segmented backbone configuration, you have a structured and modular backbone network, which gives you an incremental way to add redundancy, increase capacity, and extend the backbone as required. For example, in many large networks, Token Ring can't carry a backbone's burden, so you can replace the Token Ring segments with faster technologies with an FDDI or ATM segment (Chapter 10).

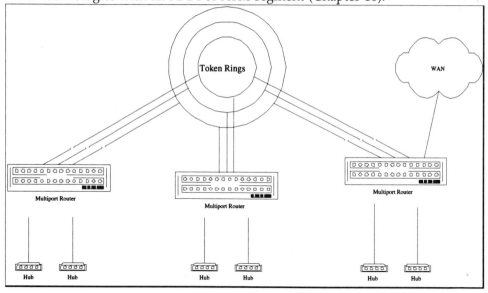

Figure 6-10   Segmented Backbone Network with Three Token Rings

Hierarchical Backbone

By adding wide-area segments, you can extend your backbone network to remote offices anywhere on earth. We enjoy a wide range of WAN choices to build the wide area segments of backbones. Like the backbones in your building, the wide-area backbone segments provide a structured yet flexible way to connect your remote networks and form the key components of your network architecture.

For large networks, you can view the WAN architecture as a hierarchy of backbone segments, as in Figure 6-11. We connect small remote networks to tertiary backbone segments, using slower and less expensive wide area technologies such as analog lines and X.25 packet switching. The tertiary

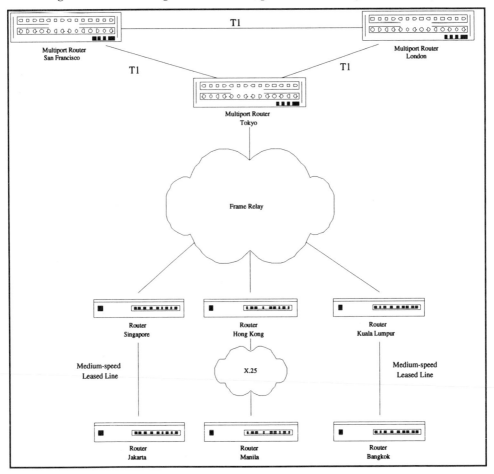

Figure 6-11   Hierarchical Wide-Area Backbone Network

segments and larger remote networks are connected to the secondary segments, using faster technologies. The secondary segments eventually link to the primary high-speed backbone.

Large building and campus network architectures have a three-level hierarchy (Figure 6-12) comprising distribution networks that provide high-speed server connectivity, lower-speed workgroup networks that connect the desktops, and a core backbone network that interconnects the distribution and workgroup levels.

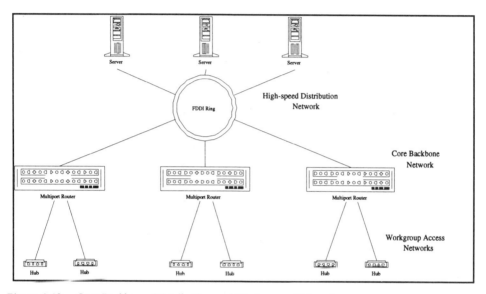

Figure 6-12   Core Backbone, Distribution and Workgroup Networks

Dividing a large network into a hierarchy makes it easier to manage. A hierarchy also makes the network more scalable. Think of the international telephone network. If it wasn't divided into a hierarchy defined by country codes, area codes, and exchanges, it would not be worldwide and would be impossible to manage.

With a well-defined hierarchy, you can address the unique requirements of each level. This allows you to select cost-effective solutions for each level without affecting nodes connected to the other levels. For example, you can implement fast 100 megabits-per-second technologies in the distribution level to provide high-speed server connections without affecting the desktop systems in the workgroup level where 10 megabits per second is often sufficient.

In the core backbone level where you require data traffic management and broadcast control, you can use routers and LAN switches to improve performance in the other levels. Similarly, you can incorporate ATM in the primary WAN backbone without affecting the secondary and tertiary levels, where frame relay or analog leased lines may be the only available and better solutions. In Chapter 10, we describe how to enhance and optimize your enterprise network by using faster technologies and switching in different levels of the network hierarchy.

Meshed Backbone

The best way to improve network reliability is to add redundancy. Using a meshed network configuration, you can build a reliable backbone network. It is common to build wide-area backbone networks by using a partially meshed configuration like the one in Figure 6-13. If one links fails, there are still alternate paths between each pair of nodes. With a fully meshed network that connects each node to every other node, you can add more redundancy. However, you need to determine if the incremental increase in reliability is worth the cost of the extra links. This depends on your applications and service objectives.

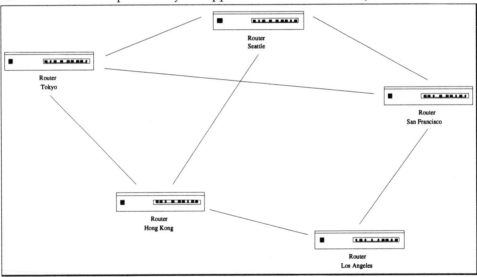

Figure 6-13   Partially Meshed Wide-Area Backbone Network

The Proof

We have implemented a number of successful—that is, high RAS—collapsed backbone networks in large complexes. In one case, the network supports an international financial institution with its headquarters in Southeast Asia. The network connects more than 2,000 desktops, mostly PCs, in a large building spanning 10 floors. It also provides access to a variety of servers that include a mainframe, 20 NetWare file servers, 15 OS/2-based Lotus Notes servers, and various UNIX systems running AIX, HP-UX, and Solaris.

Collapsed Core Backbone

Two large multiport routers, centralized in the data center, form the core of a collapsed backbone in the building. Each router offers four Token Ring and 18 Ethernet ports. The two multiport routers connect through four backbone Token Rings—each providing backup to the other.

Distribution Networks

The Token Rings that connect the two core backbone routers are the distribution networks that connect the servers. This company houses all servers in the data center where they connect to the distribution backbone Token Rings. With the servers ensconced in the data center, the company ensures the servers stay safe and sound.

Workgroup Networks

The workgroups are connected to Ethernets—usually two Ethernet workgroups on each floor are connected to the core backbone. Ethernet workgroup networks are composed of intelligent hubs. Using shared 10BaseT, the desktops are connected to the nearest wiring closets in star-wired topologies.

This solution, based on well-established and proven technologies, is simple yet very effective for many companies.

6

Extending the Network

7

By its very definition, an enterprise network extends beyond the confines of one building to span campuses and branch offices. The main problem with stretching your network, though, is LAN-WAN integration. WANs operate at slower speeds, use different protocols, and are based on different technologies than LANs. Although WAN protocols are designed to use limited bandwidth efficiently, they are still very expensive to operate.

A tough, WAN-building job is weighing the various services offered by the telephone companies. You need to analyze your data traffic patterns regarding each WAN alternative and factor in the cost of each. Each WAN offering boasts a confusing price list (called a *tariff* in the trade), which changes frequently.

Flexibility is key. We often combine several technologies, including dedicated T1 lines, ISDN, Asynchronous Transfer Mode (ATM), and Frame Relay. The relative differences between the various WAN technologies are summarized in Table 7-1.

	Dial-up	Dedicated Lines	ISDN	X.25	Frame Relay
Switched	Circuit	No	Circuit	Packet PVC/SVC	Packet PVC
Performance	Low	Medium	Medium	Low to Medium	Medium to High
Bandwidth-on-demand	No	No	Yes	Yes	Yes
Bursty data	No	No	No	Yes	Yes
Any-to-any connectivity	Yes	No	Yes	Yes	Yes
Availability	High	High	Low	High	Medium
Manageability	Low to Medium	High	Medium	Medium	Medium to High
Cost	Low to High	High	Medium	Medium	Low

Table 7-1   WAN Comparisons

Analog Connections

For most remote offices, analog data transmission by way of modems is the cheapest WAN option. It's also the slowest, but with modern, speedy, and reliable modems, throughput is not always a great concern. We typically use high-speed (28.8 kilobits per second uncompressed) modems with ordinary telephone lines to connect remote offices around the world.

For TCP/IP networks, the two common standards for connecting modems to a local network serial line are SLIP (Serial Line IP) and PPP (Point-to-Point Protocol). SLIP is the older of the two and offers asynchronous dial-up connections. SLIP does not provide error correction, so TCP/IP applications that require low-level error correction will not work very well. PPP offers a better alternative by supporting asynchronous and synchronous connections, error-correction, and the ability to use multiple high-level protocols, such as TCP/IP and IPX.

Dedicated Digital Lines

With the price of dedicated, T1 digital lines falling, we see more digital WANs deployed to carry both data and voice traffic. Integrating data and voice over a single T1 can save you money, but you need to consider several design issues.

Multiplexers combine voice and data into a single stream of bits. At 1.544 megabits per second, a T1 line can carry about two dozen, 64 kilobits-per-second (Kbps) voice channels. If you do not need a full T1, you can lease a fractional T1 for less cost by leasing 64, 128, or 256 kilobits-per-second segments.

We deploy fractional T1 lines with multiplexers (Figure 7-1) to transmit data and voice between remote offices. In some countries we use E1, which is a European version of the T1 standard operating at 2.048 megabits per second.

Figure 7-1   Multiplexed Network

Multiplexers come in three flavors; A frequency-division multiplexer (FDM) is commonly used for analog voice networks. A time-division multiplexer (TDM) offers more reliable, high-speed digital transmission. The statistical TDM (STDM) improves on the vanilla TDM. In a regular TDM, each input gets its own time slot. If an input happens to have no data for transmission, the time slot goes unused, which doesn't exploit WAN bandwidth efficiently. The STDM is more flexible and efficient, since it allocates time slots only to inputs transmitting data. STDMs can also transmit variable length frames, which also makes more efficient use of bandwidth. Finally, STDMs can prioritize transmissions, which allows you to assign business-critical mainframe transactions higher priority than file transfers.

Although STDMs use bandwidth more efficiently, we still use both TDMs and STDMs. TDMs are a better choice for transmitting voice. We use STDMs in WANs where there are highly dynamic data traffic patterns (Figure 7-2).

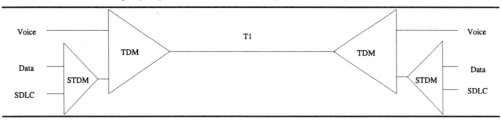

Figure 7-2   Combining TDMs and STDMs

As automobile racers say, "Speed is money, how fast do you want to go?" A WAN corollary might be, "Convenience is money. How much comfort can you afford?" Dedicated data lines cost big bucks. You pay more for dedicated than shared lines. If the dedicated link sits idle, then you are not getting what you paid for. Consider the complexity of using dedicated lines connecting many sites. For example, to connect *n* sites in a fully meshed network, you will need *n(n-1)/2* lines, or 1,225 lines to connect 50 sites. You also need many expensive ports on your internetwork devices.

Fast Switched Connections

Dedicated point-to-point network connections are permanent. You pay for them 24 hours a day, seven days a week even when they are unused. A better solution for connecting many sites is a switched network with one connection at each site. In a switched network, connections are established when needed. Two of the main switching methods are circuit switching and packet switching. In a circuit-switched network like the plain old telephone system, a connection is maintained for the duration of the call. However, once a connection is made, it operates much like a dedicated line—fixed amount of bandwidth is available even if it is not used.

Packet switching is more efficient. Data is divided into packets. Extra information is added to each packet to guide it through the network. Because packets from different sources may share the same physical links, packet switching uses network capacity more efficiently than do circuit-switched connections.

In contrast to the analog telephone system, Integrated Services Digital Network (ISDN) is a digital version of circuit switching. Another digital version is the switched 56 kilobits-per-second data service commonly used in North America. Integrated Services Digital Network is just as it sounds—a digital system designed to carry voice, data, and video. The Basic Rate Interface (BRI) is one type of ISDN service that uses three channels—two 64 kilobits-per-second B channels and one 16 kilobits-per-second D channel, which is used to set up calls and transmit signals -- disconnect, status and user information. The B channel may carry data, voice or video. Another type of ISDN, the Primary Rate Interface (PRI), has twenty-three 64 kilobits-per-second channels and one 64 kilobits-per-second D channel.

We do not recommend building a large network on ISDN alone. ISDN is not as widely available as other options. Also, once an ISDN connection is set-up it operates like a dedicated line. You pay for bandwidth that you do not use, and it can not provide extra bandwidth for bursty data traffic without setting up additional calls. If you use ISDN more than three hours per day, other options, like Frame Relay, start to become more economical.

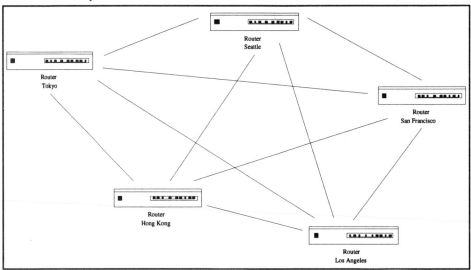

Figure 7-3   Fully Meshed Network

Some ISDN is appropriate in certain parts of your network. For example, we use ISDN to provide digital dial-up access between a LAN in a small, remote office and headquarters. ISDN lines are normally faster and more reliable than dial-up analog lines. ISDN is well suited to bring additional bandwidth when our primary network connections become congested (bandwidth-on-demand) and for emergency backup.

The X.25 Solution

For many years, the standard IEEE X.25 communication protocol has enjoyed a reputation as being a slow, typically less than 64 kilobits per second (a few devices run 256 kilobits per second and faster) but reliable and flexible packet-switching technology. While new and faster packet-switching technologies, including fast packet and Frame Relay, are now available, X.25 is still a common protocol for connecting computers in a packet-switched network.

X.25 was designed to connect dumb terminals to computers through unreliable telephone lines. Its error detection and correction abilities consume limited bandwidth and limit scalability and performance. Today's telephone infrastructure is more reliable, so the overhead devoted to error detection goes to waste.

You can build very large networks by using X.25 packet switching. If your network comprises dedicated point-to-point links between many locations

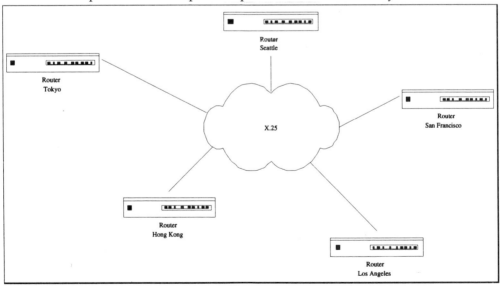

Figure 7-4   X.25 Packet-Switched Network

(example of a fully meshed network is shown in Figure 7-3), a switched network such as X.25 offers an inexpensive way to reduce complexity. Each location interconnects to the packet-switched network through one line, eliminating the cost of extra lines and router ports (Figure 7-4).

Because X.25 networks are relatively slow, we recommend that you restrict their use to secondary and tertiary backbone segments. Use X.25 in slower and less reliable networks where the protocol's extra error checking abilities are put to good use.

Flexibility is another X.25 advantage. Switched network technologies use virtual circuits to connect locations. Although virtual circuits between different locations actually share network bandwidth, they appear as dedicated channels. Using permanent virtual circuits (PVC) and switched virtual circuits (SVC), you can establish logical connections between your network nodes.

PVCs require more overhead because you must define a permanent logical channel between each pair of nodes. Use permanent channels between nodes that exchange data frequently because PVCs do not require a call setup phase, which takes time. On the other hand, SVCs set up a temporary connection between two nodes when they need to exchange data and then disconnect the channel. SVCs require less overhead because you define fewer channels.

As with ISDN, building an X.25 internetwork with routers is more difficult than using dedicated lines. You need to define additional tables for use with X.25-type addresses, which are called X.121 addresses. Routers connected to an X.25 network need the tables to translate between network (IP) and X.25 addresses.

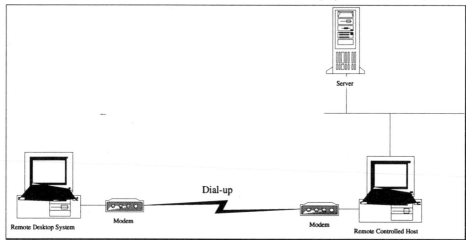

Figure 7-5   Figure 7-5: Remote Control Connection

Frame Relay

Frame Relay is an effective, standard, available, and affordable way to connect your networks across a wide area. Frame Relay works by packing data into variable-length frames, which are switched across the WAN. Although similar to X.25 packet switching, Frame Relay operates at much higher speeds—typically 64 kilobits per second, 1.5 megabits per second, and up to 45 megabits per second. Frame Relay technology also uses less overhead for error detection, correction, and flow control, making it a more efficient protocol than X.25 over modern networks.

Cost Comparison

Like X.25, Frame Relay costs less than leased lines. It is not uncommon for organizations to slash leased-line costs by 20 to 40 percent by moving to Frame Relay. Figuring your costs, however, isn't easy. Telephone companies use different methods to calculate Frame Relay's tariff. Study tariffs carefully so you pick the best yet least expensive plan for your needs. Some telcos let you choose either a fixed rate, allowing unlimited use, or a per-minute plan. Both are normally proportional to distance.

Another variable in Frame Relay's tariff is the Committed Information Rate (CIR), which is the minimum data rate your telephone company promises to provide. If you specify a CIR of 64 kilobits per second, you can install it on a 128 kilobits-per-second link and pay the 64 kilobits-per-second rate. The telephone company will allow up to a 128 kilobits-per-second rate when it has spare capacity (bandwidth-on-demand), but there is no guarantee beyond 64 kilobits per second. Depending

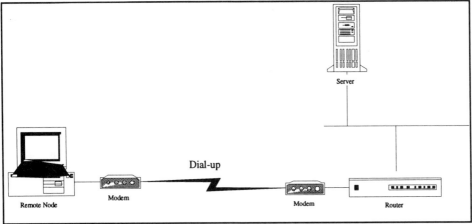

Figure 7-6   Remote Node Connection

on your network traffic patterns, it is not unusual to specify CIRs about half the port speed.

Another price consideration is the cost to setup each PVC. For a fully meshed network, you need to define at least one PVC between every two sites. This is time consuming for a network with many remote nodes. Frame Relay SVCs would provide a simpler alternative, but the standards are still in progress. ISDN signals have been proposed to set-up and manage Frame Relay SVCs. Look for them soon.

When should you replace your leased lines with Frame Relay? You need to consider five guidelines: Frame Relay is a good candidate for wide area networks that connect more than two locations, use redundant links, implement partial meshing, have link use less than 50 percent, and carry multiple protocols.

Remotely Access for the Network

In the New Enterprise, users are encouraged to roam from their offices. Many users travel with notebook computers; others work from a home office. Your enterprise network should provide nomads access to communications, information, and other computing resources so they can be productive independent of time and space.

There are a variety of ways to establish a physical connection from afar. You can use the Internet, X.25, or ISDN. The challenge is to provide a solution that is flexible and allows your users to be as mobile as necessary. For example, the Internet and X.25 often require special accounts to gain access—accounts that don't always move easily from one location to another. There are still many countries (or counties in the rural U.S.) that do not have ISDN services and probably will not for many years. You don't want to restrict access to a few locations. The most flexible solution for international remote access remains the plain old analog telephone system. As long as you have a computer, a modem, and a telephone line, you can reach your network from anywhere.

Methods for Remote On-line Access

Remote access methods vary from the mindlessly simple to unthinkably complex. Users' character-based applications have the easiest time. For example, stereotypical UNIX users use the command line to compose and read mail, edit and transfer files, read Usenet news, and even surf the World Wide Web in a text-only environment. Users of GUI-based applications, on the other hand, need high-speed connections and fancy communications software to feel at ease.

Far-flung users need special hardware to get network access, as well. Commonly, they need a modem, at least one telephone line, some remote control software, and a network-connected PC (Figure 7-5). The remote control connection enables a remote PC user to control a PC (called a host) connected to your network. All processing happens on the host, while keyboard input and screens fly between the host and the remote system. Because only the screens and keyboard input are transferred between the host and remote systems, the remote control connection works well over slow circuits. Examples of remote control software include Microcom's Carbon Copy and Symantec's pcAnywhere.

Remote control connections become increasingly expensive with the number of remote users because you need a host for each one. Host management is another expense to consider. Install hosts in a central area to manage and secure them adequately. Cubix offers a range of comprehensive, rack-mounted remote control hosts we like to use because the racks pack much hardware in a small space. Leaving hosts in users' offices is difficult to manage and creates a huge security risk.

The remote node method provides a more flexible and user-friendly approach to remote connections, but it requires more bandwidth than the remote control method. Instead of controlling another PC, which is connected to the network, remote node enables a remote computer to operate as if it were a real node connected to the enterprise network. The remote PC dials up a network router that translates between analog serial data and digital network protocols (Figure 7-6).

Dial-in and dial-out capabilities
Support for DOS, Windows, and OS/2 clients
Support for remote nodes and remote control connections
10BaseT and Token Ring connections
Multiple network protocols, including TCP/IP and IPX
Serial link protocols, including PPP and SLIP
Dial-out modem pooling
Compression
Multiple asynchronous ports
ISDN and X.25 ports
Multiple serial ports
SNMP manager
Password with password aging and time and date restrictions
Password encryption
PAP and CHAP authentication
Dial-back

Table 7-2   Remote Access Server Features

Remote node provides an effective solution for users who want to run client/server applications from remote locations. If remote client applications are installed on the remote machine and the application is designed to transfer small packets of data between the client and server, the remote node connection will be flexible and fast. However, if the client must first download the applications from the server before they can be executed then you may find the remote node connection is just too slow.

Remote Access Server

There are many ways to configure a communications server. For example, you may want to allow access by way of plain telephone lines, ISDN, or both. You may limit your users to dial-in only or allow dial-out access. You may use remote control, remote node, or both. For remote node connections, we recommend you use PPP, as we discussed earlier in this chapter. Strike a good balance between access and security for your remote users—not an easy task, certainly. We discuss security in greater detail in Chapter 11. Consider a turnkey solution that will meet all of your remote access requirements. A comprehensive remote access server that combines hosts, routing, and modems with network management will be easier to configure and support. Some products are Remote Annex 2000 and 4000 from Xylogics, Shiva Corp.'s LanRover family of remote access products and Novell's NetWare Connect. Cisco Systems and U.S. Robotics have integrated their router and modem technologies in Cisco Systems' AS5200 Access Server. Table 7-2 summarizes the key features to look for in a remote access server.

Connecting Mainframes, Servers, and Desktops 8≡

Computer companies spend millions of dollars each month hawking their wares, trying to convince you their stuff is better than what the competition has to offer. It takes discipline and dispassionate reasoning for IT managers to set aside the messages contained in slogans, the latent gratitude for a golf game paid for by the earnest computer salesperson, and the almost religious attachment some staffers may hold for (or against) a certain operating system. The sign of a professional is the ability to block out noise and focus on what is important.

Let your business requirements, applications, and other network needs drive your server configurations, not personal prejudices or advertising dogma. When considering hardware, look at memory capacity, storage options, bus speeds, CPU scalability, and high-reliability features.

More importantly, you need to pick an operating system or systems. Some applications and services work better with certain hardware and software configurations. For example, file and print sharing, application and database servers, and compute engines all carry different load characteristics. Specialty servers, such as modem, CD, and fax sharing have different requirements. Some operating systems enhance file sharing, whereas others are more naturally suited for application and database servers.

Server Connectivity

Centralizing Servers

PC-based departmental servers on LANs enabled users to share files and printers in small workgroups. These servers commonly cower in a corner or under a desk somewhere in the office, where they are subjected to the horrors of unbridled dust, spilled coffee, sticky hands, unfiltered power surges, and curiosity seekers. This is not the best environment for servers that run mission-critical applications or store sensitive corporate data.

We firmly support the notion that servers serve best when they are close to the user, physically as well as logically. Yet, as we argued in detail in Chapter 1, to deliver production-quality support to distributed systems, it is IT that must take responsibility for managing the servers properly. Wherever possible, coddle your servers in controlled environments, such as in a data center or at least in a secure equipment room.

Distributing Servers

Servers are the information hubs in our distributed-enterprise network. How we connect them to the network is therefore related to our view of workgroups. We want any server to be accessible to any user, if authorized, independent of their physical locations. In fact, the physical location of the server itself shouldn't depend solely on how we define or where we locate the workgroup.

Let's look at some alternatives: We can connect a server to the network segment where it is accessed most often. This is a good solution if workgroups are static and closely located. Figure 8-1 shows two servers isolated on two separate Ethernet segments, which are connected via multiport routers to the backbone network. In this case, the workgroup users in Ethernet X or Y generally access only the server on their own segment and only rarely (if at all) access the server in the other segment. Hence, data traffic across the network between Ethernets X and Y is minimized.

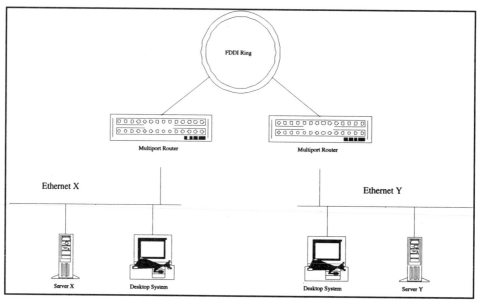

Figure 8-1   Independent Servers on Ethernet Segments

However, what if the users on one segment often need to access the server on the other segment? Data traffic, in that situation, will have to cross three networks and two routers. We can improve performance by changing the network configuration. We can relocate the server accessed from both segments to FDDI distribution backbone network like server Y in Figure 8-2. Data traffic to and from the example server Y now crosses just two networks and one router.

Whether this configuration is an improvement over the earlier isolated server case depends on the data traffic patterns. If the traffic volume between Ethernet X and server Y is high, then there may be some improvement. But what if the workgroup in Ethernet Y begins to use server Y almost exclusively? The configuration in Figure 8-2 may not be the best.

The problem with static configurations in a distributed environment is that they do not always best fit the networking conditions. Workgroups and the network data traffic patterns they create are not static; they change constantly. Some servers are accessed by users on one segment. Others are accessed by some users

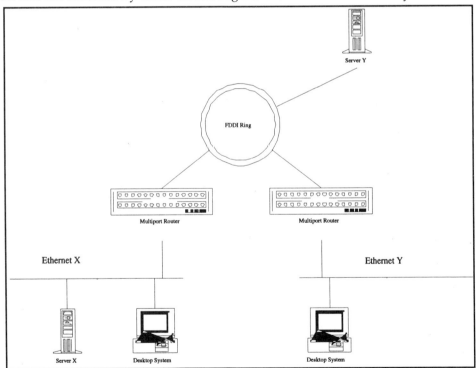

Figure 8-2   Shared Server on the Distribution Backbone Network

on several segments. And some servers are accessed by all users on all segments. That's why we connect all servers to the distribution backbone network as in the example servers in Figure 8-3.

Mainframe Connectivity

Although you can connect your mainframe to Ethernet or FDDI, we still prefer the old fashioned way—Token Ring. IBM has supported Token Ring connectivity on a wider range of devices for a longer time than any others, making it the networking technology of choice for most mainframe connectivity requirements[1].

There are four ways to connect your mainframe to your network: through a Token Ring interface, the 3172 Interconnect Controller, channel-attached routers, or through the 3746 Nways Multinetwork Controller.

Token Ring Interface

If you are using a channel-attached, front-end processor[2], such as an IBM 3745 Communications Controller, you can use a Token Ring Interface Couple (TIC) to connect your mainframe to a Token Ring network. You can also use a channel-attached IBM 3174 Network Processors with a TIC.[3] In the example in Figure 8-4, the mainframe is attached to several Token Ring networks through two 3174s. Using TICs, each 3174 links to a Token Ring. This configuration enhances reliability because enterprise network connectivity continues if one 3174 or Token Ring fails.

3172 Interconnect Controller

Another IBM device, the 3172 Interconnect Controller, provides an effective way to connect your mainframe to several types of networks, including Ethernet. The 3172 is a channel-attached device that supports TCP/IP and SNA. It offloads TCP/IP processing from your mainframe. It can also connect several networks to the mainframe.

---

1. Physical connectivity is only half of the mainframe game. You also need to integrate the mainframe's SNA protocols with your other protocols, like TCP/IP. We discuss those details in Chapter 9.
2. A channel is a fancy parallel port on a mainframe computer. A front-end processor is a fancy controller outside the mainframe that controls communications with remote devices across wide-area networks.

Beyond these features, however, the 3172's functionality is limited. Although it supports multiple network connections, it cannot route packets between different networks. Packets from each connected network must be relayed directly to the mainframe for processing or routing.

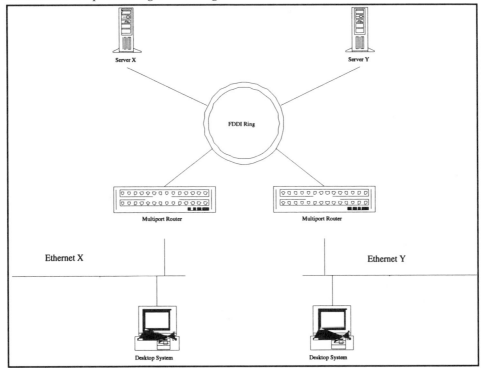

Figure 8-3   Multiple Shared Servers on the Distribution Backbone Network

Channel-Attached Routers

Channel-attached routers are another way to connect a mainframe to your enterprise network. Cisco Systems is the product leader in this area with a Channel Interface Processor (CIP) for its high-end routers. With this special interface card, you can attach a router to a mainframe's ESCON or bus-and-tag

---

3.   The 3174 has been renamed the Network Processor and Establishment Controller. It was originally called a cluster control unit because its main function is to concentrate data from a cluster of terminals before sending the data to the mainframe. A local 3174 control unit is channel-attached, whereas a remote control unit connects to a front-end processor through a WAN.

channel interfaces[4]. In many cases, a channel-attached router is less expensive and more flexible than upgrading your front-end processors. With a channel-attached router, you can bypass the 3174 and 3745 devices altogether, so there are fewer connections and fewer points of failure.

However, direct mainframe connectivity is a very complex area. Installing and maintaining channel-attached devices, particularly routers, requires specialized technical skills. Plan carefully before implementing channel-attached routers and other complex technologies.

Nways Multinetwork Controller

The IBM 3746 Nways Multinetwork Controller is intended both to replace the 3745 front-end processor and to provide an alternative to channel-attached routers. However, the initial product release still lacks a few features for enterprise networking, including bus-and-tag channel connections, IP routing, Frame Relay, X.25, and ISDN. Today, channel-attached routers still provide a more comprehensive, flexible and cost-effective solution to mainframe connectivity.

Desktop Connectivity

Desktop Network Adapter

Network-connected terminals, PCs, and workstations need a network adapter to translate the cable signal into intelligible digital bits and bytes. They also need to convert between the serial cable format and parallel computer format. Another important network adapter function is media access control, which ensures that all the nodes connected to the same network cable share the cable in an orderly way.

Although there are many fine inexpensive adapters on the market, we recommend you buy top-selling network adapters from the popular suppliers, such as 3Com and Intel. This is critical for large networks. New versions of operating systems will most likely offer drivers for popular network adapters first.

Choose network adapters that are easy to install and configure. Some have hardware switches that are difficult to get your hands on after you install the adapter and close the covers. Software-configurable adapters are easier to work

---

4.   Like PCs with different types of ports to connect external devices, mainframes have two types of channel interfaces: ESCON and older bus-and-tag interfaces.

with, but the best choice is the plug-and-play adapter. With plug-and-play hardware, operating systems like Windows 95 can detect and configure the card and install network files automatically.

Also make sure the adapters you install support a wide range of Interrupt Requests (IRQ) on your PCs. You do not want to give up parallel and serial ports to get IRQs for network adapters.

PC Network Software

PCs need special network software, which includes the network protocols needed to communicate with servers and other network citizens. Many organizations use Novell's IPX on Windows and DOS systems for NetWare file server connectivity. UNIX machines and the global Internet use TCP/IP, which has been a part of UNIX for more than 10 years.

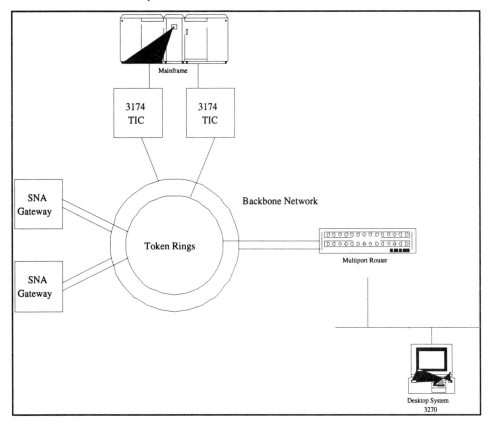

Figure 8-4   Network Connected Mainframe

8

For Windows and DOS-based TCP/IP services, you can either use a gateway or install TCP/IP on the PC. A gateway translates between server-based TCP/IP and other protocols such as IPX. With its own TCP/IP protocol stack, a PC accesses TCP/IP services directly.

Recent versions of Windows and OS/2 have TCP/IP builtin. You can also buy a TCP/IP protocol stack. There are many from which to choose, including FTP's PC/TCP OnNet, Frontier Technologies' Super/TCP, and PC-NFS from SunSoft. Another option is to download one of the free TCP/IP protocol stacks from a shareware site. However, we do not advocate that you use shareware for your production-quality enterprise network. There is no guarantee you will get support.

Compatibility is a problem. Although TCP/IP is a de facto standard, not all TCP/IP products are alike. Make sure any TCP/IP you install is compatible with the systems on your enterprise network. This also means you should standardize on one TCP/IP protocol stack for your desktops. Not all TCP/IP stacks work together, and it is easier to manage one. Winsock 2.0 currently is the de facto standard for Windows applications using TCP/IP. Make sure you choose a Winsock compliant TCP/IP protocol stack.

Don't forget applications. There are differences in the applications that come with TCP/IP packages. Choose one that supports a wide range of applications— terminal emulation, Telnet, FTP, remote execution, Trivial File Transfer Program (TFTP), Ping, Finger, Traceroute, Talk, and Network File System (NFS) just to name a few. (See Chapter 13 for more information about Internet applications.) Another TCP/IP application to consider is X Window System. WRQ, Netmanage, and Hummingbird Communications offer respected PC X Window System software.

If you run more than one protocol on your PCs, beware. Load them up with sufficient memory to run the extra protocols. Also you will need to use one of the standard network drivers such as Network Driver Interface Specification (NDIS) from Microsoft or Open Data-link Interface (ODI) from Novell. We have no preference, but NDIS is more common. Most protocol stacks and network adapters support both interfaces. NDIS and ODI offer a common way for network protocols and other software to interface with different device drivers that control different types of network adapters. Both let you install and use more than one protocol at a time.

Integrating Platforms and Protocols 9 ≡

Which operating system is the best for your applications? It depends. None are perfect and some are better at some tasks than others. For example, NetWare's strength is in file and print services while Windows NT and UNIX are better at multiprocessing and multitasking. UNIX has emerged as the OS of choice for fast transaction processing, while the AS/400 remains one of the easiest-to-maintain computers around. Your business requirements, applications, and services should drive your operating system selections. From the networking standpoint, expect to support more than one connected operating system.

You should be able to access any operating system from anywhere on your network. On the other hand, operating systems management and maintenance swallow an inordinate amount of time and money. Your ability to manage declines as you add variables. From a manageability perspective, you need to set standards that limit the operating systems you allow.

Serious operating systems—NetWare, Windows NT, OS/2, Vines, and UNIX—offer the features you need to build a network with high RAS. And don't forget OS/400, MVS, and VMS, which are still important in many organizations.

Protocols, Addresses, and Logical Networks

So far we have focused on the physical portion of network connectivity. The other half involves the logical network architecture, which consists of implementing the network protocols—in other words, configuring software on desktops, servers, and routers. You need to set the address space for your network, assign addresses to devices, and define packet routing.

Addresses and routing relate closely. Nodes use addresses to send packets to other nodes. You, or management software, assign each node a network address that contains two parts. The first part identifies the network. The second part defines the node. If the sending and receiving nodes are on the same network, the packet is sent directly. However, if the nodes live on different networks, the sending node must send its packets through one or more intermediate routers and networks to reach its destination. The sending device needs to know the address of the appropriate router to send the packet for further processing. Note that a router has an address for each network to which it connects.

Guidelines for a TCP/IP Address Space

Before you define your TCP/IP address space, you need a unique network identifier or address. You can use any handle you want, though there is one big reason not to. If your organization is as security conscious as the Central Intelligence Agency and absolutely, positively will never connect to the Internet, you are free to pick your own network address. If, on the other hand, there is a chance your organization will join the wired world, you should get a unique network number from an organization called the InterNIC.[1] If you choose to pick your number now, and decide to connect to the Internet later, you face some nasty expenses, which we will mention later in this chapter.

There are a variety of ways to define your address space and allocate addresses to your nodes. Plan this carefully, since it will be difficult and costly to change addresses later, particularly for large networks. The two issues you need to consider are the size of your address space and how to subdivide it. For TCP/IP networks, you choose one of three types of network addresses—Class A, B, or C.

An IP address consists of a network identifier and host identifier. Each class allocates the bits in the 32-bit IP address to the network and host identifiers differently (Table 9-1). The first few bits of an IP address determine the class to which the address belongs. A Class A address uses 8 bits to identify the network, leaving 24 bits for hosts. Sixteen bits are allocated to the network identifier in a Class B address, and the remaining 16 bits are allocated to hosts. Class C uses a 24-bit network identifier, which leaves 8 bits for host identification. Eight bits means a Class C network is limited to only 254 nodes plus two for broadcast and

	Class A	Class B	Class C
First byte	1—126	128—191	192—223
Bits in first byte	0nnnnnnn	10nnnnnn	110nnnnn
Network identifier bits	8	16	24
Host identifier bits	24	16	8
Number of networks	126	16,400	2.1 million
Number of hosts	16.8 million	65,500	254

Table 9-1   IP Address Summary

---

1.   http://rs.InterNIC.net/

other purposes. We discuss Internet basics and IP addresses more in Chapter 14.

While every network serves different needs and requires different addressing schemes, we recommend keeping an address structure as simple as possible. The simplest structure is to use one Class A, B, or C address where all of your nodes use the same network number. However, this flat structure only works for the smallest networks. To ensure reasonable performance, you need to divide large networks into smaller subnets and throttle traffic (particularly broadcasts) between them. Two problems loom. Thanks to the Internet's rapid growth, IP's addressing scheme is hitting a brick wall. You have better chances striking it rich at the lottery than acquiring a unique Class A or B address from the InterNIC. Because it can address only 254 hosts, a single Class C address does not meet the requirements for large networks.

One solution is to reserve a range of Class C addresses. You can assign different Class C addresses to different subnets in your organization. The main disadvantage is that rather than using one address, other organizations must maintain a range of Class C addresses for your network, which takes space in router tables.

Unregistered Addresses

Another solution is to use a private, unregistered address. RFC (Request for Comment) 1597 describes using Class A, B, and C addresses for private use.[2] With a gateway, you can use a single, registered Class C address to uniquely identify your network to other networks and translate between your "legal," registered Class C address and the free-range, unregistered addresses roaming your network prairie.

Such a gateway carries other implications. Since the rest of the Internet sees only a single Class C address, you effectively hide your enterprise network behind a veil. Remapping shields internal IP addresses, which, if otherwise exposed, the malevolent might use to hack into your network. To external users, all outbound traffic appears to come from a single address. When the gateway receives an inbound packet it routes it to the correct internal subnet.

Subnetting

You do not *need* to divide your network into subnets, but you should. It's easier to manage traffic on several subdivided networks than on one massive network.

---

2. Information about RFCs is available at http://ds.internic.net/ds/rfc-index.html and http://www.cis.ohio-state.edu/hypertext/information/rfc.html

There are two ways to divide your address space. One method, called subnetting, adds a subnet number to a network's unique number. To the outside world, your network is still known by its single, unique network number. Your network routers, however, use the subnet number to identify specific subnets. Subnet addresses are implemented by using part of the host identifier in the network address. The subnet mask determines which parts of the host identifiers are considered part of the subnet address. The subnet mask is usually specified in each network node when you configure its TCP/IP software. In some cases—for example, diskless computers or X terminals—the subnet mask may be requested by a network node by sending a broadcast message across the network. If you need to do this, you must configure a device to recognize the request and send the correct information.

Multiple network identifiers is the other way to subdivide network address space. You request a range of unique network numbers from the InterNIC. Instead of using a single network number that is divided into subnet numbers, you just use multiple network numbers. The downside to this is it wastes scarce Internet addresses and bloats routing tables—not just for your organization but for the entire Internet. We recommend subnetting for its easier management and environmental friendliness. In reality, many enterprises use a combination of methods to divide the address space.

Allocating Network Addresses

After you decide how to subdivide your address space you need to allocate network addresses. In most cases, you will allocate a subnet address or network number to each physical network in your enterprise. There are special situations where you may want to allocate more than one address to a physical subnet. We recommend this if you plan to segment the physical subnet into smaller networks in the future. This way, you will not have to reassign network addresses and reconfigure your nodes later.

RFC 1219 describes a straightforward method to ensure you can accommodate future subnets with different address lengths. The bits of subnet identifiers are identified by a subnet mask, so the bits do not have to be contiguous. We recommend that you use contiguous bits in the most significant bits in the host identifiers.

We recommend that when you assign a network address to devices on a subnet, you start with "1," the lowest host identifier and then count up normally in binary. For subnet identifiers, you should start numbering from the most significant bit, using the mirror image of normal binary counting. For example, you would start numbering 10, 01, 110, 001, 101, 011 and so on. This will make it easier to increase the number of bits in your subnet mask if you need more subnets in your network later.

Managing Network Names and Addresses

It takes a long time to assign and configure a unique IP address for each node, especially on large networks. If a computer moves from one subnet to another, you must reconfigure the IP address again. You also need to reconfigure other parameters, such as default routers and subnet masks.

Several technologies allow network nodes, such as PCs and X terminals, to get their IP address and parameters automatically. RFC 903 defines the canine-sounding RARP (Reverse Address Resolution Protocol). It was designed for diskless workstations to find their IP addresses. It lacks some of the features we need to manage wide-scale IP configurations. BOOTP, defined in RFCs 1533 and 1542, exchanges additional IP parameters. However, as with RARP, BOOTP uses static tables and does not allocate addresses dynamically.

Dynamic Host Configuration Protocol

We recommend Dynamic Host Configuration Protocol (DHCP) for allocating and managing IP addresses centrally and dynamically (see RFCs 1541 and 1533). Every computer using TCP/IP needs a unique IP address, which depends on where it connects to the internetwork. DHCP assigns IP addresses to DHCP-friendly computers automatically when they connect to the network. IP addresses are allocated from a pool, so besides easier address management, DHCP lets mobile users tap into the network from various locations. DHCP-assigned IP addresses are also reusable, so your organization can make more effective use of limited IP addresses.

Address allocation can be dynamic, static, or some combination of the two. Using the dynamic allocation scheme, DHCP assigns a unique IP address to a computer from a pool of IP addresses for a fixed time. When time runs out, the computer may renegotiate for an additional period. When the computer is finished, the IP address is released back to the pool. DHCP is a feature of the OnNet TCP/IP protocol suite from FTP Software and is found in other operating systems, including Windows NT.

Because DHCP depends on special broadcast messages, ensure that your network routers can forward DHCP requests, otherwise you will need to install a DHCP server on each subnet. A DHCP server for each subnet is better than none at all, but a centralized DHCP server is easier to manage. While centralization is admirable in theory, you should plan for some decentralization. DHCP products are new, so there has not been time to test them in large networks. In practice, the best solution is to configure a DHCP server for small groups of subnets.

Names and a Naming System

Whereas computers use numeric IP addresses, humans prefer names. You can assign names to the nodes on your enterprise network and then use the Domain Name System (DNS), an Internet staple, to associate names and addresses from one location. In UNIX, the alternative is to associate names and addresses in the *host* file on servers and desktops. Obviously, this becomes a nightmare as you connect more devices to the network. Since DNS is critical to normal network operations, we recommend you configure two DNS servers—one primary and another for backup.

You need to worry about name formats. TCP/IP networks with DNS servers use a hierarchical naming format to identify a specific node. (See Chapter 14 for more information about domain names.) We recommend using a naming format that is meaningful and reflects the node's function and your organization's structure. For example, if your naming format is *nodename.department.organization*, then we know something about server *accounts.controller.asiahq* and it is easy to remember. Also with central naming systems and format, we can ensure that common names are not duplicated inadvertently, which takes time to unravel.

Guidelines for TCP/IP Routing

There are several methods for configuring the tables in your routers. One method uses a static configuration whereby you set the tables in each router and they remain the same until you change them manually. Obviously, this is not very flexible. A better method automates the task so that routers dynamically detect network changes and update their tables without intervention. Dynamic routing makes the networks easier to manage and more reliable, since routers can start redundant paths automatically if the primary path fails.

For dynamic routing, routers depend on one of several special routing protocols to exchange information about their environment. They maintain a complete map of the network so they can determine the optimal paths between different nodes.

Routing Information Protocol

Routing Information Protocol (RIP) is a widely used Interior Gateway Protocol (IGP). IGPs exchange information between routers in an "autonomous network." In the networking world, a single organization owns and controls an autonomous network. For example, the networks in two organizations are considered two autonomous networks. The boundary between autonomous networks is important because you do not want misconfigured routers elsewhere to affect your network.

RIP employs a simple distance-vector algorithm whereby each router keeps a table of the estimated distance to other nodes. How does RIP estimate distance? It uses the hop count, which is the number of routers in the path. RIP-based routers broadcast their router tables every 30 seconds, even though no changes have taken place.

RIP works well for smaller networks but falls down as networks scale up. Complete news broadcasts from every router every 30 seconds consume bandwidth. RIP is also slow to *converge*. In convergence, all routers update their tables so they have a common view of the network. For example, if a router broadcasts just before one of its network links fails, it can take at least 30 seconds before this information is relayed to the other routers in the network. Actually, the minimum time to converge will take about 90 seconds, because RIP-based routers normally wait for three change notifications before updating their tables.

Calculating distance based on hop counts is another weakness. Simple hop counts do not consider many important inter-router link characteristics, such as speed, congestion, and cost. Since RIP cannot handle networks with more than 15 hops, it is limited to small- to medium-sized networks. Furthermore, RIP does not use parallel paths efficiently, and it does not adapt well to networks with dynamic traffic patterns and a variety of line speeds.

Cisco Systems' Interior Gateway Routing Protocol (IGRP)—and, more recently, Enhanced IGRP (EIGRP)—overcomes some of RIP's disadvantages. IGRP uses a more efficient distance-vector algorithm to calculate the best path (least delay or least cost) in large networks with a variety of inter-router links with different speeds and costs. However, IGRP is still slow to converge, and only Cisco Systems routers support it today. In contrast to RIP, IGRP supports load balancing. With load balancing, you can spread data traffic across multiple links to balance traffic, which improves reliability and performance. Load balancing is a very effective way to avoid the problem of slow convergence. Others take over immediately when one link fails.

Open Shortest Path First

For large networks, Open Shortest Path First (OSPF) offers a scaleable and flexible alternative to RIP and IGRP. OSPF uses something called the link-state algorithm, which allows a router to send updates about any changes to its links as they occur. This contrasts with RIP's broadcast of the entire routing table every 30 seconds. Compared to RIP and IGRP, OSPF converges quickly. Rather than waiting for three updates such as the distance-vector algorithms, OSPF can use information about network changes immediately.

OSPF's sophisticated shortest-path algorithm calculates the optimal network routes by using a variety of metrics, including the cost of each link. Each OSPF router keeps a complete and accurate map of the entire network, which allows the router to identify alternative paths quickly when a link fails.

For really large networks comprising hundreds of routers, OSPF updates are an important concern. As the size of the network increases, so does the bandwidth consumed by update messages. It also takes longer for the network to converge. With its hierarchical structure, OSPF was designed to handle these problems. You can divide your network into areas, with border routers connecting groups of OSPF routers in each area. Hierarchy boosts performance and scalability because you confine router updates to each area.

For example, if your network comprises 200 routers, you can divide the network into four areas with 50 routers each. The routers in one area do not exchange updates with routers in other areas, which reduces the data traffic that flows across the enterprise network. Interarea updates are summarized and managed by the border routers. We recommend that you divide enterprise networks with more than 50 routers into OSPF areas and restrict the maximum number of routers in each area to 50.

Exterior Gateway Protocols

Exterior Gateway Protocols (EGP) exchange routing information among autonomous networks. Instead of passing all the routing information in an autonomous network, EGPs pass only selected information to outside networks. One of the original exterior gateway protocols was (not surprisingly) called EGP. EGP scaled poorly and was replaced with the newer Boundary Gateway Protocol (BPG). We recommend the latest version of this protocol, called BGP4.

Selecting Routing Protocols

The best routing protocol for your network depends on your unique needs. For smaller networks, RIP is simple and effective. But for larger networks where you need performance and scalability, you need an efficient link-state routing protocol. We recommend OSPF for large, heterogeneous networks with different types of routers. Another option is to use more than one routing protocol. Protocols can coexist, but a multiprotocol network begs for management headaches.

Another option is boundary routing, a low-cost internetworking option for small, remote offices. With single LAN and WAN ports a boundary router operates like a bridge. Any network traffic that is not local is forwarded across the WAN to a fully functional router for further processing. While they cost less than a normal router, boundary routers offer few functions and limited scaleability. Boundary routers may not always make effective use of limited WAN bandwidth, which wastes money.

NetWare Protocols and Routing

Although we focus on TCP/IP, other important protocols carried by enterprise networks—IPX, DECnet, AppleTalk and others—cannot be ignored. Each protocol has unique characteristics that affect your network design. For example, NetWare networks depend on IPX. Unlike TCP/IP, Novell did not design IPX to run on slow WANs but, instead, intended it for faster Ethernet and Token Ring LANs. NetWare servers use the Service Advertisement Protocol (SAP) to announce their presence to the network. You need to design your network to restrict SAP broadcasts so they do not clog lethargic (or busy) segments.

One solution is to filter SAP broadcasts in the network routers. Although effective, filtering limits your network design options. It is difficult for clients and servers on different segments to exchange data. Another solution is to use a more efficient protocol. Novell intends NetWare's Link Services Protocol (NLSP) routing to replace SAP and RIP for IPX. SAP and RIP make periodic broadcasts to inform of routes and services available to network users. Broadcasts are made every 60 seconds, whether changes are detected or not. On a large network, these broadcasts consume much bandwidth. NLSP sends only routing and service information when a link changes or a service becomes online or unavailable. For NLSP to be used, it must be supported by all routers on the network.

As with TCP/IP, you need to centrally manage IPX addresses because IPX network addresses must be unique within a NetWare network. Without centralized control, you are sure to have problems. In many organizations, it is common for departments to select IPX network addresses, randomly, for their NetWare LANs. No problem as long as they don't connect to the enterprise network. Eventually they will, and you know who will have to sort out the mess: you will. You had better plan to gain control now.

Like IP addresses, the IPX network addresses you assign to your network devices must be unique. Fortunately, it is easier to administer IPX addresses than IP addresses. In most networks, you only need to assign IPX network addresses to file servers and routers. The problem is the lack of tools. There is nothing like

DHCP to centrally allocate IPX network addresses. You need to develop your own standards to centrally manage IPX network addresses and ensure each one is unique.

One technique is to use network addresses assigned by the Novell NetWare Address Registry.[3] Similar to the InterNIC's IP address service, the Registry allocates IPX addresses. This method is useful if you intend to connect your NetWare network with other organizations. IPX addresses from the Registry are guaranteed to be globally unique (as long as everyone follows the standard). Another method is to "hexify" your IP addresses. For example, the IPX network address of a server with IP address 206.151.138.87 would be CE978A57. If the IP address is unique, it follows that the IPX address will also be unique (as long as everyone follows the standard).

Implementing Multiple Protocols

Devices must use the same protocol to communicate and exchange data. Management is a breeze on networks where devices share one protocol. However, if you own devices that use different protocols, then you need to find a way to install, integrate, and manage several protocols. We recommend you only use one: TCP/IP. We realize, however, this is not always possible. For large enterprise networks, you will likely deal with several, including SNA, DECnet, IPX, NetBIOS, and others.

We can choose from several multiple protocol options. One is to run multiple protocol stacks, such as TCP/IP and IPX, on each desktop computer. The advantages of a client-based multiprotocol approach include performance, flexibility, and reliability. The local computers communicate directly by using the servers' native protocols, so nothing hinders performance. Reliability is good because a failure at one client computer does not affect others.

Manageability, however, ranks as the top disadvantage of client computer-based protocol stacks. Centralizing configuration management is difficult unless you use special tools, like DHCP, which we discussed earlier. Figure on visiting each PC to resolve configuration problems. Additional protocol stacks require more local RAM, which always seems scarce.

The second option is to load multiple protocols on a gateway. Here, the client runs one protocol: usually TCP/IP or IPX. In this configuration, traffic between an IPX-based client and TCP/IP-based UNIX server would use IPX between the

---

3.   See Novell NetWare Address Registry at http://iamg.novell.com/iamg/products/ bizinet/nnartoc.htm

client and gateway and IP between the gateway and the UNIX server. One gateway is easier to manage than a fleet of PCs. The disadvantages of gateways are performance and reliability. Passing traffic through a gateway takes time. Furthermore, a gateway presents a single point of failure, making it a good idea to configure multiple gateways that take over automatically when one fails. A common use of gateways is to connect non-TCP/IP networks to the Internet. For example, an IPX-TCP/IP gateway, such as Novix Elite from Firefox, can give IPX-based NetWare clients TCP/IP connectivity on the corporate network or Internet. Another common use of gateways is to provide access to mainframes, which we discuss in the next section.

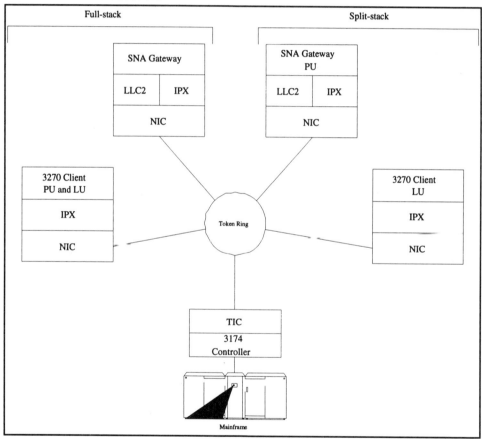

Figure 9-1   Full-stack and Split-stack SNA Gateways

The third option is to run multiple protocols on your servers. For example, with SunSoft's PC Protocol Services, you can use your IPX-based PCs to access the file and print services on your heavy UNIX iron.

For most organizations, TCP/IP is the strategic direction, even in long-time SNA shops. While TCP/IP is the proven, de facto standard for linking mixed computer brands, the problem of TCP/IP management remains. By that we mean implementing centralized management with automatic IP address allocation and IP address sharing and minimizing the number of different protocols.

Integrating SNA

Often, organizations build separate networks for their SNA and non-SNA data. This, of course, may double the support staff and other costs. Consider the potential of combining your SNA and enterprise networks for reducing the cost of equipment, communications links, and operations.

You need to answer a range of complex questions when connecting your SNA-based mainframe to your network. Plan accordingly. Your users are accustomed to SNA networks carrying mission-critical data with fast and predictable response times. Your enterprise network must provide the same, or better, levels of RAS.

Another concern is investment protection. Your SNA integration should protect your organization's installed base of equipment and applications.

SNA Gateways

Gateways offer a simple and popular way to access SNA-based mainframe applications from your enterprise network. SNA gateways translate between the SNA protocols and other common protocols such as IPX and TCP/IP. A common use of SNA gateways is to transmit 3270 SNA traffic between your mainframe and desktops, which are emulating 3270 terminals. You can implement your SNA gateway architecture in several ways. Take a look at the full-stack and split-stack methods shown in Figure 9-1.

With the full-stack method, you place the entire SNA protocol stack on each desktop, allowing each to communicate directly with the mainframe. The split-stack method splits the SNA protocol stack between a gateway and desktop. In both cases, the gateway communicates with the host, using LLC2 (Logical Link Control). It also communicates with the desktops, using common network protocols such as TCP/IP and IPX. If your gateway runs TCP/IP you can use TCP/IP's TN3270 to establish a 3270 session with your mainframe computers. The advantage of the split-stack scheme is that it simplifies network management. With the full-stack method, you must define a PU (Physical Unit) in VTAM

(Virtual Telecommunications Access Method) on the mainframe for each desktop that emulates a 3270 terminal. This can be a time-consuming task for a large network. Using the split-stack method, you define PUs only for the gateways.

Running on the mainframe, VTAM is a complex program where the devices in the SNA network are centrally defined and controlled. A PU is an SNA device that controls other devices. For example, a 3174 controller for 3270 terminals has a PU definition in VTAM. An SNA gateway may be a controller for desktop systems acting as 3270 terminals. Using the split-stack method each SNA gateway has a PU definition in VTAM. The alternative is to add the controller function—the full stack—to each desktop system that acts as a 3270 terminal. With the full-stack method the SNA gateway simply translates between network protocols, and each desktop has its own PU definition in VTAM.

Some SNA gateways come as turnkey systems that combine hardware and software. Others are software only. Although the turnkey variety performs well, the hardware is often proprietary. This could be costly if you need to upgrade the capacity of your SNA gateways in the future. The software SNA gateway is a more flexible solution. With software gateways, you can choose one to run on any hardware and operating system you like—486, Pentium, RISC, Windows NT, OS/2, UNIX. When you need more capacity you can simply buy a bigger machine—a standard one that is widely available and cost competitive.

SNA is still the predominant protocol used to carry mission-critical data in many enterprises. Your SNA gateways must be manageable. As with other important network devices, make sure the SNA gateways you choose can send information to your central management system by using SNMP. It is common for enterprises with mainframes to manage their SNA networks with NetView. If your enterprise is one of these, you will want to consider SNA gateways that are NetView compatible.

Architecture	Split-stack, hardware and software, software only
Mainframe interfaces	Token Ring, Ethernet, SDLC, ESCON, bus-and-tag
Network interfaces	Token Ring, Ethernet, FDDI
Protocols	TCP/IP, IPX
Fault tolerance	Load balancing
Number of sessions	256 concurrently
Types of devices supported	Mainframe, AS/400, PU2.0, PU2.1, LU0 through 3, LU6.2
Management	SNMP, NetView, centralized and distributed

Table 9-2   SNA Gateway Features

Another management issue is location. Some SNA gateways are designed to be centralized near the mainframe, whereas others are supposed to be distributed near the desktops at remote locations. With some gateways, it doesn't matter. They can be centralized or distributed. As you most likely guessed, we recommend that you centralize your SNA gateways in the data center. This is the best way to protect and manage critical network devices.

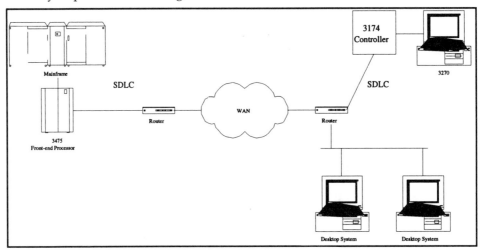

Figure 9-2   SDLC Passthrough

With your SNA gateways centralized in one location, fault tolerance becomes a major concern. Make sure you use multiple gateways, in case one has a problem. Also, choose a gateway with fault-tolerant features. For example, we use SNA gateways that can automatically balance the load if one fails or becomes congested.

Before selecting your SNA gateways, weigh your requirements and options carefully. Your mission-critical data depends on it. Table 9-2 summarizes the SNA gateway features you should look for.

SDLC Passthrough

For large WANs, simple SNA gateways are not always the right choice. Although SNA gateways offer effective ways to provide mainframe access from desktops emulating 3270 terminals, organizations often have other types of SNA connectivity requirements. For example, you may need to link several front-end processors or connect remote control units to front-end processors. With SDLC

(Synchronous Data Link Control) passthrough and SDLC conversion, you can connect existing SNA/SDLC devices, such as cluster control units and front-end processors, to your network.

In Figure 9-2, a remote 3174 using SDLC is connected to a router's serial port. On the mainframe side, the mainframe connects to the WAN through a front-end processor and a router. Using SDLC passthrough, the routers accept the SDLC data through a serial port and encapsulate it in another network protocol, such as TCP/IP, for transmission across the WAN. Although this is a simple solution to implement, it is sensitive to network congestion. Being a connection-oriented protocol, SNA/SDLC depends on acknowledgments, keep-alive messages, and timers, which are affected by other data traffic.

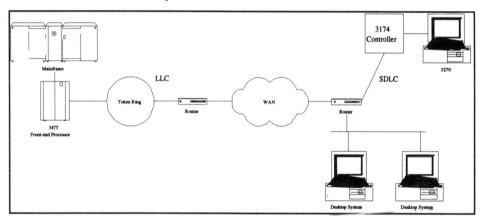

Figure 9-3   SDLC Conversion

SDLC Conversion

For many years, SDLC has been the primary, wide-area, data-link transport protocol used to carry SNA data over point-to-point serial lines. LLC2 is a common connection-oriented data link protocol for Token Ring and Ethernet-connected SNA devices. Using SDLC conversion, you can convert serial-based SDLC to LLC2. This can be done internally, as is the case for a Token Ring-connected 3174 cluster control unit. You can also use external conversion devices, such as the routers shown in Figure 9-3.

With SDLC conversion, you can minimize the cost of expensive front-end processors. Regular SDLC and SDLC passthrough use more expensive front-end processor ports than does SDLC conversion. Each SDLC link and each control unit using SDLC passthrough require a separate front-end processor port. Each active connection places an additional load on the front-end processor's CPU and memory. With SDLC conversion, you can consolidate the remote connections to your front-end processor into a single Token Ring connection, as shown in Figure 9-4. SDLC conversion provides another important benefit. You don't have to regenerate new VTAM and NCP definitions—a complex time-consuming task for large SNA networks—when you add, move or delete network devices.

By using a Switched Major Node, you only define the Token Ring connection once in VTAM and NCP. You can add and delete devices without making software changes.

Local Termination

An SNA session depends on keep-alive messages, acknowledgments, and timers to ensure the link is available. If the link fails, SNA executes recovery procedures. In a large, router-based WAN using SDLC passthrough, these link-control packets consume bandwidth. It is difficult to avoid time-outs on congested WANs. Local termination addresses these problems with acknowledgments, timers, and keep-alive messages.

Some routers boast local termination, which blocks SNA control messages from crossing the WAN. Figure 9-5 shows how the routers on each side of a WAN simulate link control messages so the WAN stays unsullied. TCP/IP connectivity is maintained between the routers, so they can exchange information about the SNA/SDLC devices connected to each side of the WAN.

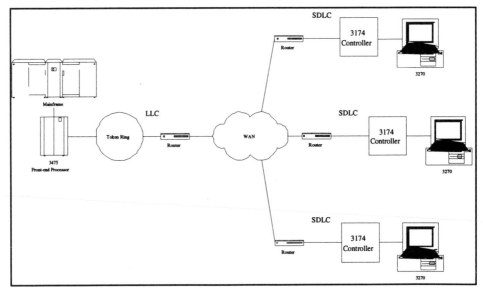

Figure 9-4   Consolidating Remote SNA Connections

SDLC passthrough and conversion with local termination are methods you can use today to integrate SNA and IP over a common network. An important problem, however, remains—congestion.

To overcome this problem, several router features allow you to prioritize mission-critical data, such as SNA, and reserve minimum bandwidths to ensure predictable response times. Prioritization, bandwidth reservation, and dial-on-demand routing are some of the router features you can use to optimize the performance of your enterprise network (see Chapter 10).

Data Link Switching

SNA and IP integration suffer from a lack of standards. SDLC passthrough, SDLC conversion, and local termination use proprietary methods. Data link switching (DLSw) emerges as a likely standard to integrate SNA and IP on a backbone.

DLSw promises to overcome the limitations of IP encapsulation on SNA performance and provides a common method for local termination and caching to reduce SNA and NetBIOS discovery traffic. DLSw ensures that SNA sessions do not time out when the routers find new paths around failed WAN links. Internetwork suppliers now offer DLSw, and several have added new features. For example, one problem with DLSw is scalability. In practice, DLSw is limited to networks with fewer than 100 routers. Cisco Systems' proprietary DLSw+ is designed to overcome the 100-router limitation. Keep in mind these nonstandard additions, as useful as they are, force you to buy all routers from one vendor.

Frame Relay Encapsulation

SDLC passthrough, SDLC conversion, and DLSw depend on TCP/IP protocols and IP encapsulation. RFC 1490 defines a more efficient and standard way to encapsulate SNA traffic in Frame Relay. Unlike DLSw, Frame Relay can transport

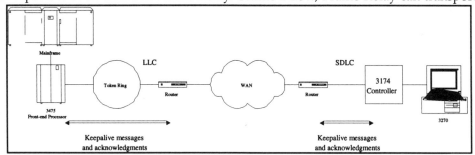

Figure 9-5   Local Termination

other protocols along with SNA. If your WAN is based on TCP/IP, then DLSw is an effective option to integrate your SNA traffic in a multiprotocol environment. If you are not a TCP/IP shop, however, DLSw introduces TCP/IP's performance and management overhead.

Frame Relay encapsulation does not need TCP/IP, and data traffic overhead is much less than that of DLSw. Frame Relay does require you to define virtual circuits between your network routers, but the work required is still less than configuring a TCP/IP network for DLSw. If you plan to implement a Frame Relay-based WAN, we recommend you consider using it to transport SNA traffic.

The main problem with RFC 1490 Frame Relay encapsulation is it is a level-2 protocol. You give up some of the level-3 advantages of TCP/IP-based routers.

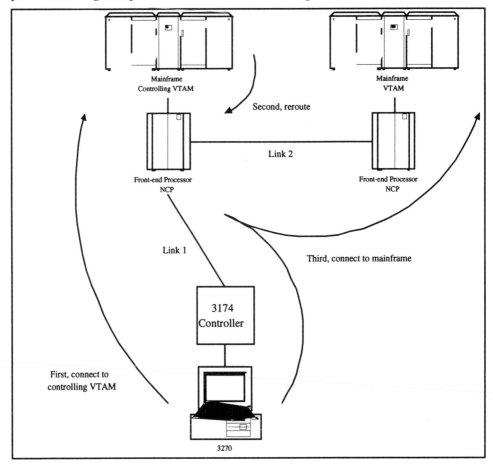

Figure 9-6   SNA Rerouting

SNA Routing and APPN

SNA transport methods such as SDLC passthrough, SDLC conversion, DLSw, and Frame Relay encapsulation do not address SNA routing. SNA is often thought unroutable, but it really is. Static routes in the mainframe control SNA routing—classic, centralized SNA. APPN is the new SNA that distributes routing information around the network. While both live in the same SNA family, classic SNA and APPN are very different.

The classic, centralized SNA is based on subareas managed by the mainframe. VTAM running on the mainframe contains tables of routes between SNA network nodes. Many switching functions are offloaded to the front-end processor running NCP (Network Control Program). NCP controls the communications to groups of terminals (called "subareas" in SNA-speak). VTAM manages the communications and flow of data between subareas.

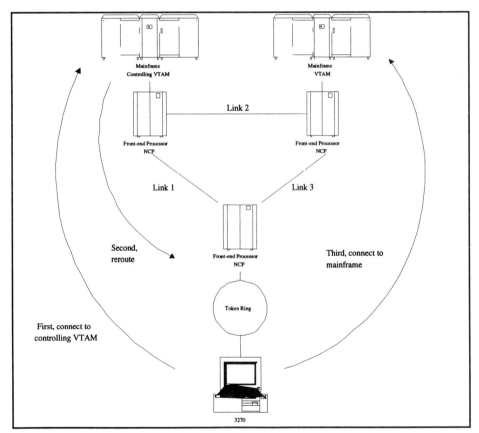

Figure 9-7   SNA Rerouting Between Front-end Processors

In an SNA network, mainframe-based VTAM establishes a session between desktop clients and servers. If several mainframes are connected to a network comprising several subareas, each mainframe-based VTAM is responsible for a different set of subareas. Another way to look at it is each subarea has a controlling VTAM. This means that a client must establish a session with its controlling VTAM before it can communicate with mainframe or servers in other subareas. Figure 9-6 shows how a client first establishes a session with its controlling VTAM, which then reroutes the session to a mainframe in another subarea.

SDLC passthrough, SDLC conversion, DLSw, and Frame Relay encapsulation are not substitutes for SNA rerouting. Without careful planning, replacing the front-end processors with routers can lead to unexpected results. For example, in Figure 9-7, after the client establishes the session with the second mainframe

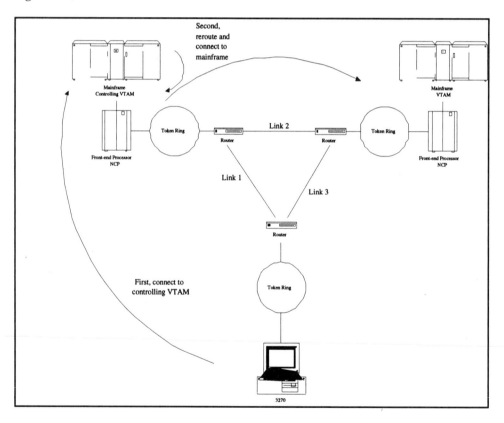

Figure 9-8   SNA Rerouting Between Routers

through link 2, all wide-area communications flow through link 3. In Figure 9-8, where routers connect the three sites, communications pass through links 1 and 2. If links 1 and 2 are more expensive than link 3, this will not be a cost-effective solution.

In contrast to classic SNA, APPN establishes direct routes between clients and servers without involving a mainframe. It uses IBM's Advanced Program-to-Program Communication (APPC) and Logical Unit (LU) 6.2 protocols for peer-to-peer networking. In the APPN architecture, network nodes can be End Nodes (EN), which are normally clients and servers, or Network Nodes (NN), which can act as routers. It is common to read about comparisons between IP and APPN, but such comparisons are irrelevant. APPN and IP, like other protocols, are effective solutions for different applications. For example, APPN is a good idea if your enterprise network is predominately SNA. We think it likely APPN will dominate the SNA backbone over the medium term. However, APPN will not replace other protocols such as TCP/IP.

Today, APPN suffers a number of limitations. That's why the longer-term direction points away from APPN to High Performance Routing (HPR) and APPN+. The original versions of APPN are suited to small networks using static routing, called Intermediate Session Routing (ISR). HPR and APPN+ use dynamic routing and scale up to faster networks. Also, unlike IP devices, APPN-compatible devices are not yet widely available. Even among IBM's product lines, important APPN functions are still missing.

We recommend that you avoid using APPN in the near-term unless it satisfies specific requirements. In most organizations, SNA data traffic is still predominately 3270 data streams, for which APPN does not offer many advantages. A better strategy is to wait until APPN products mature. Over the long haul, plan to use both IP and APPN. It is most likely that APPN and IP will share the enterprise backbone network. This means you should look for internetworking devices that can support IP and APPN routing. Several network suppliers, such as Cisco Systems and Bay Networks, have routers with APPN (and some APPN+) network node capability.

9

Networking the New Enterprise

Enhancing the Network 10

Critical devices, including hubs, routers, and switches, drive your network. If one fails, all or a major portion of your network goes dark. One way to reduce your network's vulnerability is to buy reliable devices. While an array of consolidating suppliers offer a panoply of devices at discount to premium prices, we recommend you spend what it takes to get quality equipment. The amount you lose to downtime will be many times higher than the extra amount you pay for reliable components.

How is the average network administrator supposed to discriminate between a "high-quality" device and one he should avoid? The type of quality we suggest is not the kind that appears in a magazine review, which usually compares feature checklists. The best way to ensure you get high-quality components is to select network suppliers that have proven they can build production-quality networks with their products. Another way is to turn to other users. Find out what others use to build their production-quality networks.

Special fault-tolerant devices harden your network. By definition, you may not shut down critical devices. Hot-swappable components let you add and replace modules without turning off the device. Fault-tolerant devices usually sport extra fans and power supplies, the very subcomponents most susceptible to failure.

Flash EPROM makes routers more reliable and easier to manage. You can quickly reload software on routers to Flash EPROM to resolve software problems. For remote routers, Flash EPROM allows you to download software updates from a central site.

Reliable, fault-tolerant, properly managed devices still fail. The ultimate (but not extreme) way to protect your network is to duplicate critical devices, such as backbone routers. In Chapter 6 we described how to build redundancy into your backbone network by using multiple routers in a collapsed backbone.

For critical subnets needing high availability, we recommend you connect these subnets to two routers, a technique called dual-homing. This allows fast, automatic cut-over and continuous service if one router fails (Figure 10-1).

How does dual-homing work? The subnet has primary and secondary connections to two routers. Only the primary connection stays active. If the router for the primary connection fails, the router for the secondary connection detects the failure by means of the hot-standby routing protocol, assumes the primary router's MAC address, and provides a connection for the subnet.

For the WAN, we recommend you establish backup communications for critical links. These additional channels provide extra capacity as well as fault tolerance.

Dial-on-Demand Routing

In Figure 10-2, remote subnets connect router-to-router by way of dial-up lines instead of more expensive dedicated lines. With dial-on-demand routing (DDR), routers establish dial-up connections to the core backbone network when there is data to transmit, then disconnect when there is no more data to transmit. You can use the analog telephone system or, better yet, ISDN.

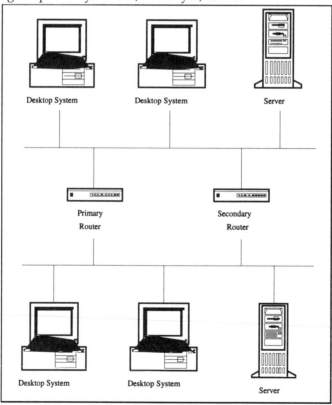

Figure 10-1   Dual-Homing with the Hot-Standby Router Protocol

There are a number of issues to consider for dial-on-demand routing. First, you need to configure an extra table in each router that lists the telephone numbers of the destination routers. Another issue is security. Like other dial-up connections, use security methods—Password Authentication Protocol (PAP) and Challenge Handshake Authentication Protocol (CHAP)—to ensure dial-on-demand connections are secure. We discuss dial-up security in Chapter 11. The last issue concerns routing. Dynamic routing is not appropriate for a network of routers using dial-up connections. Using RIP, OSPF and IGRP, routers exchange frequent updates. Each update requires a network connection. In the case of ISDN, each connection costs money. Although they require more effort to configure and maintain, use static routing tables.

DDR with Load Balancing

Along with establishing connections between remote subnets and the backbone, dial-on-demand routing backs up primary, dedicated links as shown in Figure 10-3. If a primary link fails, a dial-up link automatically maintains connectivity. DDR also allows additional WAN capacity. With load balancing, the routers can use

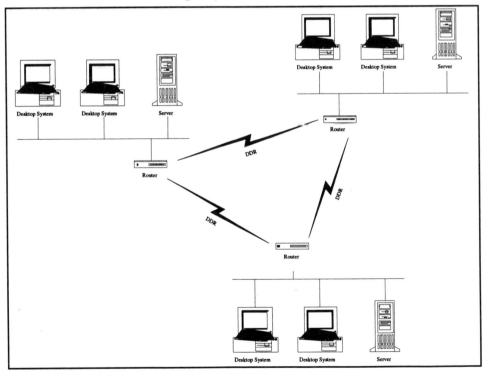

Figure 10-2   Dial-on-Demand Routing

the primary and DDR links together, so the two physical links appear to operate as one faster link.

In practice, both links should have similar characteristics for load balancing to operate in most routers. For example, the links should operate at similar speeds. Another important factor to consider is the protocols. Use OSPF, IGRP, and EIGRP because they balance loads more effectively than RIP.

Quality-of-Service

Quality-of-service is a new idea in the networking world and is one that has a chance to become a household phrase. In router-based networks, quality-of-service depends on two routing mechanisms: custom queuing and priority queuing. Custom queuing uses a bandwidth reservation scheme that ensures performance for time-sensitive data. For example, you can guarantee a minimum level of bandwidth for business-critical data such as transaction processing, while lower minimum levels of bandwidth are allocated to other data traffic, such as file transfers. With three applications—A, B, and C—you can assign 50 percent of

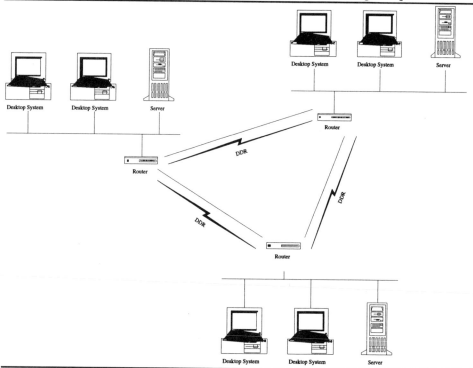

Figure 10-3   Dial-on-demand Routing with Load Balancing

network bandwidth to A, 30 percent to B, and the remaining 20 percent to C. If all three applications are sending data, each is ensured a specific minimum quality-of-service. If A and B become idle, C can use 100 percent of the network bandwidth.

Another method is to assign higher priorities to critical data traffic. Priority queuing allows you to assign priorities to different types of data traffic competing for limited WAN bandwidth, so critical data enjoys preferential treatment. For example, if several applications use the network at the same time, critical, response-time-sensitive data can be given priority over other data traffic (e.g., file transfer and e-mail) transmitted across the WAN. Priority queuing does not guarantee minimum bandwidth for lower priority applications. You can prioritize traffic by protocol, physical port, and message size.

Why might quality-of-service become the next household buzzphrase? The Internet! Pundits suggest quality-of-service will allow the Internet to continue its rapid growth by making high-volume, time-sensitive users (e.g., consumers of video or audio) pay more for service than do casual e-mail users.

Compression

Compressing data in routers or external devices reduces bandwidth requirements for WAN transmission, which boosts throughput. While router vendors claim 4-to-1 compression ratios, it is more reasonable to expect ratios closer to 2-to-1. Compression can be integrated with the routers or implemented in separate devices.

There are several compression methods: header, data, and link. With header compression, only the TCP/IP header of the data packet is compressed. Depending on the applications you use, header compression can improve throughput by 20 to 50 percent. You can probably guess that the data method compresses the data in the data packet. It is used in switched networks like X.25, Frame Relay, and ATM. The header is uncompressed because it switches the packet through the network. Link compression provides the best throughput because it compresses the entire packet—header and data. Link compression is best for point-to-point links.

≡ 10

The Proof

A department store chain in the Visayan region of the Philippines depends on a router-based WAN to connect three stores, one warehouse, the central office accounting department, and several merchandising (order) units. The business depends on a point-of-sale (POS) application that runs over a distributed network connecting the three stores and the central office.

In each store, a Token Ring network connects approximately 80 POS terminals to an OS/2-based POS store controller. The POS store controllers communicate with UNIX-based DBMS applications containing customer data in the central office. The desktops in the warehouse, accounting department, and merchandising units are connected to Ethernet networks. The remote merchandising units outside the central office are small, with Ethernet networks comprising only a handful of desktop systems.

Key Network Requirements

The mission-critical POS applications capture sales transactions in each store and process information from the DBMS application in the central office, so fast response times and high availability are essential. During normal business hours, the POS applications must be available 100 percent of the time. If customers have to wait at the checkout stand they will shop somewhere else.

The merchandising and warehouse applications are other business-critical systems requiring high levels of performance and availability. Ethernet-connected desktop computers at each retail outlet and other remote locations access merchandising applications on the DBMS server in the central office. The warehouse applications also run on the central DBMS server.

Logical Topology

The logical topology revolves around a backbone. Using routers and WAN links, the basic core backbone network ties together distributed Ethernet and Token Ring networks, which connect servers and desktops.

WAN RAS is a key requirement but it is also a major constraint. The WAN links are 64 or 56 (depending on the country) kilobit-per-second dedicated lines—often the best we can do in remote areas of developing countries. Another problem is reliability. Although major projects are underway to upgrade the telecommunications infrastructure in many developing countries, the remote areas outside the major urban sites are usually the last to reap any benefits. Unusual constraints mean we must devise creative solutions.

Remote Access to the Basic Core Network

The remote subnets in the merchandising units connect router-to-router through dial-up lines instead of more expensive dedicated lines. Using dial-on-demand routing, the routers establish dial-up connections to the backbone when there is data to send and hang up after the transmission completes. ISDN is not available, so plain old analog telephone lines are used. Fewer than 10 connections are made per day and traffic volumes are low, so the low speed analog lines are adequate. They provide the connections when needed, which is the key requirement.

Redundancy and Backup

Because WAN RAS is a major issue, we need to find creative ways to handle the major problems: reliability and speed. Besides establishing connections between remote networks and the backbone network, dial-on-demand routing also provides backup for the primary 64 kilobits-per-second links. If a primary link fails, a dial-up link automatically maintains connectivity.

Compression

The limited bandwidth of the lower-speed, 64 kilobits-per-second wide-area links is a problem. The best way to improve WAN throughput without buying more capacity is to use compression. With compression devices between the routers, we realize higher data throughput—two to three times faster than the normal 64 kilobits per second.

Quality-of-Service Application

We are also exploring how other router features, such as quality-of-service, can be used to enhance the network's reliability and performance. Quality-of-service depends on two routing mechanisms: custom queuing and priority queuing. We can use custom queuing's bandwidth reservation scheme to ensure high levels of performance for time-sensitive POS data. For example, a minimum bandwidth is guaranteed for business-critical data, such as POS data, and lower levels are allocated to other traffic such as file transfers.

Using priority queuing we can assign priorities to different types of traffic so critical data is given preference. For example, critical, response-time-sensitive POS and controller-to-DBMS traffic enjoy priority over more pedestrian traffic, such as file transfers and e-mail.

10

Other Performance Enhancements

There are a variety of ways to cure different types of bottlenecks and increase the capacity of your network. An obvious solution is to buy more bandwidth, which we discuss later. But more bandwidth usually means more money. You will be more popular with your boss if you can make a more efficient use of your existing capacity. Since WANs are slow compared to LANs, WANs are likely to create bottlenecks. We already discussed several methods to optimize wide area bandwidth—compression, DDR, and load balancing. We have also discussed how efficient protocols such as OSPF can provide better performance than other protocols.

If there is a router bottleneck in your network, we recommend that you disable extraneous router features to ensure your router's processing power is dedicated to routing data packets. For example, you can disable event logging, data recording, and other debugging features until you need them to resolve a problem. Restricting the use of these tools leaves more processing power to normal routing functions. Bridging can hurt routing performance, too. If you need to integrate bridging and routing, we recommend that you use routers with multiple CPUs and buses designed for high-speed bridging and routing.

Increasing Network Capacity

For most users, shared Ethernet networks still suffice. But be ready. Sooner or later, users will want to run the latest applications. The latest applications, including engineering, imaging, and client/server applications, require higher speeds than before. Furthermore, delay-sensitive applications, such as voice and video, continue to gain in popularity.

Fortunately, we enjoy many performance-boosting choices. Besides switching and full-duplex Ethernet, we can pick one of two new 100 megabits-per-second LAN standards: 100BaseT and 100VG-AnyLAN. Other fast alternatives include FDDI and ATM. You should select the technology that will protect your installed base and not become obsolete too soon.

High-Speed Performance, Scalability, and Manageability

When evaluating high-speed networks, consider how your network will use its bandwidth bounty. For example, FDDI with dual ring fault tolerance, management features, and large packet size makes for an effective backbone.

100BaseT interconnects existing 10BaseT networks with aplomb. For multimedia applications, deterministic access methods make FDDI and 100VG-AnyLAN effective choices.

While performance reigns as the top priority, you also need to consider scaleability and manageability. As we mentioned earlier, the cost of a network is more than hardware and software acquisition costs. When buying high-speed technologies that are not scalable or manageable, we pay a premium for them with each passing day. Any new high-speed solution must support additional network nodes and more bandwidth-intensive applications.

Depending on your network configuration, some high-speed technologies integrate easily into your existing network, whereas others require complex and time-consuming reconfigurations. There can be significant network management costs associated with installing and configuring drivers and hubs and reconfiguring cables. Furthermore, some high-speed technologies using new protocols may require costly retraining. Because changing bandwidth requirements and data traffic patterns are difficult to predict, whatever high-speed solution you implement must be flexible.

Network Switching

Although Ethernet's theoretical throughput is 10 megabits per second, the actual throughput you see in real-life networks is about 3 megabits per second. Because Ethernet employs a contention-based protocol, Ethernet becomes congested as you add more nodes. Using well-known standards and existing cable and equipment, Ethernet switches improve network performance while avoiding expensive modifications, which protects your installed base and allows you to keep your options open as new standards emerge.

Ethernet Switching

An Ethernet switch works like a bridge. It has multiple ports (8, 16, or more) that connect to Ethernet segments. If the sending and receiving nodes (designated by the MAC addresses in the data packet) are connected to the same segment, the switch simply drops the packet so the other segments think they're living on the quietest Ethernet in town. Where the nodes are connected to different segments, the switch establishes a temporary high-speed connection between the segments.

The Ethernet switch minimizes network media sharing. Data traffic is restricted to the segments connecting the sending and receiving nodes. In effect, the switch divides the network into discrete segments so one large data flow is divided into smaller independent data flows. The switching backplane becomes the shared media. Instead of many computers sharing a single 10 megabits-per-second

Ethernet, each system or small group of systems share a dedicated 10 megabits-per-second segment connected to the switch's gigabits-per-second backplane. Along with improving performance, another switching advantage is that we can avoid making modifications to cables, network interfaces, drivers, and systems software.

Besides multiple 10 megabits-per-second ports, many switches have ports for Fast Ethernet, FDDI, and ATM. Typical computers connect to the 10 megabits-per-second ports directly or through 10BaseT hubs, whereas the faster pipes connect backbone networks and servers. The result is a scalable and cost-effective solution using easy-to-install switches that boost bandwidth where it is needed most.

Beware, some switches support only four or fewer MAC addresses per port. This may be adequate for some applications. If four do not meet your requirements, look for a switch that supports the number of MAC addresses you need.

Three Types of Ethernet Switches

There are three main types of Ethernet switches: cut-through, store-and-forward, and error-free cut-through.

Fast, nonblocking backplane (2-4 Gbps)
Stackable bandwidth for Ethernet, Fast Ethernet, and ATM
Support for error-free cut-through switching
Manageable as a single entity
Virtual LAN support within the stack
Network analyzer port
Full-duplex support on Ethernet, Fast Ethernet, and ATM
IEEE 802.1d spanning-tree protocol support
Address filtering
Full-duplex 10BaseT ports
Full-duplex 100BaseT ports
ATM ports
Automatic address aging
Telnet access
SNMP MIB II support
Flash PROM for software updates
Network management applications

Table 10-1   Switch features

The faster cut-through switch does not buffer incoming packets. It simply forwards a packet when it reads the destination MAC address in the packet header. While fast, the cut-through switch may propagate error-filled packets because the error-correction codes in the packet trailer are never verified. If errors are propagated too often, network performance may deteriorate, which negates switching's advantages.

The store-and-forward switch buffers each incoming packet, checks the error-correction code, and forwards the packet to the proper destination. The store-and-forward switch uses its buffer to flip packets between 10 and 100 megabits-per-second segments.

The error-free cut-through switch combines the advantages of cut-through and store-and forward switches. Operating in the normal cut-through mode, the switch transfers packets between same-speed segments. However, if the network data error rate increases, the switch changes to the store-and-forward mode automatically.

We list the features you should consider for your network switches in Table 10-1.

Switched Internetwork Scalability

For maximum scalability, we recommend switched internetworks—with a few provisos. Many vendors advocate replacing your routers with switches. We're not sure this is always a good idea. Do your homework first. Understand your network data traffic before you believe the vendors' promises. While you can build a fast switched internetwork using only layer-2 switches, a flat structure is not scalable. Like bridges, switches propagate network broadcast messages such as ARP requests and service advertisements. For this reason, we advocate deploying switches locally and building a backbone network with routers. The routers control inappropriate broadcasts and manage network bandwidth effectively.

Virtual LANs (VLANs) are an emerging technology that is supposed to address the problem of switched internetwork scalability. VLANs allow you to define workgroups in a manner independent of your network's physical layout. This lets you assign related users, who might work in offices on separate floors, to one (virtual) LAN. VLANs use fast switches linked with a 100 megabits-per-second network, resulting in better performance than a router-connected segment.

While VLAN products work well in small LANs, the jury is still out on how VLANs work in large multiprotocol networks. Today, vendors offer their own vision and architecture. The schemes integrating layer 2 and 3 functions with VLAN capabilities in the same device are still proprietary. For example, each vendor uses different signaling methods to convey VLAN information between switches. Also, some switches function at layer 2, and offer varying degrees of layer 3 routing capabilities. Some layer 3 switches use OSPF but most still depend on RIP. The range of network protocols supported by layer 3 switches is still limited.

Perhaps VLAN's greatest weakness is manageability. Most still require a lot of manual configuration. The IEEE has started the standards process for VLANs, but do not expect to see any standards in place soon. Without standards and management tools you will want to consider enjoying the first half of the game from the sidelines.

Full-Duplex Ethernet

Plain vanilla Ethernet is half duplex—traffic flows in one direction at a time. As its name implies, full-duplex Ethernet connections allow simultaneous two-way traffic, which increases capacity. If data traffic flows predominately in one direction at a time, upgrading to full-duplex connection will not boost performance one whit. Full-duplex Ethernet works wonders between switches, since traffic between switches is usually symmetrical. Another good spot to use full-duplex is the connection between a server and switch, where oceans of data flow between the server and many clients. Over on the client side of the switch, full-duplex rarely exists, since traffic flows usually from the server to the client.

How does full-duplex work its magic? Star-wired 10BaseT and 100BaseT networks use two pairs of wires: one pair for transmitting and one pair for receiving. Transmission and reception cannot take place at the same time. Full-duplex Ethernet, on the other hand, allows transmission over one pair of wires and reception over the other pair simultaneously. Full-duplex Ethernet dovetails nicely with plain (half-duplex) Ethernet and uses existing 10BaseT wiring.

Full-duplex Ethernet has a few drawbacks. You need to buy NICs, hubs, switches, firmware, and drivers that support it. Full-duplex makes sense only in point-to-point connections with heavy enough traffic, such as in backbones or between servers.

While pundits suggest ATM will eventually rule the backbone, we think plain and switched Ethernet will continue to provide inexpensive desktop connectivity for years to come.

Faster Network Technologies

If you need high-bandwidth networks down to the desktop, you need to consider the alternatives—Fast Ethernet, switched Token Ring, FDDI, and ATM.

Faster Ethernet

Compared to other high-speed alternatives, 100BaseT is easy to implement and manage, which saves you time and money. It uses the same CSMA/CD found in 10BaseT, so it merges nicely into existing 10BaseT networks. Although 100BaseT requires new 100 megabits-per-second network adapters and hubs, the components are widely available, so, along with moderate management costs, purchase costs are also affordable.

100BaseT uses the tried-and-true CSMA/CD protocol for good and ill. The contention-based CSMA/CD limits 100BaseT's scalability, since adding busy nodes increases network collisions, which throttles performance. As with 10BaseT, however, 100BaseT switching and full-duplex transmission help to ease scalability problems. 100BaseT switching allows you to dedicate 100 megabits per second to high-bandwidth devices, and with full-duplex you can double throughput to 200 megabits per second.

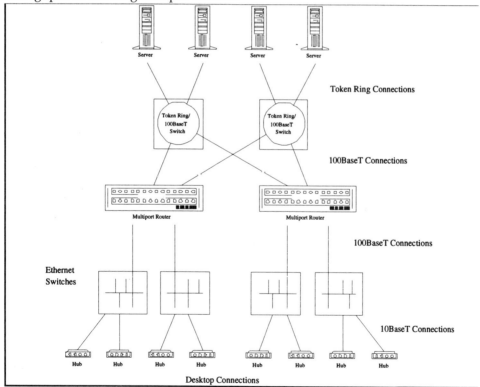

Figure 10-4   Token Ring and Ethernet Switching with a Core Router Backbone

As 100BaseT's detractors point out, CSMA/CD isn't very efficient at 100 megabits per second. CSMA/CD is limited by a short collision window, which is the mechanism a node uses to detect collisions. While 100BaseT is 10 times faster than 10BaseT, collision windows are the same. This means 100BaseT's maximum cable length is shorter than 10BaseT. Where 10BaseT hubs are connected with 100 meter UTP cable, 100BaseT must make do with 10 meter UTP connections. Furthermore, 100BaseT allows only two repeater hops between two network nodes, whereas 10BaseT allows four. If you are considering a change to 100BaseT, be sure to take a close look at your cable. There are several 100BaseT variations. The more common variation, 100BaseTX, uses two-pair Category 5 cables. 100BaseT4 uses four-pair Category 3, 4, or 5 UTP cables, while 100BaseFX uses fiber-optics.

100VG-AnyLAN is another speedy LAN option described in IEEE 802.12. Refer to IEEE's Web site[1]. In place of CSMA/CD, 100VG-AnyLAN employs a new, arguably superior, protocol called Demand Priority Queuing (DPA). DPA uses special signal techniques to provide better performance than contention-based CSMA/CD. With a deterministic scheme, it handles time-sensitive information such as voice traffic. However, DPA is a new protocol, which means you need to spend time and money on extra training. Also, compared to 100BaseT, DPA is not as widely available and there still are not many applications that take advantage of the deterministic protocol. Remember, use widely available, standards-based products because they ensure that you can implement new solutions in the future that are cost-effective and compatible with your existing network.

Common 100BaseT is still an effective solution for most network configurations where you need a 100 megabits-per-second link to connect a server or router to a switch or interconnect switches. Network contention is not an issue when 100BaseT connects one device to a switch. 100VG-AnyLAN and other fast technologies provide a better solution when several devices share a 100 megabits-per-second link or when you need to transmit voice or video.

As with 100BaseT, 100VG-AnyLAN uses four pairs to transmit data over Category 3 cable. In many organizations, the Category 3 UTP has only two pairs. For Category 5 cable, two cable pairs are sufficient for DPA. Using a scheme called quartet coding, DPA transmits four parallel data streams at 25 megabits per second. Two faster parallel data streams are transmitted on higher-quality, Category 5 UTP cables.

---

1.   http:// www.ieee.org

Token Ring Scalability

You can turbo-charge a Token Ring network two ways: switching and full duplexing (sound familiar?). In Figure 10-4, the enterprise servers are connected to a distribution network comprising two Token Ring switches. Dual Token Ring switches provide better performance and reliability than a single switch. Two collapsed backbone routers are connected to both switches, so the network stays alive if one switch dies.

FDDI Scalability

With built-in management and fault tolerance, FDDI makes a dandy backbone that spans several buildings. Besides better performance, FDDI also supports 500 nodes on a single segment, which may extend several kilometers. While you can use your Category 5 cabling to run FDDI to your PCs and workstations, FDDI remains a pricey proposition, since you need to buy FDDI hubs and adapters for each device.

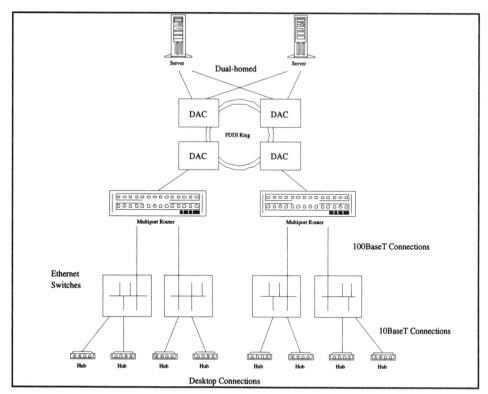

Figure 10-5   FDDI and Ethernet Switching with a Core Router Backbone

FDDI operates effectively at 80 percent of its capacity, making it a more stable high-speed backbone than CSMA/CD-based 100BaseT. An FDDI backbone is modular and scalable, so FDDI can be implemented easily. In Figure 10-5, an FDDI ring replaces the distribution backbone Token Rings. There are several physical FDDI configuration options, which include a physical ring, an FDDI concentrator, and multiple, interconnected concentrators for redundancy. For additional fault tolerance, you can use dual-homing, that is, you connect critical network servers to two FDDI concentrators in case one fails.

FDDI has deterministic and bandwidth allocation schemes, which enhance performance and scalability. Using a prioritization scheme called Synchronous Bandwidth Allocation (SBA), FDDI enables you to assign a fixed amount of bandwidth to a network node or a group of nodes. FDDI can allocate the bandwidth that is not used by SBA so that it is divided among the other nodes on the network equally. Unfortunately few, if any, applications take advantage of these features.

FDDI also has a number of built-in management features, and with modern hubs and switches, it is easier to integrate FDDI into Ethernet and Token Rings. FDDI's dual counter-rotating rings enhance reliability because tokens can travel on either ring. Network nodes can be connected to the two rings. If a break occurs in one network ring, the problem can be bypassed so the token can travel in the opposite direction in the other ring. (See the description of FDDI's wrap-around capability in Chapter 6.) FDDI's Station Management (SMT) monitors the network and controls this fault-tolerant process.

FDDI is also commonly used to connect centralize servers, or server farms, to the backbone. However, when many users begin to access a large number of high-performance backbone servers, even FDDI becomes a bottleneck. Like Ethernet and Token Ring, you extend FDDI's life with (expensive) switches from such vendors as Alantec and Digital Equipment.

The Proof

An international insurance company with offices in major Asian cities asked us to review their network architecture. The network links 500 desktops, mainframes, and 30 UNIX and Windows NT servers scattered throughout a building in Hong Kong. It was planned to connect at least 500 additional PCs in the near future. And there were plans to provide access to remote users and to interconnect other offices in Asia.

Initial Analysis

Although the network was based on a collapsed backbone architecture, there were several critical problems. First, the network seemed to be growing out of control. Performance was becoming a problem as more client/server applications were deployed. The network lacked structure, which made it difficult to analyze. The lack of structure also affected scalability—it was difficult to implement enhancements.

Structured Hierarchy

We redefined the network architecture. The physical network is divided into three well-defined areas: workgroup, the core backbone, and server distribution networks. This approach makes the network more incrementally scalable so capacity can be added where needed. Servers are most likely to place high-bandwidth demands on the network. With the busy servers isolated on a small number of distribution networks, we can add higher bandwidth technologies into these well-defined areas without having to make costly upgrades to desktops and other undemanding devices.

Core Backbone Network

The core backbone network consists of two multiport routers. The backbone network is configured in a collapsed backbone architecture where the high-speed router interconnects the workgroup and server distribution networks. This centralized configuration provides high levels of performance and manageability. To incorporate full redundancy, two collapsed backbone routers are interconnected. Two routers in a collapsed backbone also provide additional capacity and allow more efficient use of the switches.

Switched Distribution Networks

All servers connect to the distribution network switches. Two switches provide a combination of Token Ring, FDDI, and 100BaseT connections for servers. The mainframe requires Token Ring access, and the HP UNIX server requires fast, 100 megabits-per-second capacity, which this user answered with FDDI. 100BaseT is intended for other servers centralized on the distribution network.

Switched Workgroup Networks

The workgroup networks use a combination of shared and switched Ethernet. Groups of desktops attach to 10BaseT hubs. The 10BaseT hubs are connected to dedicated 10 megabits-per-second switched segments on workgroup switches. The 10 megabits-per-second desktop segments are switched between 100 megabits-per-second segments that connect to the core backbone routers.

Asynchronous Transfer Mode

Asynchronous Transfer Mode (ATM) is a promising but unfinished network technology controlled by a group called the ATM Forum. It is supposed to integrate everything—LANs, WANs, data, voice, and video on a single network running at speeds of 25 megabits to 2.4 gigabits per second.

Where traditional networks used variable-length packets, ATM uses short 53-byte cells. Each cell consists of 5 bytes of header material and 48 bytes of payload. By contrast, an Ethernet packet can range in size from 64 to 1,500 bytes. ATM uses a quality-of-service scheme to distinguish between cells requiring a constant bit rate (for voice or video) and those that don't (e-mail).

Organizations invested big money in current networks, which are still adequate for most needs. ATM is a new technology with many critical standards issues yet to be resolved. Nevertheless, keep a weather-eye on ATM.

We expect that integrating ATM with existing networks will be a headache for many. The ATM Forum says it is trying to resolve the issues surrounding how to execute current LAN and WAN technologies over ATM. There are still many ATM standards to work on, and until standards are set, ATM products from different vendors will likely be incompatible.

A connectionless TCP/IP network uses large address tables to independently route each packet to its destination. A large network address in each packet must be processed independently by each router in the data path. This means each router must do a separate table lookup for each packet.

By contrast, ATM is connection oriented, so a connection is negotiated before data is transmitted. To establish a connection, each intermediate point in the network between the sending and receiving nodes must be identified. A connection number in each cell identifies the connection for each node. This connection setup process happens once. After the connection is established, all cells flow through the same connection path, so only simple cell-switching operations are performed. Using small connection numbers, which conserve network bandwidth, and small tables in the switches, ATM switching is simple and fast. Simplicity allows ATM switching to be done in hardware, which also enhances its capacity.

Along with providing very high data throughput, ATM-aware applications can negotiate for quality-of-service. Different types of applications require different types of network resources. Where voice and video applications depend on low delays to ensure that the special timing relationships between cells remains constant, routine traffic (e-mail, for example) does not require a constant bit rate. Data applications with bursty data traffic require variable bit rates. ATM can satisfy application requirements for both constant and variable bit rates.

Besides incomplete standards, another problem with ATM is a lack of APIs (Application Program Interface) and ATM-aware applications. Once you complete end-to-end ATM connectivity from desktop to desktop, you will still need network layer protocols, such as TCP/IP, and internetwork devices such as routers, for your existing applications. This means you need to find ways to integrate ATM with your existing network technologies, which is not straightforward.

Cost is another constraint to ATM networking. Compared to other options, ATM is still expensive for what you get. With 100 megabit-per-second Ethernet, LAN switching and emerging gigabit Ethernet, users have a good reason to delay their ATM plans. Some organizations are planning to connect switched Ethernet workgroups to gigabit Ethernet backbones through 100BaseT, although it will not be ready until 1997. This architecture will provide a common technology end-to-end, which is what ATM is supposed to do. Ethernet may work better at a lower cost.

Integrating ATM and LANs

User-to-Network Interface (UNI) is an ATM software service that defines the interface between an ATM user node and an ATM switch. With UNI, network nodes discover the layout of the network and calculate effective routes. This network interface is important because it defines how a switched virtual connection is made in an ATM network. It also defines how the connection is concluded.

Because ATM networks differ from your existing Ethernet and Token Ring networks, you need an interface that defines how local Ethernet and Token Ring networks communicate over an ATM network. Enter the LAN Emulation (LANE) protocols. LANE is an important part of UNI because it emulates Ethernet and Token Ring networks, and bridges them across ATM networks.

Since ATM is a connection-oriented protocol, you need LANE protocols to support connectionless network layer protocols that depend on broadcasts. LANE is a layer 2 function that makes a connection-oriented ATM network look like a connectionless Ethernet or Token Ring. Because LANE is similar to bridging, it has many of the same scalability problems that bridges do. You can implement LANE in any ATM-connected network device. It runs in LAN switches, routers, and the network adapters of servers and desktops connected to an ATM switch.

Choosing LANE products—routers, switches, and network adapters—can be tricky. Even though LANE is a standard, there are several incompatible versions—UNI 3.0 and 3.1, and upcoming 4.0—each providing different capabilities. Adding to the confusion a number of suppliers have developed their own proprietary LANE versions. Also, be forewarned that LAN emulation limits some of the key benefits of ATM, including the capability to negotiate for quality-of-service guarantees.

Another method of running LAN protocols over ATM is to modify network-layer protocols to operate directly over ATM in native mode. The Internet Engineering Task Force (IETF) has published a specification for running IP with ARP over ATM in RFC 1577. Such native-mode protocols are important, because they will allow direct use of the quality-of-service guarantees of ATM by higher-layer protocols when these acquire multimedia capabilities. This is more difficult with a LANE-based network.

Looking toward the future, the ATM Forum is working on a standard called Multiprotocol over ATM (MPOA), which allows network-layer protocols to run on ATM. We expect MPOA to be a standard in the next generation of multilayer switches.

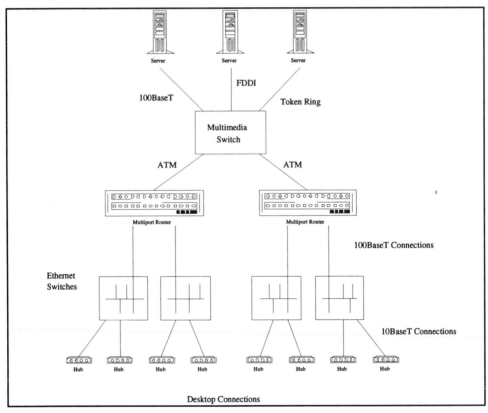

Figure 10-6   ATM Switching with a Core Router Backbone

Migrating to a Switched ATM Network

Your organization, like many others, will likely deploy new client/server, image-based, and other bandwidth-intensive applications in the future, so it is important to have a well-defined plan for a scalable network. This means you need to develop a phased transition to a fully switched internetwork with ATM. In other words, you had better plan for ATM.

Emerging high-performance switched internetworks are based on an ATM backbone. Combining ATM switching and routing, an ATM backbone provides high-bandwidth connectivity between switched workgroup networks. The routers provide broadcast control and traffic management to prevent broadcast messages from propagating across the switched internetwork and slashing performance.

You will probably migrate from a router-based network that interconnects shared Ethernet and Token Ring networks to a fully internetwork and, eventually, end-to-end ATM. You need to juggle this migration in a controlled and cost-effective manner while protecting the installed base.

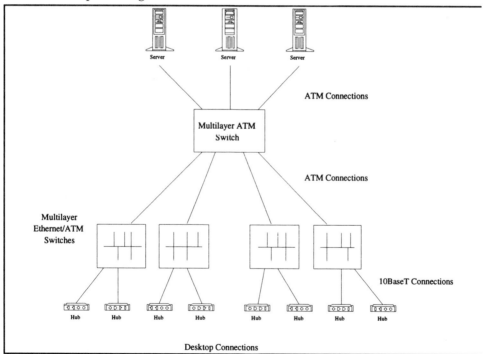

Figure 10-7   Multilayer Switched Network

We recommend a three-phased migration plan to a fully switched internetwork. The first phase is feasible and workable today.

In the first phase, introduce ATM into the backbone between the routers in Figure 10-6. The routers connect shared and switched Ethernet networks. Bringing ATM into the WAN backbone provides the advantage of efficient use of bandwidth, where capacity is often limited and relatively expensive. Although ATM uses limited WAN bandwidth more efficiently, the routers still represent a potential bottleneck where high-bandwidth applications are implemented. The routers introduce latency, and their connectionless nature means that other potential delays are introduced because the routers process each data packet separately.

We find that implementing ATM between the core backbone routers is an effective and manageable way to introduce the high-bandwidth technology in an enterprise network. We designed a large network for a communications company in an island-country in Asia. The network spanned more than 150 locations. We used ATM in the core backbone WAN to connect the four key sites—all within the capital city. Secondary networks—Frame Relay and dedicated lines—from

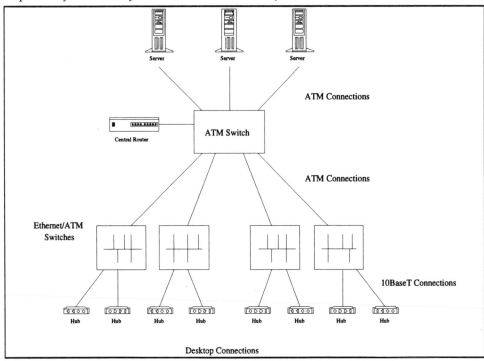

Figure 10-8   ATM Backbone with Central Routing

other remote areas around the country all fed into this small core ATM backbone. This configuration is providing a number of important benefits to the client. ATM provides a high-performance solution in an important part of the network where high bandwidth is required. ATM is restricted to a small part of the network, so it is easier to manage in the beginning. This allows the client to acquire hands-on experience with the technology before extending ATM throughout the rest of the network.

In several other companies, we used ATM to connect the collapsed backbone routers in large building complexes. Again this configuration allows us to introduce ATM into a part of the network where high bandwidth is required but to restrict its scope to an area where the new protocol can be managed easily.

In phase 2, shown in Figure 10-7, the routing functions are distributed across multilayer switches. This is becoming feasible as suppliers begin to combine layer 2 and layer 3 switching functionality in their routers and switches. Layer 3 switches allow switching based on network addresses. With less latency and cut-through capabilities, the switches can transfer data packets between networks faster than routers. However, bringing the routing functions into the switch, with all the complex calculations, introduces additional overhead. You should be aware this is still not a proven standard-base solution for networks. There is no guarantee that products from different suppliers will interoperate.

In Figure 10-8, the routing functions are moved out of the switches to a central router, so there is supposedly less overhead in the switches. The router calculates optimal paths and provides the results to the switches. This configuration is still in the future, so there are still many issues to be resolved.

Managing ATM

How do you plan to manage an ATM network? As we discussed earlier, network management is often an afterthought. With ATM it is essential to make network management a No. 1 priority. ATM is different from the Ethernet and Token Ring networks we are familiar with. Connection-oriented ATM has its own set of limits—cell delay, cell loss rate, cell error rate, and call setup time. This means that ATM network management is different. Because ATM networks are still new and unfamiliar, no guidelines exist for the limits and criteria needed to monitor and manage large networks.

Although there are tools to analyze and monitor ATM networks, they are new and still need work. Tools for 100 megabits-per-second networks are still lacking. The ones that are available are expensive. Unlike Ethernet and Token Ring that depend on shared broadcast media, ATM uses virtual circuits. For shared Ethernet and Token Ring networks, you can connect your analyzer to any point on the network to monitor all traffic. This is not possible with ATM networks and

10

LAN switched networks. With switched networks, you can either monitor one interface at a time, or you need a method to summarize the traffic passing through a switch. Some ATM and LAN switches come with special monitor ports that summarize data traffic. We recommend that you choose switches with this feature.

Securing the Network 11 ≡

It's harder to secure a distributed-computing network than a mainframe computing environment. Client/server applications, Intranets, and PCs scatter your data into uncontrolled areas, traveling over wires outside your organization. The job is difficult but not impossible, though.

Securing the enterprise network is more than a technical problem. You also need cooperation from users. Network security depends on people, policies, and technology. For each area of the computing environment, consider different layers of security. A multi-layered approach combines security measures to enhance the security of the enterprise network. Security measures should include:

- Risk assessment
- Physical security
- Secure operating systems
- Encryption
- Eavesdropping/intrusion protection
- Authentication and access controls
- Password management
- Virus protection
- Secure dial-up access
- Firewalls
- Packet filtering
- Application security

Assessing Your Risks

Start with an accurate risk assessment since many security neophytes focus on the wrong risks. A risk assessment forms the cornerstone of the security policy we discussed briefly in Chapter 3. With so much media attention given to break-ins from external hackers, many managers forget that the greatest security losses come from honest employees failing to follow procedures and malcontents on the inside bent on revenge or personal profit. This does not mean it is safe to ignore outside threats—they are real. You should analyze risks dispassionately so that you spend your money on the appropriate countermeasures.

Ask yourself, where does your organization keep its crown jewels? High-tech companies, for example, shield their engineering groups' networks behind several firewalls, among other countermeasures. Identify your business-critical data and network devices. Calculate the damage done if this data or control of these devices fell into a rival's hands.

For highly confidential systems, you will want to ensure that these use special password controls, are logically isolated on the network, use security logging for auditing, encrypt data, and so on. For your nonconfidential and non-business-critical systems, simple password controls may suffice.

Physical Security

As with the mainframe, place critical devices, such as important servers and backbone routers, in a safe place. Without physical security, other countermeasures make little difference. Put critical network devices under lock and key in monitored data centers, equipment rooms, and wiring closets. We discuss important elements of secure physical facilities in Chapter 7.

Secure Operating Systems

When selecting servers for applications, you need to consider security as well as many other features. There are three important security areas: features, management, and updates/fixes. With increasing attention given to network security over the past several years, lack of security features is not a major problem. The predominate network operating systems—UNIX, NetWare, Windows NT, Banyan Vines, and OS/2—have the important features you need to build a secure network. A number of organizations have also defined guidelines for secure systems. The best known is the U. S. Government's Orange Book, which defines four security levels. *A* is the high security level and *D* the lowest. The levels are divided into classes such as *A1, B1, B2, B3, C1,* and *C2*. Most experts agree C2 security is adequate for most commercial organizations.

While most network vendors claim to have C2-compliant products, we prefer to take a more thoughtful approach to security. The Orange Book is complex, difficult to understand, and focuses on standalone systems. It is not relevant to many distributed-network security issues. For example, a number of companies claim their well-known operating systems are C2-compliant—that is as long as you don't connect them to the network. When you do, all bets are off. (They don't always tell you that part.) We recommend that you choose operating systems with good logon and file access control procedures and user accounting that are easy to use and manage.

Most network operating systems have these features. An important difference is the way they are managed. On systems such as NetWare 3.X, you need to manage security on each server separately. For example, if a user needs to access five different servers, you must enter the user's ID and so on in each server separately. This is a time-consuming task for a large enterprise network and prone to errors, which are security risks in and of themselves. Other operating systems let you define in a single transaction a user who has access to several servers on a network. The methods to do this vary among operating systems—some are more flexible and scalable. Nonetheless, when you select operating systems, consider how you will manage security. If security is not easy to manage, you probably won't have any.

Even if an operating system is C2-compliant, has all the features to build a secure network, and is easy to manage, it still may not be secure. Because operating systems are complex programs, they usually have bugs that open security holes. Install the latest version of the operating system and all its security updates. Get more information about security problems and updates from the suppliers. The CERT (Computer Emergency Response Team) Coordination Center also issues security alerts.[1]

Consider the interaction of applications with the operating system on the servers. Even though the operating system may be secure, hackers can exploit applications, such as FTP and NFS to compromise the security on the servers. For example, to secure a UNIX environment, consider:

- Restricting Simple Mail Transfer Protocol (SMTP)
- Using versions with higher security levels
- Installing security updates
- Restricting FTP
- Disabling NFS
- Disabling group accounts
- Restricting root passwords and permissions
- Using TCP Wrapper

---

1. http://www.cert.org/

11

Encryption

Encryption is one of the most versatile methods to ensure that data remains confidential and in good order. We use encryption in several layers of the network, depending on applications and policies.

WANs extend the backbone to remote sites over telephone lines that are often exposed to tampering. One of the telephone companies' dirty little secrets is the susceptibility of WAN links to undetected eavesdropping. This is not to say that eavesdropping runs rampant, but since it is so difficult to detect, who knows? We recommend encrypting WAN links by placing encryption devices at each WAN access point. Encryption may be integrated within the router or by external devices.

At the operating system and application levels, we encrypt sensitive data before it is stored on disk or tape. For example, we encrypt all password and private encryption key files, as well as all data on backup tapes stored off-site. We also encrypt sensitive messages, for example, cash transactions, before transmitting them across the network.

Eavesdropping Protection and Intrusion Detection

It is easy to configure a notebook computer as a protocol analyzer that monitors Ethernet or Token Ring traffic without detection. You may want to use secured hubs. Many hubs protect against this type of eavesdropping and intrusion by noting each device's MAC address. The concentrator keeps track of the MAC address of the device attached to each port. When a data packet is transmitted on the network, the concentrator checks the destination address in the header and sends the data packet to the correct port. The concentrator also sends the data packet to the other ports, but it overwrites the data field with alternating 1s and 0s. Only the device with the correct destination address can read the data.

Since the concentrator keeps track of the MAC addresses of the devices on each port, it can also detect an unauthorized device. When it finds a rogue device, it partitions the port and sends a message to the network management system.

Authentication and Access Controls

All operating systems designed for distributed-enterprise computing have authentication mechanisms. Most systems use passwords to authenticate and/or identify users. Although this may be adequate for most basic security requirements, we recommend a more sophisticated authentication mechanism to protect business-critical applications, particularly where the network extends access to uncontrolled areas. Password management depends on users to control their passwords properly. This usually does not work well, since users tend to select passwords that are easy to guess, or write them down, or share them with others. Business-critical applications need a more secure mechanism, such as a one-time password.

With a token-based authentication system, users carry a credit card-like token. Each minute the token generates a new password that is synchronized with the passwords on the remote server. When initiating a connection to the network, the user enters a secret personal identification number (PIN) and the valid password displayed on the token. SecurID from Security Dynamics is a token-based security system that is compatible with a wide range of servers, routers, modems and other network components.

For business-critical applications, we restrict access to isolated and secured desktops on specific days and times.

Password Management

The most basic security measure is the password. The weak link in password-based security is the user: it is mainly a people issue. While we always invoke operating system features that require users to change their passwords periodically and select passwords with at least six characters, it is difficult to encourage users to select hard-to-guess passwords, to avoid sharing passwords, and to ban writing passwords down where others can see them. Through security policies, security awareness seminars, and electronic mail, we periodically remind users of the importance of network security and password management.

Virus Protection

There are thousands of computer viruses that can shutter the network. New strains appear daily, so you must take ongoing precautions to protect the applications and data on the network. A number of products, including NetShield from McAfee Associates and NET-PROT from Command Software Systems, automate virus scanning on NetWare servers, which are most susceptible to viruses. We have also used Intel's LANProtect. These products scan your server periodically and send messages to network administrators if they detect a virus.

Some of these products also scan desktop systems. For example, we use LANProtect on all NetWare servers to scan desktops once a week. Virus scanning is initiated automatically when the PC starts up.

11

Like password management, virus protection is more than a technology problem—it depends on the users. Without good security awareness it is difficult to prevent users from using unsafe software from unknown sources on their desktop systems. We give them tools to detect viruses in their desktop systems and notebooks, and in our security awareness programs and electronic mail reminders, we encourage them to use these tools.

Dial-in Security

There are several methods to secure dial-in access. First, restrict access to a centralized communications gateway, such as a Livingston Portmaster. A central access point is easier to manage and control than scattered access points. Use authentication on the communications gateway. The gateway should require a valid password before permitting access to the network.

Another technique that better secures dial-in access is the dial-back method. A remote user dials into the system, supplies a password, and then disconnects. Moments later, the system calls back to the predetermined phone number and reestablishes the connection. This way, remote connections are restricted to a list of trusted phone numbers. A more flexible method is the one-time password for dial-in security.

One big problem with many password schemes is that passwords are sent across the network as clear text and can be easily copied. Password Authentication Protocol (PAP) and Challenge Handshake Authentication Protocol (CHAP) are two ways to secure dial-in connections using the PPP. Of the two, CHAP provides better security. PAP transfers a clear-text password one time when you make a dial-up connection. CHAP transfers passwords at different times during a dial-up session and each time the password is encrypted differently. We recommend using remote access devices, including routers, remote access servers, and PCs, that can be adapted to use CHAP.

Be aware of emerging security software. Several network companies are beginning to adopt TACACS (Terminal Access Controller Access Control System) and RADIUS (Remote Authentication Dial-in User Service) in their products. TACACS and RADIUS are designed to be used with a broad range of network products for enterprise-wide remote access security.

Firewalls

If the idea of using the Internet and the telephone network to provide network connections does not set off warnings in your head, then you are probably the wrong person in your organization to worry about security. Hackers can see and tamper with data crossing the public networks. The public network can be turned against you to break into your network

Your security job here has three parts. First, you must ensure that incoming data traversing public networks is really coming from authorized users. Second, you need a way of making sure the data is not modified. And third, you need to keep confidential data away from prying eyes. Using firewalls with other security countermeasures such as encryption and authentication, you can establish a potent defense.

If you connect your network to the Internet, you open an unsecured channel that can be used to attack your data and applications. Common Internet protocols have weaknesses that hackers can use to get inside the network unless you take special precautions. One of the main security countermeasures to protect your corporate network from the Internet and other networks is the firewall. A firewall is a computer or router that stands between the network and the Internet.

A variety of commercial firewall products and routers with built-in security capabilities are available. However, simply implementing one of the commercial firewalls is not enough. You must remain aware of new ways that hackers use to break security and understand how your firewall protects the network. There are different types of firewalls with different strengths and weaknesses. The exact requirements for the firewall depend on your network security policy.-

Packet Filters

Packet filters enhance regular IP-based routing. With packet filters, you can identify certain types of packets based on their content and then take some specific actions. For example, you can define router filters that discard ("drop") packets with certain MAC, IP, or port addresses. A simple packet filter is shown in Figure 11-1, in which network 192.168.1 can access network 192.168.2 and the Internet, network 192.168.2 can access network 192.168.1 but not the Internet, and no incoming connections from the Internet can pass to network 192.168.1 or 192.168.2. By checking the destination IP address of each incoming packet on each, the packet filter can decide if the packet should be forwarded or dropped.

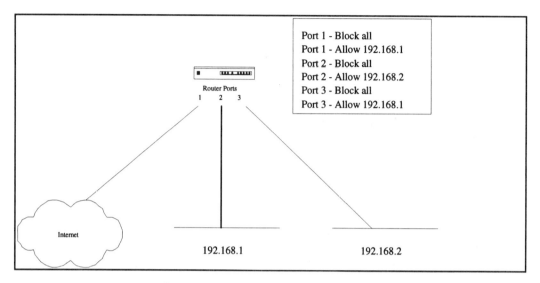

Figure 11-1   Figure 11-1: Packet Filter

Because packet filtering depends on the contents of the data packet, it has some limitations. For example, packet filters depend on port numbers to identify different network applications. Because the association between applications and port numbers is not always fixed, packet filtering is not always the best solution.

Some packet filters are also subject to address spoofing. Using address spoofing with source routing and information about your internal network, an attacker on the Internet can impersonate an authorized IP address on your network. A better solution is to combine packet filters with application gateways.

Application Gateways

Figure 11-2 shows one way to combine packet filters with application gateways to build a secure firewall. The exact configuration will depend on your security policy. The external and internal routers are configured as packet filters. Each application gateway is assigned to one or more network applications. (An obvious, more manageable solution is to combine the application gateways in one server. Many commercial firewall products do this.) The application gateways are installed on an intermediate network, called a Demilitarized Zone (DMZ), between the internal enterprise network and the Internet. The name indicates the DMZ is not guaranteed safe. Passing through the external packet filter, an incoming session from an Internet host must first log in to an application gateway. The external packet filter verifies the IP destination and source addresses. The destination should be that of an application gateway in the DMZ. The source should not be a source address on your enterprise; otherwise, this may indicate trouble.

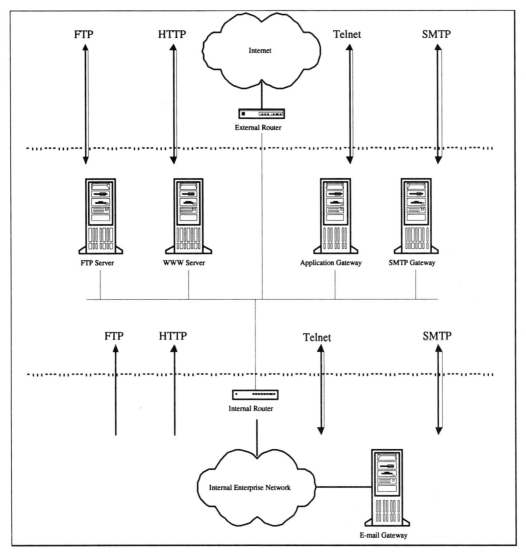

Figure 11-2   Figure 11-2: Secure Firewall Combining Packet Filters and Application Gateways

Depending on the corporate security policy, after an Internet host is authenticated by an application gateway, you may allow a session to be established between the application gateway and a host on the network. Passing though the internal packet filter, the IP source and destination addresses will be verified again. This time the source address should be the address of an application gateway that is authorized to communicate with a host on the network. Similarly, the destination address should be the address of a network node that is authorized to communicate with an application gateway.

Depending on the security policy, you might not allow connections from the Internet to pass through the application gateway to a network host. An alternative would be to place information that is to be accessed from the Internet on an application server connected to the DMZ. A typical example of data that flows between the network and the Internet is electronic mail. There is no application gateway login procedure, but electronic mail is controlled strictly by specially designated gateways—one connected to the internal enterprise network and the other connected to the DMZ.

Deny all services except those explicitly permitted
Use an application gateway architecture
Provide a graphical interface for configuration management
Support a wide range of IP protocols
Reject unknown protocols
Hide the structure of the internal enterprise network
Prevent dynamic routing
Prevent external users from logging on as root
Provide logging, reporting, and auditing
Provide external DNS service for internal enterprise network
Provide SMTP e-mail gateway
Provide strong authentication method
Provide encryption
Be transparent to internal enterprise network users
Offer high performance

Table 11-1   Firewall Requirements

Securing Application Gateways and Other Hosts

Application gateways are important points to verify authorized users and control the flow of data between the network and the Internet. As with any other important host connected to the enterprise, you must ensure that the application gateways are secured. This means configuring the application gateways so they are hardened to withstand a hacker's attack. For example, remove or disable any applications and systems software that are not needed by the application gateway to perform its main functions. You should also implement strict password and file access controls.

Firewall Logging

Event logging is another key part of the firewall. You cannot manage what you cannot measure, and log files are one way to measure security. The firewall should log all connections and connection attempts. The log should show the source and destination addresses, time, and protocol being used. Certain critical conditions should trigger an alert to notify the security administrator. Check the security logs frequently and systematically.

Firewall Guidelines

There are a variety of excellent commercial firewall products. We recommend BorderWare Firewall Server from Border Network Technologies, FireWall-1 from CheckPoint Software Technologies and Raptor Systems' Eagle, among others. Table 11-1 summarizes important requirements for an enterprise network firewall.

_11_

Managing the Network

The management tenet "You cannot manage what you cannot measure" holds true for enterprise networks. As grizzled veterans in the enterprise networking game, we have a veritable catalogue of processes you should follow, not to just keep your network under control, but to make it operate as a competitive asset.

In this chapter we discuss at length our recommended network management processes—adapted from the PRINCE methodology discussed in Chapter 2—and their interrelationships, as shown in Figure 12-1. You may wish to add more of your own.

Start by defining network management processes, though it is tempting to do otherwise. Network management tool sellers would rather you shop first, then fit management processes to their wares. Resist this strategy! Armed with a management processes checklist, you can compare network management applications and tools, not just to each other, but to how they satisfy your needs. Try not to compromise configuration, performance, and problem management requirements.

Process Input Documents

Network operational processes depend on several design and planning documents. These include network strategies, project plans and schedules, network designs, floor layouts, and service level agreements.

Change Management Process

Change management plays a central part in the overall operations and management of the network. It ensures network alterations take place in a structured and controlled manner. Since you are dealing with mission-critical devices, changes need to be understood properly, planned conservatively, and implemented safely. The change management process should register, document, and plan proposed changes. It should, when appropriate, evaluate options, estimate costs, and apply priorities.

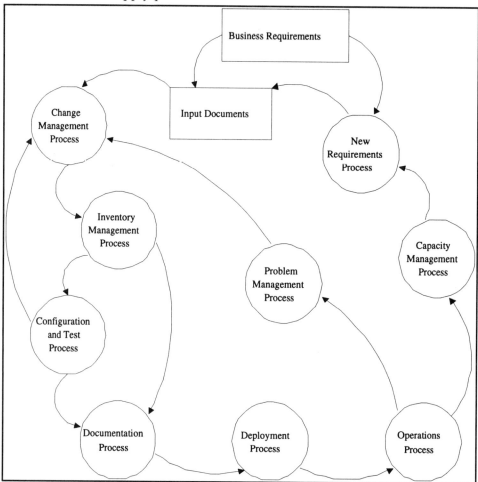

Figure 12-1   Network Management Processes

Inventory Management Process

The inventory management process ensures accurate records are kept of the physical equipment and software, their location, and modification level. Update the inventory *before* installing equipment and apply software modifications. We use three main documents: Network Inventory (Table 12-1), Network Map, and Cable Configuration (Table 12-3).

The Network Inventory	
Device type	Model number
Serial number	Purchase order
Hardware configuration	Software configuration
Exact location	Maintenance agreement
Network name	Addresses
Cables used	User contact
Other helpful data and comments	

Table 12-1   Your network device inventory list should include these 13 fields.

The network map is our graphical representation of where everything is connected logically as well as physically. It shows how the routers, concentrators, gateways, and servers are physically connected to the network, and it contains the name and address for each network device.

The Cable Configuration	The Network Map
Location	Topology
Outlet label	Device type
SNR (signal-to-noise ratio)	Model
NEXT (near-end crosstalk)	Network name
Attenuation	Address
Cable length	Location

Table 12-2   Recording cable and network details will pay big dividends by eliminating headaches.

Configuration Testing Process

Before a new configuration (combination of hardware and software) is installed in its intended location, it is assembled in a network test lab and checked to see if it meets requirements. If a change is needed, the change management controls are applied and, when appropriate, the inventory records are updated. Configuration testing is carried out according to formal testing plans that are subject to quality assessment.

Documentation Process

Documentation is produced according to defined standards. A document librarian is responsible for tracking the production of all required documentation and its subsequent storage, issue, and amendment. Along with the input documents, other important documents describe different processes.

12

Deployment Process

Deployment can consist of the physical transportation and installation of equipment or the electronic distribution of software and configuration changes. Before deployment, configuration testing, change management, and inventory management are verified. Keep an up-to-date status description of all changes that have been completed successfully.

An Installation Guide

- Systems overview, including network diagrams
- Installation instructions
- Installation test instructions

Operations Process

Hand-off maintenance and management of new network equipment to the operations staff only after completing successful installation tests. Operation of the network is carried out in conformance with an Operations Guide, using the facilities provided by the network management system.

Operations Guide

- Instructions for corrective actions in the case of problems requiring operator intervention
- Guidelines to extract management information on a scheduled basis
- Guidelines to extend the scope of the management system
- Roles and responsibilities of operators, administrators, and managers
- Security procedures for control of passwords
- Problem reporting and escalation procedures
- General maintenance tasks
- Analysis of event and error logs
- Threshold notification actions

Problem Process

Problems that require support go through the central help desk and are resolved within agreed-upon times. The help desk allocates resources and monitors the progress and resolution of problems. This process keeps network staff informed of progress at predefined intervals and automatically invokes escalation procedures if expected resolution times are in danger of being exceeded. In line with a policy of setting service levels, the help desk carries out trend analysis of escalated incidents and identifies procedural and other changes to maintain or improve service levels.

Capacity Process

Part of the task of the network management system is to monitor predefined performance traits and to report on trends and changes. We use this information to predict potential bottlenecks and to allow timely upgrades of the network as use increases over time. We also use the capacity information to estimate the effect of introducing new applications to the network.

Designate a network management leader responsible for the production and automation of standard capacity reports. In addition, set thresholds and alarms at appropriate points around the network to provide early warning of unexpected increases in traffic.

New Requirements Process

Assess new requirements, considering information gathered from the network management system. A clear understanding of the current capacity of the network allows us to conduct effective cost/benefit analyses for proposed applications. A clear process for the submission, assessment, approval, and planning of new requirements is also important. New requirements, from whatever source, are conveyed by way of change proposals. If these changes do not affect the network and require no additional resources, the change proposals may be accepted and implemented. Otherwise, the changes are referred to the change control manager, who organizes change control reviews.

Organizing for Network Management

To effectively implement and support network management processes in a large complex network it is essential for everyone to have a clear understanding of who is responsible for what. Without a well-defined organizational structure with clear responsibilities, it is impossible to manage and control changes to the network.

Our tried-and-true organization structure for network management is shown in Figure 12-2. It consists of several roles and functions, some shared by the same person and others requiring two or more people for the same task—depending, of course, on the size and complexity of your enterprise network.

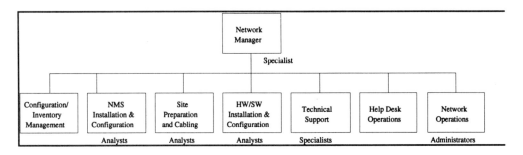

Figure 12-2   An organization chart for an effective network management organization.

We define these positions and responsibilities for our personnel:

Network Specialist

- Define network requirements
- Develop network strategies, plans, and designs
- Evaluate new network technologies
- Develop network standards and procedures
- Ensure adequate network capacity
- Interface closely with other planning staff

Network Analyst

- Develop network procedures
- Make network configuration changes
- Install and configure network equipment
- Perform first-line hardware and software maintenance
- Produce and interpret network performance reports
- Perform fault analysis and resolve problems
- Perform internetworking trouble shooting

Network Administrator

- Start up and shut down network components.
- Enable/disable network devices
- Implement network procedures

Inventory Manager

- Establish inventory management process
- Adherence to the inventory management process
- Maintenance of the inventory management process

Change Manager

- Establish change management process
- Adhere to the change management process
- Maintain of the change management process

Help Desk Operator

- Operate the help desk service
- Carry out first-line problem diagnosis
- Update and maintain the incident database
- Prepare reports

Developing Network Standards

To manage a complex network you must use standards—industry standards, naming standards, and consistent configurations. This is the best way for you to leverage the experience and knowledge of your technical staff. By using network components that conform to industry standards, you can be sure that the components you buy today and in the future will be compatible and will interoperate. This is an important way to ensure high levels of reliability and ensure you can protect your organization's network investment in the future.

Implementing standards also means developing naming standards for your network equipment and selecting standard configurations. Using standard names and addresses is important in a large network to ensure that names and addresses are unique. Standard names are also important in maintaining documentation for a large network inventory.

Centralizing and Automating Significant Processes

Along with standardizing, you must also centralize and automate, which are the only ways a handful of people can control a large network. Centralizing and automating network management and administrative tasks allows us to take advantage of limited staff at a central site rather than relying on technical staff at remote sites. In most cases, it is either very expensive or impossible to distribute support staff across our network. Maximizing their time requires the use of network management applications and tools. We believe automating three processes—performance, problem, and configuration management—yields the biggest return on your network management tool expense.

Performance Management

Accurate capacity planning depends on network performance information collected over time. Then, process and analyze this information to determine how well the network has been performing regarding response times, availability, and downtime. We also factor in new requirements to determine what investments are needed to make for future network capacity. This is an ongoing and time-consuming process, so we use tools to help us collect data and perform trend analysis for different periods of time. We use trend reports that are generated automatically daily and weekly for day-to-day-operations and short-term capacity planning. For longer-term capacity planning we automatically generate monthly trend reports.

Identify key network parameters that will be used to measure network performance. Useful limits include response times, network utilization, packet transfer rates for internetwork devices, error rates, and packet loss rates. For each parameter you also need to define the criteria for measuring it. Ethernet use, for example, should not exceed 40 percent and peaks should not exceed 70 percent. Token Ring use should not exceed 50 percent and peaks should be less than 80 percent. For FDDI, maximum use should be 80 percent. WAN use should never top 85 percent. Error rates should never exceed 1 percent of total bandwidth.

Problem Management

The network is going to break someday. How fast can you respond, identify, and resolve the problem? Can you consistently respond quickly? Large heterogeneous networks are complex, and complexity makes it more difficult to identify and resolve problems, especially without causing other problems. Ideally, we want to identify and correct problems before they harm the network and our users. The causes of most network glitches are hardware failures, congestion, software bugs, human errors, and disasters. Although some problems are obvious and simple to solve, many will require network management applications and tools, diagnostics, and documentation.

To stay on top of network problems, automate common tasks. Problem management is one area most network management tools automate effectively. We recommend setting thresholds and automatic alarms for significant network events, such as high network utilization, errors, and lost connections.

Diagnostic tools are important tools for problem management. Using facilities in network management platform and applications, we test connectivity, run debugging programs to resolve configuration problems, and run packet traces to follow packets routed through the network.

Configuration Management

To automate configuration management, we need to set the network management system to discover and display network components automatically. An accurate and detailed map of the network topology is essential for performance monitoring, problem solving, capacity planning, and network design.

We configure and test every networking device in a central facility before we distribute it on the network. After configuring routers and concentrators, we store copies of their configuration files centrally on the network management system. Using DHCP, we centralize and automate important TCP/IP administration tasks.

Integrating Network Management

Managing Systems

Systems management is different from network management. Along with managing network devices, we need standards and processes to ensure that servers are performing properly, that each has sufficient capacity, and that we can identify and resolve server problems. Don't ignore the desktops. These are important components of your distributed enterprise network—from the user's view, the most important. You have to manage them. In our second book, *Managing the New Enterprise*, we devoted a substantial portion to systems management in distributed-computing environments. Please read that book for more information.

The main problem with systems management in a heterogeneous environment is that each server is monitored differently. Each depends on a different set of utilities and configuration schemes to define the server operating environment, files, programs and users. For example, NetWare uses *SYSCON, FCONSOLE, PCONSOLE*, and *FILER* for configuring and administering the server. UNIX, Windows NT, and Banyan Vines use their own utilities. One way to alleviate this problem is to use one or two server configurations throughout the enterprise. Another way is to use third-party tools, such as Computer Associates' CA-Unicenter, Tivoli, OpenVision, to automate processes common to all servers.

Managing Network Backups

We need to protect the enterprise from data lost because of a security breach, server failure, errors, or other disasters. A sure-fire way is to schedule backups often and store them in a safe archive at an off-site location.

Centralization is the only way to control and manage backup on mission-critical servers. It is impossible to ensure that backups, tape management, and off-site tape storage are carried out properly if you have to physically visit the site of each server to perform this crucial task.

Products such as Legato's Networker enable us to centralize data backup for different types of servers connected to the network in different locations.

Managing Software Distribution

Installing applications, operating systems, and software upgrades on servers and desktops is a never-ending, time-consuming, and costly endeavor. You can save time and money if you automate. By automating software distribution with products like Microsoft Windows NT-based Systems Management Server (SMS), we schedule jobs at a central location to distribute specific files to designated systems at appropriate times.

Managing the Desktop

Because many users depend on their PCs for business-critical tasks, we must find a way to manage these desktops, even if they are not connected to the network. Like other management activities, the key to network management is centralization and automation.

Policies & Standards

Policies and standards are the best way to centrally control the desktop. With standard desktop configurations, the task of configuring and supporting the desktop is simplified, which saves time and money. Implementing standards at the desktop, however, will raise red flags for some users. This does not have to be the case. First, give the users several standards from which to choose, so they do not feel handcuffed to one operating system.

Standard configurations are not always the best idea for every organization. For example, where the nature of the work is fairly consistent, one standard works well. Where the nature of the work is more dynamic, however, it is better to offer flexibility. Keep in mind the idea is not strict regimentation for its own sake, but for maximizing users' productivity.

If users insist on nonstandard configurations, give them the option to acquire their own support. They may develop their own technical experience or they may contract for outsourcing. At least we have a clear policy and have given them a choice. Now it becomes a business decision within the business unit. The key is to find the right mixture of centralization and user independence.

Consider using servers to store standard software. We often install Microsoft Windows on desktops, but place applications on servers where they can be accessed by desktops across the network. This simplifies desktop management because you support a small number of applications in a handful of places. We have seen some companies that have virtually eliminated the disk drives in desktops by installing all software on servers or use puny local drives for temporary and swap files.

Asset Management and Software Distribution

Desktop management comprises several processes, including asset management, software distribution, and software metering. These processes only work if desktop configurations are standard.

We recommend automating the management of desktop configuration, software distribution, and version control. With business-critical client/server applications running on distributed desktops, their management is essential. The two key areas of desktop management where central control is important are configuration management and software distribution. In many organizations, inconsistencies and uncontrolled changes in desktop configurations cause problems. It is essential to ensure that desktop configurations are standardized and controlled from a central point to avoid network management problems from occurring in the future. Central control of desktop configurations, software distribution, and version control depends on processes and tools.

The Paucity of Tools

While we seemingly enjoy a cornucopia of desktop management tools, we suffer a drought of *comprehensive* management tools. Most are "point solutions" addressing specific areas. Vendors need to go back to the drawing board and pay more attention to integration and ease of use. All have been slow to offer software based on standards, such as the Desktop Management Task Force's Desktop Management Interface (DMI).

Several popular desktop management products are LANDDesk Management Suite from Intel and Microsoft's SMS. LANDDesk Manager is modular, with components covering software distribution, software metering, asset management, desktop diagnostics, and remote control.

Virus Control

Another important desktop management task is antivirus control. Since viruses usually enter the network through desktops themselves, you need local virus detection software on all PCs and Macintoshes. Microsoft, Intel, McAffee, IBM, and others offer effective antidotes.

Managing the Help Desk

We often think of the help desk as a noisy, busy place where staffers struggling to be patient answer a never-ending string of telephone calls from hapless users. The prototypical telephone-based help desk is not the most effective way to provide this important service. First, the help desk should revolve around a database containing descriptions of every problem it meets. This allows the staff to follow the status of unresolved incidents, search for solutions to similar problems, and track historical information for trend analysis. The help desk database needs current information about the configurations of all desktops.

The only way to maintain an accurate incident database is through automation. You can create an incident database by using one of the server-based DBMS packages, REMEDY, or Lotus Notes. We created an effective incident-reporting system using templates supplied with Lotus Notes. Problems reported to the help desk over the telephone are entered manually at the time they are reported or users themselves can report problems through Lotus Notes or REMEDY.

Keeping an accurate hardware and software inventory is the Holy Grail of many IT managers. The effective help desk knows exactly what is installed where. A variety of products purport to automate inventory management, but in our experience they do not scale up to large enterprises. None closely integrate with other applications, such as help desk management. Other tools useful for help desk management are centralized desktop diagnostics and remote control. These form a portion of several desktop management suites that let you review desktop configurations and run diagnostics from a central point. Remote control software lets you change configurations from one place.

So Where's the Integration?

Good question. Users have wanted to know this for a long time—and they still do. A number of companies claim their products fully integrate network and systems management tasks, but many pieces of the integration puzzle are still missing. As we mention in earlier chapters, an important piece of the puzzle is the common management platform such as OpenView and SunNet Manager. If third-party network and systems management applications are compatible with these platforms, they will provide a common way to collect information centrally. Many third-party applications still have a long way to go before they interoperate with common management platforms. Rather than using the widely available platforms, some companies have tried to create their own, which adds to the complexity of managing distributed systems.

Another important puzzle piece is comprehensive management applications like CA-Unicenter. Without well-defined standards for systems management, these applications are the only way to have a common view of network traffic and systems information from different servers. Comprehensive applications that are compatible with common management platforms will provide the best way to integrate network and systems management in the future.

Internet 101: Introduction to Internet Technologies 13 ≣

In the age of global information, the New Enterprise is not defined by the confines of a company's WAN. In hindsight the evolution of its network comes clear; first there was the LAN. Then we connected LANs to form the WAN. Local networks were no longer confined, and the "IT enterprise" was born.

The enterprise has business requirements to use and share information across all boundaries, company to company, nationally and internationally. The New Enterprise must connect to the Internet to complete its connectivity puzzle.

Once connected to the Internet, employees will take advantage of communications and information on more than 40 million computers around the world, by using the functions we describe here.

This chapter offers a brief overview of popular Internet software tools and technologies available today, including electronic mail, Telnet, Finger, FTP, Gopher, Usenet, and the World Wide Web.

Electronic Mail

This is the most basic, and perhaps valuable, function on the Internet. Not indigenous to the Internet, e-mail was used in the enterprise long before the Internet became popular. However, the Internet turns e-mail from an office convenience to a powerful tool that provides a cost-efficient, instantaneous, and somewhat scalable method to exchange notes, ideas, plans, and formal documents around the globe.

Many e-mail tools are available, providing easy-to-use graphical user interfaces. The tools vary to serve different computer platforms, with the popular packages offering versions for DOS- and Windows-compatible personal computers, Macintosh, and sometimes UNIX.

In choosing e-mail tool options, priorities in your selection criteria should center on two things: a friendly user interface and compatibility with other systems. If you find yourself in a situation in which you have to give up a little of one to get more of another, the top priority should be compatibility. Systems chosen should handle SMTP, POP, and MIME messages with relative ease, transparently to the user. The big issue is how to handle outgoing and incoming attachments.

Though they can come in simple ASCII/text format, many attachments will come in more complex formats, such as word processors, spreadsheets, and programs. Different e-mail systems treat these formats differently when sending or receiving. Some e-mail systems do a better job of this than others. Make sure the system you choose to handle your mail demonstrates the ability to read incoming attachments from different mail systems with no pain to the user.

Another way to solve this problem is to leave everything to your servers. Innosoft[1] and Clarity Software[2] offer different server-based approaches to solving the e-mail attachment problems. In a nutshell, both translate attachments passing through the server to a file format the recipient can understand.

If your enterprise is not using e-mail to connect your computer users, you are missing an opportunity to save money. Facsimile broadcasts and constant voice communications over the telephone are sucking money from your bottom line. Is it smarter to fax 50-page documents between offices or click a few buttons and send e-mail? The answer is obvious to all but the many firms that still rely on fax machines today for routine correspondence. Electronic mail can't solve every communications problem your organization may have. With that in mind, we'll take a brief tour of the popular communications tools available. Some, you won't need. Others, your organization may not know how it functioned without.

Telnet

Telnet is a standard, command-line UNIX tool used to log on to a remote computer. It is bundled or otherwise available on most other operating systems. Before the advent of Web browsers and Java, the only way users could run remote applications was to log in to them with Telnet and run them from afar. Today, Telnet is still the best way for UNIX users to check their e-mail while traveling.

Using Telnet, you can also offer more complicated and interactive services. It provides a remote character terminal over the net and thus can be set up to appear as a normal UNIX-prompted user or can take the user directly into a customized procedure or program. Since Telnet can provide almost all services that can be served to a VT100 character terminal, it is an option for cursor-screen handling packages and escape sequences that provide basic graphical effects.

---

1. http://ww.innosoft.com/
2. http://www.clarity.com/

Telnet has a dark side, however. Allowing Telnet for friendly users also exposes you to the risk that a malevolent hacker might use Telnet to attack your network. For this reason, many systems administrators configure firewalls to block incoming Telnet attempts.

File Transfer Protocol (FTP)

FTP is an ancient program that allows users to copy files from one machine to another. Many technology companies set up "anonymous FTP servers" that allow anyone to log into a server and copy online documentation, software updates, drivers, and help files. The World Wide Web has gussied up anonymous FTP servers by making them easier to use, but hasn't changed their underlying function one iota. If you need to broadcast multimedia, software, or text to many users, you should consider a dedicated, anonymous FTP server.

You might want a password-protected FTP server for internal use. For example, many engineering groups need to acquire data from remote sites or share their data with off-site contractors. FTP servers can be ideal for large projects that require the sharing and editing of large documents such as CAD files, software builds, financial records, and complex documents. Web browsers are making it easier to perform FTP by papering over FTP's command-line heritage with friendly graphical interfaces.

In setting up your FTP server, you can make a variety of data types available for transfer, including text and software binaries, regardless of platform and operating systems. You can also control the number of users that connect to your server simultaneously, as well as control access to various files and directories.

FTP's limitations include sluggish directory browsing and no inherent feature to describe files or data. Once configured, an FTP server is a breeze to maintain for systems administrators. Keeping its content current, however, is a different story.

Gopher

Gopher is an information retrieval program that offers the administrator and user a structure for providing information navigation of a site. It also provides the user with searchable indexes. All in all, Gopher is a useful way to provide data when organized and maintained well.

But no one uses Gopher anymore. Gopher is a text-based program for displaying text files transferring binary data that preceded the World Wide Web and Mosaic. Accordingly, Gopher sites have become less popular. A well-designed FTP and Web site, combined with a search engine, has quickly become the de facto methods of serving information to the Internet, as well as within the enterprise.

Finger

As a simple utility, the Finger service comes with most operating systems and was designed to provide useful information about a user. A common use for this is to provide the full/real name of a user. Finger will provide basic information about users, such as login name, how long they've been logged in, etc. The neat thing is that any users on a system can set up a *.plan* file within their home directory and provide information about themselves. This may not be an acceptable process for information sharing, depending on how security conscious you are. Hackers use these profiles to learn who's who on the network.

Before the surge of the Web, the Finger service was a useful way to provide tidbits of information, such as stock quotes. It can even be set up to update information every time the system is queried. But again, the popularity of the Web has buried the use of Finger. Since most people surfing the net these days are doing so with a Web browser, static and dynamic information can be easily hosted on a Web server with a much prettier interface.

Usenet Newsgroups

Before the advent of the Web, Newsgroup activity was heralded as the most heavily trafficked function on the net. Newsgroups are, in essence, focused electronic bulletin board systems that allow users to post information, tips, rants, and bonmots for anyone interested to read and respond to. Beware: most Newsgroups are unmoderated and uncensored, for better and worse.

Special interest Newsgroups range from cooking, where culinary masterpieces are posted for all to try, to job postings, where employers and employees can post available positions. In early 1996 the number of Newsgroups totaled more than 14,000, not including private Newsgroups run behind firewalls.

Access to Newsgroups can be easily restricted to provide your enterprise with business related topics, filtering out all other activity (the home can be similarly restricted.) Administrative processes to request, approve, and add specific Newsgroups can be set up. You can even piggyback on similar request and approve processes already in place, such as security administration.

World Wide Web

The Web was envisioned as a separate and new use of the Internet. Special Web sites were set up, providing content in textual and graphical formats, allowing the reader to view both simultaneously. Web browsers read the content provided by the Web server. This opens a brand-new world to Internet users. The result has been a staggering growth in Web content, creativity, and tools. The Web browser is a point-and-click window that displays content from anywhere on the Internet.

Figure 13-1   Netscape Navigator is a popular Web browser

≡ 13

The Web's popularity has spawned newer versions of software that now combine the standard Web browsing and viewing with built-in e-mail, Telnet, FTP, and Newsgroup reading capabilities.

For instance, for the Web browser to display an FTP site, it simply lists its directories, subdirectories, and files as a series of hypertext links. Clicking on a

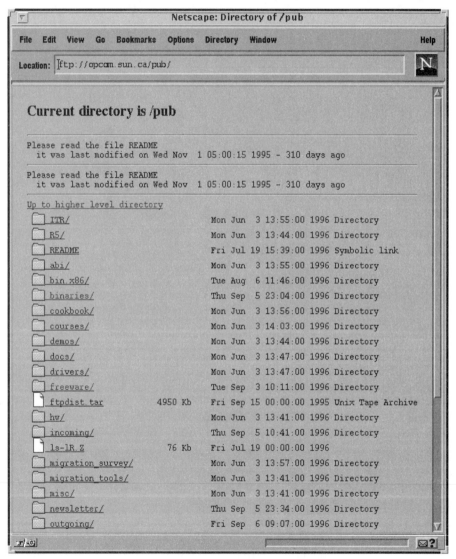

Figure 13-2   Web browsers allow users to download files by way of the FTP protocol

subdirectory within the site will take you to its contents and display them as links as well. If you click on a file link, the browser will attempt to display the file. Whether you can read will depend on a great many things, not the least of which is the data format of the file and whether you have the ability to read that format on your machine. As you guessed, text files are easily displayed. The other option when you've reached the data file you are looking for is to transfer it to your local computer. You can use FTP from the site to do so.

Internet Futures

Some things to look for soon on the Internet and how it will affect you:

High-Bandwidth Internet Services to the Home

There is currently a feverish race occurring in the industry to bring consumers high-speed data communications services through cable and telephone lines. The cable and telephone companies hope to deliver, for prices near a mere $20 per month:

- Voice and facsimile (telephony) services
- Internet services
- Unidirectional and interactive services
- Video services
- Information services

In fact, this paradigm of combined services is currently being tested by cable and telephone ventures. Trials underway in New York and Boston, for instance, are delivering a service community while providing high-bandwidth (over T1) service to the Internet via a cable modem. This community is similar to that of, say CompuServe, but adds features like interactive video, high-bandwidth Internet access, and telephony services to the residence, all provided by one company. In addition, this cable modem model is providing the customer with the same cable feeds as always.

Similar trials using fiber, provided by telephone companies, are underway to accomplish many of the same services to the home. The race and competition between the two for your business will provide interesting and exciting opportunities for consumers and businesses.

13

Wireless Technology

The wireless technologies to look forward to in the near future are wireless campus and regional network solutions. Look for affordable new products and services to provide a line-of-sight, high-bandwidth connectivity. New technology and services will provide more than just campus-wide connectivity, as installed in many places today; they will provide more regional solutions for the New Enterprise.

In essence, these products and services will compete directly with local telephone companies for local-loop business. For a larger investment up front, the New Enterprise may save thousands in recurring carrier charges in the years to come.

Internet 102: Getting Connected 14

As with every other connectivity decision, you must balance cost and capacity when connecting the organization to the Internet. The first task is to calculate how much Internet connectivity is required. Or, depending on the nature of the organization, your first task may be to find what your monthly connectivity budget is and then, using the completion backward principle, find the fastest and most affordable connection.

The Internet connectivity business is new and changes rapidly. Small Internet Service Providers (ISP) are being gobbled up by larger ISPs, and larger ISPs are the prey of long-distance telephone companies. Prices vary by area, and in some countries finding an Internet service provider (or even a telephone line) is impossible at any price.

As we write this in 1996, a constant comment we hear from network managers is a general dissatisfaction with the technical support offered by ISPs. Most ISPs are startups and have invested their funds in capital equipment, not customer service. As competition increases and the technology improves, service will presumably improve, too. Although it may prove a depressing exercise, contact your counterparts in the area with an informal poll of how well they rate local ISPs. This may alert you to an egregious ISP.

Connection Types and Options

Keep in mind you need to pay connect fees and monthly charges to *two* service providers: the carrier (usually your local telephone company) and the ISP. As we learned in Chapter 7, in theory we enjoy a cornucopia of connection types. Internet connectivity usually falls into two categories, static and dynamic.

Static connectivity occurs at predetermined intervals. This offers managers, who are not yet comfortable with the security and productivity-loss-potential aspects of full Internet access, a way of dipping their toes in the Internet waters. A static connection usually uses an analog POTS (Plain Old Telephone Service) line and a modem. To establish this service, you need a modem-equipped server on your premises configured to dial the service provider at certain intervals (e.g., once every 15, 30, or 60 minutes). Your server contacts the ISP, uploads and downloads data, and then hangs up. The data usually consists of e-mail and Usenet Newsgroup verbiage.

Since the connection time is intermittent and only established for a short time, the threat of security breach is virtually nil. However you'll note that real-time activities, such as "surfing the Web" are not possible, as that would require full-time (dynamic) connectivity.

For the most common types of Internet functions we identified earlier in Chapter 13, use Table 14-1 to determine which can be used with static-only connectivity.

Option	e-mail	Telnet	FTP	Newsgroups	Web
Static	Yes	No	No	Yes	No
Dynamic	Yes	Yes	Yes	Yes	Yes

Table 14-1   Static vs. Dynamic Access Capabilities

As you can see, dynamic access will not hinder you from using any functionality. Dynamic access is simply full-time connectivity to the Internet. The issues and decisions to be made regarding this type of access are discussed below.

Service Providers

When dealing with WAN connectivity, you are familiar with the local and long-distance carriers that provide the line or lines between local and remote sites. That model may look something like that in Figure 14-1.

Figure 14-1   Private WAN Connectivity Model

The only variable in the model shown in Figure 14-1 is the long-distance carrier. In the case of Interlada connectivity, the local carrier may suffice. In the Internet connectivity model, the "remote site" becomes the Internet provider, or what is commonly referred to as the Internet POP (Point of Presence). This model is shown in Figure 14-2.

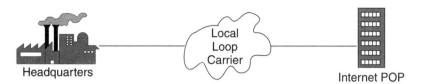

Figure 14-2   Internet Connectivity Model

Yes, the Internet connection is very much like WAN connectivity. It is WAN connectivity in the broadest sense.

Remember, you are dealing with two service vendors now. This means two setup fees, two monthly fees, and two technical support groups. Even today, large telephone companies that have jumped into providing Internet and carrier services, they are still run by two separate operations. These companies may act as a single point of contact for you, and single-vendor-minded companies will find that attractive. Long distance telephone companies, such as MCI, still must go through a local-loop service provider to make the "last mile" connection to your site.

Even now in the US, with the recent 1996 Telecommunications Bill signed into law, allowing both the long distance carriers and Regional Bell Operating Companies (RBOCs) to compete in each other's playground, a seamless service model to you, the customer, is still a ways out in the future. This service model will simply combine your local loop, long distance, and Internet access into one operational mold. Note: you are more likely to see a seamless billing model long before a seamless service model. This is already evident in the many monthly residential telephone bills we pay today, where long-distance and local services are bundled into one invoice. However, today, when you have issues with the service of one carrier or another, a single point of contact does not exist, such as one calling card, one customer service number to call, etc.

No matter how "one-stop-shopping" your carrier model seems to be, two service providers or operations will dictate, or at least influence, the decisions in selecting network protocols, hardware, etc. For example, not all telephone companies offer ISDN in your neighborhood. Your Internet provider may offer ISDN, but if the carrier cannot support it, you will not be able to take advantage of the service, and vice versa. Additionally, cost factors, such as packaging and pricing, affect what the carriers are willing to offer. For example, you may be interested in Frame Relay at 256 kilobits per second, but your local-loop carrier may only offer it at 128 and 384 kilobits per second.

14

Bandwidth Requirements

Bandwidth is the size of the pipe from the internal network to a service provider. Bandwidth directly affects the speed of connectivity. Estimate bandwidth requirements by forecasting throughput. Of course, the bigger the pipe, the bigger the bill.

Bandwidth is measured in fractions or multiples of megabytes. The fractions of megabytes are measured in kilobytes. Analog modem speeds range anywhere from 1.2 to 33.6 kilobits per second. You may hear talk about compression capabilities, but ignore those for the time being. More advanced types of telephone connections bring bandwidth speeds from 56 kilobits per second to the heralded T1 (1.5 megabits per second) and from the T1 to the T3 (45 megabits per second). The quote is based on the amount of data a pipe can push through per second. Thus, a T1 will allow you to move 1.5 megabits of data per second through its pipe.

Within these bandwidth sizes, you can pick from a variety of choices in network protocols. Again, these protocols fall into two categories: analog (POTS lines) and digital services. Fortunately, protocol choices, as noted earlier, will be guided by your local telephone company. The choice of analog versus digital will be automatic after you choose your bandwidth and protocol requirements.

The most common connectivity options are summarized in Table 14-2.

Bandwidth	Analog	Digital	SLIP/ PPP	ISDN	Frame Relay	Clear Channel
1.2 to 33.6 kilobits / s	Yes	No	Yes	No	No	No
56 kilobits per second	Yes	Yes	No	Yes	No	No
64 kilobits per second	No	Yes	No	Yes	Yes	CD
128 kilobits per second	No	Yes	No	Yes	CD	Yes
256 kilobits per second	No	Yes	No	Yes	CD	Yes
384 kilobits per second	No	Yes	No	Yes	CD	Yes
1.5 megabits per second (T1)	No	Yes	No	Yes	CD	Yes

Table 14-2   Common Internet Connectivity Options

How do we choose the correct pipe size? This is a difficult question when you are getting started but there are some rules of thumb you can follow. As we will see in more detail in Chapter 15. the first rule of thumb is this: if you plan to host an external Web site for the company, don't even bother with any connection smaller than a T1. Easy. Also, if the enterprise employs more than 500 people within a WAN and they regularly use and maintain desktop access to the network, go with an initial T1 installation. Another rule that we touched on earlier: if you plan to perform functions on the Internet beyond e-mail and Newsgroup activity, static connectivity is no longer an option.

If you are not hosting a Web site, are larger than 500 network-active employees, and will use dynamic Internet access, the choice about your starting level is complicated. We recommend that you work closely with the providers at this point to make the appropriate choice. Getting started on the right track will include an investment in scalable hardware and protocols, allowing you to grow incrementally without making significant changes in your infrastructure to do so. For instance, an investment in a T1-capable router and CSU/DSUs (Channel Service Unit/Digital Service Unit to connect to digital lines), with a circuit rate of 156 kilobits-per-second Frame Relay could be a good starting choice. This would allow you to upgrade your circuit rate to a T1 when it makes sense, simply by arranging it with the providers. Once the initial connectivity model is implemented, your network administrators should work cooperatively with the providers to monitor:

- Overall percentage of network usage
- Peak network usage and effects
- Usage conflicts and effects

Regular statistics and trending around these measurements will provide you with clear data with which to make good decisions as to impending growth requirements for additional bandwidth.

Domain Names

Connectivity solutions in play, we need to choose a domain name for our enterprise. Your domain name is the name by which people all over the world will recognize you. You've seen a typical e-mail address:
washington@fusion.com

In this e-mail address "washington" is the name of the user of the address, "fusion" is the name of washington's host (e-mail server). The name "com" is an Internet standard domain name extension. Representing "commercial," com is the standard extension given to for-profit enterprises. These extensions are used to distinguish the type of entity that owns the domain name. Other Internet domain extensions used by the Internet are listed in Table 14-4.

.com	Common or commercial
.net	Network providers (Internet Service Providers)
.edu	Education (schools, colleges, universities)
.us, ca	Two-digit country/state codes (Post Office codes)
.gov	Government
.mil	Military

Table 14-3   Internet Domain Name Extensions

URLs (Uniform Resource Locator) are similar to e-mail addresses and are used by the Internet to find Web pages. A standard naming convention for a Web page is: www.sun.com

The full URL used in a Web browser uses a syntax like the following:
```
http://www.fusion.com/
```

Again, it is the hierarchy of domain names and extensions that is important. The "www" is a name recognized within the "fusion" domain and "fusion" is recognized by the Internet extension of "com."

Within the extension of the Internet domain (com, net, edu, etc.), domain names are unique. There can only be one "fusion.com." Another company with a name that includes the word "fusion" (Fusion Dental Services, for instance) must choose another domain name within the Internet's "com" extension. Fusion Dental Services might want to consider using the word "dental" as its domain name. If that name is not taken, this company's domain name will be "dental.com"

The InterNIC is the entity that administers domain names on the Internet. Its primary functions are to provide, administer, and maintain domain names and IP (Internet Protocol) addresses.

How do you know if a given name is taken? Here's one service your ISP should provide; ask the ISP during the sales and subsequent hook-up phases to check names for you. However, if you have access to the Internet through a personal account, you can conduct your own research. Use your Telnet application to access *internic.net*. Once there, you can look up domain names by using the UNIX command
```
prompt> whois -h dental.com
```

If no dental.com exists, you will receive the message that says, "Unable to find selection." If dental.com is already taken, you will receive back all the registration information of the entity that owns that domain name. This information includes company name, administrative contact and e-mail address, technical contact name and e-mail address, host machines, domains, and other technical information.

If you are fortunate enough to find that your desired domain name is not taken, you can register it to your company by using your ISP or by filling out the registration form yourself and e-mailing it to the InterNIC. You must coordinate this effort with your ISP, as you will need technical information, such as its DNS and IP address. If you find that your desired name is taken, you can always contact the owners of that name (from the information received from whois) and explore the possibility of a deal.

You can also visit the InterNIC at its home page. There you can get information about their enterprise and how to work with them. You can even perform the whois command, point-and-click-style, and register for your domain name right off the page.

IP Addressing

Internet Protocol addressing drives the Internet. As we learned in Chapter 9, a computer uses IP to address, find, or talk to another computer. Every node on the Internet has a unique IP address assigned to it.

As an enterprise connected to the Internet, you will need registered IP addresses to broadcast your presence on the net. Closely related to domain name registration, IP addressing at the Internet level is also run by the InterNIC. At a high level, the InterNIC is responsible for distributing addresses. However, for most cases, Class C addressing can be obtained through your Internet provider, as these providers generally own a corral of Class C addresses for their customers' use. Moreover, IP address resolution will take place between you and your provider. (See Chapter 9 for a more detailed discussion of IP addressing.)

Internet Security Basics

Treat security seriously, but do not panic. The seriousness of your security measures should reflect the value of your company's data or the embarrassment your organization would suffer if your executives' e-mail was put on the front page of tomorrow's newspaper. Keep in mind that your greatest security threats are from disgruntled or dishonest employees. See Chapter 11 for more on network security.

14

Networking the New Enterprise

Spinning a World Wide Web Server

Not since the introduction of Windows 3 in 1990 has the world devoted so much interest to a single piece of software—the World Wide Web browser. Enjoying 80 to 90 percent market share, Netscape Communications' Navigator[1] also leads the pack (including Microsoft's Internet Explorer[2]) in features and performance. At least, it does as we write this in mid-1996. By the time you read this, the tables may have turned on Netscape in the fast-changing Internet world.

The Web browser allows users to surf the Internet and, among other things, read daily newspapers on other continents, get play-by-play reports on professional sports contests in progress, glance at catalogs touting everything from airplanes to underwear, search technical journals for background information, and view travel photographs taken by 12-year-olds.

Most large organizations offer a public Web server with content ranging from boring brochureware to elaborate, animated destinations offering contests, chat rooms, and original short stories. While public Web servers garner most of the attention from the popular press, a Web-inspired revolution *behind* the firewall is also sweeping the globe. Compared to conventional client/server application construction, Web development takes less time, requires less specialized knowledge, needs no cross-platform conversion, and costs little, relatively speaking, to develop and deploy.

Setting up external and internal Web servers varies only in the space the servers occupy and the amount of paranoia you need to apply to each type. We will begin with an external Internet server and conclude with an internal Intranet server.

---

1. http://www.netscape.com/comprod/mirror/index.html
2. http://www.microsoft.com

External Web Server

The first question to tackle here is whether to host your Web server or to outsource the server needs to a third-party. That provider might be the same outfit providing your Internet POP, or it could be one of the many startups specializing in Web server creation and hosting.

The matter comes down to cost and control. What will it cost to set up a Web server? It adds up quickly. If this price seems too steep for the return, consider outsourcing. A company that does this professionally can leverage an installed infrastructure that includes connectivity, servers, and software. This provider can host many customers from one server, creating an economy of scale. But before you outsource, check to see if you can create your own economies of scale. For example, if your enterprise has already implemented high-bandwidth (T1), dynamic Internet connectivity, you may not need a second line. In this case, you probably have employed a firewall already and won't need another.

Start by sketching the network and hardware you need (Figure 15-1).

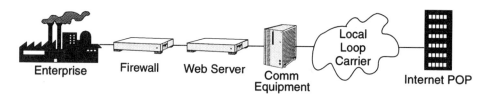

Enterprise   Firewall   Web Server   Comm Equipment   Local Loop Carrier   Internet POP

Figure 15-1   Web Server Configuration

Working from right to left in Figure 15-1, we start with Internet connectivity to an Internet POP. The Web server bandwidth requirements will probably be greater than you experience for your routine enterprise connectivity needs. Most Web servers need a T1 or multiple T1s, depending on the expected traffic and how rich the graphics, Java applets, and other large files (such as try-n-buy software or patches) the server will carry. Also keep in mind the target audience. If your customers (and potential customers) are few and tend to use dial-up accounts, then a fractional T1 may suit your needs. But this is probably not the reason you decided to host a Web site to begin with, and, therefore, this requirement for lower bandwidth is a low priority.

If your company is like most companies and your and the target audience is in the millions, or if your users will otherwise not tolerate sluggish Web service, then you need more help in analyzing the expected traffic. If a T1 sounds expensive or overkill, you are probably a good candidate for a third-party Web host service.

Why worry about a Web server's bandwidth? Users enjoying quick response times tend to visit more pages, which gives your organization more opportunities to serve its customers. Put another way, would you rather a potential customer spent more time visiting your pages or those of a competitor? Most Web browsers have a very important icon-button labeled STOP. This icon can be clicked to abort the visitation of a site you have selected, but have changed your mind, most often because a transfer takes too long.

If you are starting from scratch, you will need the telecommunications equipment required to host a T1. This consists of a CSU/DSU unit and a router, in addition to the systems and software you will be implementing.

Working our way left in Figure 15-1, we come to the system and software required to host the site. Again, the issue of performance rears its head. As of mid-1996, SPARCstations running Solaris dominate the Internet in general and Web servers in particular.[3] Silicon Graphics gear falls in second, with Windows NT farther back in the pack, though gaining in popularity. We find RISC-UNIX Web servers a winning combination, thanks to their free-breathing I/O designs and mature, multi-processing operating systems. It is not a good idea to run a Web server on an old 386 desktop computer, for example.

If the Web server is considered mission critical, as it is at some big companies, you should consider buying a pair of Web servers. With failover software, one server can carry on if the other crashes. For true redundancy, link your servers to separate ISPs so if one goes dark, your Web site stays open for business. As you do with all mission-critical equipment, cloister your Web servers in your data center and maintain them with the same discipline you use on your mainframes and applied in your new networked enterprise. Getting the server into the production space will expose it to management processes, such as change control, problem management, backup schemes, etc. You can then rest assured that the basic production needs of your server are met.

You also need an internal Web development server. This server should be identical to the public Web server in directory configuration, Web server software revision level, and operating system level. Why? You don't want to experiment or develop your Web pages on your public server, and the internal development machine offers your operations staff a safe sandbox in which to play, experiment, and brainstorm wacky ideas.

A Web server needs Web server software, which answers hypertext transfer protocol (HTTP) requests and logs all HTTP-related activities. As with most UNIX-related software, you face many shareware servers and a handful of

---

3.   http://www.webcrawler.com/WebCrawler/Facts/Servers.html

commercial choices. The shareware leader is Apache, while Netscape Communications offers a popular suite of servers. The Web server market is new, hotly competitive, and will have changed radically by the time this book leaves the printing press. We recommend you visit your favorite Web index and conduct a search on *Web servers*, and visit the many Web pages following servers.[4]

Once the system and software components are in place, you must consider the staff time needed to install, configure, and maintain your Web page. Marketing people will need reports to see which pages are visited most often, so be sure to budget a staff member's time for log file analysis.

Continuing left in Figure 15-1, you see that you must now invest in and implement a firewall to protect your network. The Web server sits naked outside the firewall with almost all network services and ports shut off to ward off attacks from the malevolent. Never place unprotected, proprietary information on your external Web server. Assume it was compromised the moment you opened it for business, and that even cloaked files on non-public directories are dancing across the screens of your competitors.

Depending on what you pick up as shareware or purchased software, a firewall usually consists of a router teamed with a dedicated machine. We heartily recommend a RISC-UNIX workstation for the same reasons we recommended this combination for a Web server—throughput and lots of it. For more on firewalls, see Chapter 11.

External Web Server Hardware, Software, and Services Checklist
Router
Carrier (installation and monthly fee)
CSU/DSU
ISP (installation and monthly fee)
Host computer (hardware and operating system)
Web server software
Content creation and maintenance

Table 15-1   External Web Server Checklist

---

4.   http://www.yahoo.com/text/Computers_and_Internet/Internet/World_Wide_
     Web/Servers/
http://www.netcraft.co.uk/Survey/
http://webcompare.iworld.com/

Web and FTP Server in One!

The Web server, once installed, can also double as an anonymous FTP server. Properly configured, anonymous FTP poses a slight security threat. Placing logically similar functions (exposed server offering files to a hostile public) on one machine makes sense. That many Web browsers now support FTP downloads somehow makes this decision even easier.

Internal Web Installation—The Intranet

Often, the difference between a successful endeavor and failure is follow-through. Throughout history, great organizations were founded on great ideas. In time, however, these organizations maintained their leadership by executing their great ideas routinely. Some management experts call this institutionalizing a drive to excellence.

Will an Intranet make your organization excellent? Not in itself, but it does provide an infrastructure to enable excellence An Intranet makes it easier and cheaper for departments to share documents and procedures, such as personnel manuals, price lists, customer-contact information, competitive analysis, schedules, press releases, memos, reports, checklists, newsletters, and almost any other "one to many" document distributed throughout an organization.

Intranets are also good replacements for process-oriented paperwork, such as forms. These could be requests for purchases, facilities, system administration, employee opinion surveys, and expense reports.

E-mail answers many of these needs today; however, e-mail has a weakness in that people are often bombarded with unsolicited information that is difficult to manage. E-mail also does not provide a quintessential front end to the database.

Intranet Web Server Hardware, Software, and Services Checklist
LAN (installation and monthly)
WAN ISP (installation and monthly) (optional)
Host computer (hardware and operating system)
Web server software
Content creation and maintenance
Browser software for clients

Table 15-2   Intranet Web Server Checklist

Intranets, on the other hand, are libraries in which there is always one more copy of every file on hand. The Web and browser concepts provide a dynamic infrastructure in which content can be easily produced and maintained in creative fashion.

From a hardware and software standpoint, Intranet server requirements differ slightly from Internet Web server requirements. Since the server nestles safely inside the enterprise, you do not need rigid security measures. We summarized cost components for the Intranet Web server in Table 15-2.

One of the great aspects in dealing with an Intranet installation is the response time users enjoy. This is especially nice compared to Internet Web browsing. Intranet servers are usually installed on your LAN. This means 10 megabits per second of throughput or better, compared with 32.2 kilobits-per-second dial-up connections or shared T1s (1.5 megabits per second) and fractional T1s, if you are lucky.

In WAN-equipped enterprises, where you could be connected to an Intranet server over a 156 kilobits-per-second Frame Relay, the performance may initially resemble a typical Internet connection. However, unlike the Internet, the enterprise controls its own WAN, has the ability to manage the network for better performance, and can lease more capacity where necessary.

Content, Operations, and Java

IT is responsible for the maintenance of the platform and its administration. The platform includes the hardware, its operating system, the network, and the application software. In addition, as an architect you may provide leadership regarding technology and direction. You are not responsible for the content of that server, except the "IT Production Control" home page you create for your department.

Web content belongs in the hands of its owners, as the model was designed. This means individuals and departments creating information and processes are responsible for keeping the Web site accurate, whether it is the external or internal Web site. These department representatives have been dubbed "gatekeepers" of sorts at certain operations. Gatekeepers possess file permissions allowing them to alter their pages, but not the pages outside their purview.

As part of your production processes, set up a gatekeeper workspace in the Web server's environment. One of the links on your Production Control home page gives gatekeepers a form they can fill out, requesting workspace for their department. When delivered, that form sends an e-mail to your Web administrator, who then processes the request. Here is the process:

- Create a directory for the requester's department (this is where their Web pages will be created).
- Create user IDs for the requester.
- Give the requester write access to that directory only.
- Send the requesters this information, how to logon, etc., and some "boilerplate" helpful hints on how to get started.
- Wish them luck.

Beyond these operational processes, you as an IT organization should consider forming an Internet/Intranet task force team. The objective of this function is to provide leadership to the company with direction and architecture. This team should:

- Look at changes in the industry, including direction and technology.
- Evaluate new tools.
- Use technology to model new paradigms.
- Disseminate information and training to the enterprise.

An example of technology paradigm shifts to keep a close eye on is the emergence of applets. The Java[5] programming language and its supporting technologies may emerge as the new software distribution method. The applet-on-demand paradigm overthrows the notion of loading mega-software into every local machine, taking up local disk space for functionality never used. An applet is simply a small piece of software served to the user only when needed, and then discarded.

Java, though widely accepted, is at the start of its maturity cycle, so expect rapid changes and lurches forward and back as toolmakers learn more about this powerful, yet clean, language.

In the end, the IT organization provides the enterprise with sound production-quality architecture, operations, and maintenance of the intranet platform, as well as providing high quality leadership in technology and direction.

---

5.   http://www.javasoft.com/

≡ 15

Appendix: IT Questionnaire A

1. What is your job title?
2. Briefly describe your job function.
3. Do you understand your IT technical architecture vision, objectives, and goals?
4. Do you understand how client/server, distributed, or network computing fits into the IT technical architecture vision?
5. Is there a process for selecting new technology architectures?
6. How are technology architecture decisions currently made (based on your understanding)?
   a. - By business need?
   b. - By business system/application?
   c. - To try new technologies?
7. Are technology decisions made by IT, Corporate, Regions, or Divisions?
8. Does the technology decision affect how you perform your job?
9. Will your group/job function be involved in supporting distributed, client/server solutions?
10. What are the 4 or 5 major issues that should be resolved to help your group/job function support or be involved in supporting distributed, client/server solutions?
11. Do you understand the interaction between your group/job function and other groups/job functions related to supporting distributed, client/server solutions?
12. Have your group's job functions and competencies been defined for distributed, client/server computing?
13. Do you understand where your support requirements begin/end versus other support groups?
14. How is the communications between your group and:

a. - Other groups within IT?

b. - Regions?

c. - Divisions?

d. - Users?

15. Related to distributed, client/server computing, what are the 4 or 5 top issues that must be resolved for you and/or IT to be successful?

16. From your perspective, what are the benefits of distributed, client/server computing at your company?

17. Do you see any risks?

18. From your perspective, what are the benefits of having a common IT support plan for all architectures/platforms?

19. From your perspective, what are the current levels of service provided by your group to:

a. - Other IT groups?

b. - Users of IT services?

20. Have you specified and selected your system management processes and tools?

Appendix: Production-Computing Disciplines

1. Disaster Recovery
   a. Disaster Recovery plan
   b. Recovery Facilities
   c. Recovery Testing
   d. Compliance
   e. Metrics (Time to recovery)
2. Security
   a. Security Policies
      i. Network
      ii. Desktop
      iii. Application Server
      iv. Remote Access
   b. Security Methodologies and Tools
   c. Audits
   d. User Access and Control
3. Performance and Tuning
   a. Resource Utilization
   b. Performance Monitoring
   c. System Optimization
   d. Stress Testing
4. Workload Balancing
   a. Application Scalability
   b. Configuration Scalability
   c. Batch Job Scheduling
5. Data Management

a. Storage Management

b. Backup and Restore

c. Database Management

d. Data Availability

e. Data Integrity

6. Network Management

   a. Network Planning and Architecture

   b. Network Management Strategy and Tools

   c. Network Implementation

   d. Network Operations

   e. Network Availability

7. Business Systems Management

   a. Client/Server Production Acceptance (CSPA)

      i. Deployment Checklist

   b. Configuration Management

      i. Standards

   c. Version Control

   d. Software Distribution

   e. Service-level Monitoring

8. Capacity Planning

   a. Capacity Planning Methodology

   b. Capacity Modeling

   c. Capacity Forecasting

   d. Capacity Acquisitions

9. Management Reporting

   a. Metrics

   b. Security Violations

   c. Problem

   d. Change

   e. Training

10. Change Management

a. Production Control Procedures

b. Certification Process

c. Compliance

11. Problem Management

a. Procedures

b. Help Desk

c. Escalation Procedures

d. Customer Satisfaction

e. Quality Assurance

f. Problem Isolation

g. Tracking

12. Asset Management

a. Asset Tracking and Reporting

b. Resource Accounting and Procurement

c. Charge-back

13. Service Level Agreements

a. Documented and Approved (CSPA)

b. Metrics and Review

c. Customer Satisfaction

d. IT Roles and Responsibilities

14. Organizational Structure

a. Organizational Chart

b. Job Descriptions

c. Charters

15. Staffing

a. Training/Education

b. Mentor Program

c. Career Path Planning

d. Motivation and Morale

16. Facilities

a. Physical Plant and Location

b. Power and Uninterruptable Power Supplies (UPS)

    c. Air Conditioning

    d. Security

    e. Expansion Potential

    f. Showcase Command Theater

    g. Telecommunications Facilities

    h. Footprint (Floorspace) Management

17. Sustaining Operations

    a. Documented Production Procedures

    b. Operational Standards

    c. Operations Management Tools

    d. Automated Operations

    e. Preventive Maintenance

18. Event Management

    a. System Monitoring (Network, Database, Application)

    b. Automated Event Notification

Glossary

10Base2

IEEE 802.3 standard based on thin coaxial cable. Also called "thinnet."

10Base5

IEEE 802.3 standard based on thick coaxial cable. Also called "thicknet."

10BaseT

IEEE 802.3 standard based on unshielded twisted pair cables.

100BaseT

IEEE 802.3 standard for 100 megabits-per-second Ethernet.

100BaseT4

A variation of 100BaseT that uses four pairs of wires in UTP cables.

100BaseFX

A variation of 100BaseT that uses fiber-optics.

100BaseTX

A variation of 100BaseT that uses two pairs of wires in Category 5 UTP cables.

100VG-AnyLAN

IEEE 802.12 standard for a 100 megabits-per-second LAN that is compatible with Ethernet and Token Ring.

3172

A channel-attached controller that connects the mainframe to local area networks and offloads TCP/IP processing from the mainframe. Also called an Interconnect Controller.

3174

A terminal cluster controller that provides terminals access to the mainframe computer. Also called an Interconnect Controller.

C

3270

A type of device, like a terminal and printer, used to communicate with mainframes.

3745

A front-end processor that offloads communications processing for remote devices from the mainframe. Also called a Communications Controller.

3746

Next generation replacement for the 4745 Communications Controller. Also called the Nways Multinetwork Controller.

62.5/125

Refers to a type of multimode (can transmit many rays of light) fiber-optic cable with inner and outer diameters of 62.5 and 125 microns.

access control list

A file used to control access. In a computer, it controls access to files. In a router, it filters data entering or leaving an interface.

access method

A protocol that controls which device accesses the shared network medium and the way a device accesses the network.

address

With respect to networks, a unique code that identifies a node in the network.

address resolution

A method to determine a layer-2 MAC address based on a layer-3 IP address.

Address Resolution Protocol

A TCP/IP protocol that allows a node to determine a layer 2 MAC address based on a layer 3 IP address.

administration

See *system administration and network administration.*

Advanced Peer-to-Peer Networking

A protocol from IBM for computer-to-computer networking and distributed routing in SNA networks.

Advanced Program-to-Program Communications

A protocol from IBM for peer-to-peer communications for SNA applications. Also known as LU6.2.

agent

A distributed process that collects and processes information about network data traffic and sends the results to a central network management system.

AIX

A version of UNIX from IBM.

American National Standards Institute

An organization that reviews and approves product standards in the U.S. In the electronics industry, its work enables designers and manufacturers to create and support products that are compatible with other hardware platforms in the industry.

American Standard Code for Information Interchange

The standard binary encoding of alphabetical characters, numbers and other keyboard symbols. Synonymous with "text" encoding, such as ordinary word processing files.

ANSI

See *American National Standards Institute.*

API

See *application programming interface.*

APPC

See *Advanced Program-to-Program Communications.*

applet

A small piece of software served to the user only when needed and then discarded.

AppleTalk

A suite of network protocols from Apple Computer.

application

A software program specifically designed for a particular task or the specific use of a software program.

application gateway

A firewall that implements security at the application level.

C

application layer

> Layer 7 of the OSI reference model, comprising network applications like Telnet, electronic mail, and file transfer.

application programming interface

> A set of calling conventions defining the interface to a service.

application server

> Server on a distributed network that provides access to an application.

APPN

> See *Advanced Peer-to-Peer Networking*.

APPN+

> An enhancement to APPN with dynamic routing. See *Advanced Peer-to-Peer Networking*.

architecture

> The specific components of a computer system and the way they interact with one another.

ARP

> See Address Resolution Protocol.

AS/400

> A mid-size computer system from IBM.

ASCII

> See *American Standard Code for Information Interchange*.

asynchronous

> A method of communications with no timing relationships between devices. Start and stop bits are used to identify the beginning and end of bytes of data.

asynchronous gateway

> A gateway that provides desktop systems access to modems and communications through the telephone network. It also allows remote desktop systems to dial in to the network.

Asynchronous Transfer Mode

> A standard for cell relay networks where different types of information such as data, image, voice, and video are transmitted in fixed-size cells. Also called cell relay and Broadband ISDN.

ATM

> See *Asynchronous Transfer Mode*.

ATM Forum

> An organization that coordinates development and acceptance of ATM standards. http://www.atmforum.org/

attenuation

> The loss of electrical signal energy.

authentication

> Verification of who the user really is.

autonomous system

> A set of networks under the same administration.

B channel

> An ISDN channel for transmitting information such as data, voice and video.

B-ISDN

> See *Broadband ISDN*.

backbone network

> A network that interconnects other networks consists of a collection of internetwork devices (routers) and the connections between them.

backup

> A copy on a diskette, tape, or disk of some or all of the files from a hard disk.

bandwidth

> A range of frequencies; also refers to the capacity of the network or the rate that data can be transmitted across the network.

bandwidth-on-demand

> A network service that increases bandwidth for a limited period to accommodate bursty data traffic.

bandwidth reservation

> A method to reserve bandwidth for high-priority data. See *custom queuing*.

C

Basic Rate Interface

An ISDN service comprising two 64 kilobits-per-second B channels for information and one 16 kilobits-per-second D channel for signaling.

BGP

See *Border Gateway Protocol*.

BOOTP

A TCP/IP protocol for a device to determine its IP address.

Border Gateway Protocol

A routing protocol used between autonomous systems. BGP4 is the latest version.

border router

(1) A router used to connect autonomous systems. (2) A router used to connect OSPF areas.

boundary routing

A low-cost internetworking option for small, remote offices. It operates like a bridge. Any network traffic that is not local is forwarded across the WAN to a fully functional router for further processing.

BRI

See *Basic Rate Interface*.

bridge

A device that connects two or more physical networks and forwards data packets between them. Bridges operate at the data link layer.

broadcast

Data that is sent to all devices on the network.

Broadband ISDN

A high-speed network that uses ATM. See *Asynchronous Transfer Mode*.

Browser

A graphical user interface to read sites on the Web. The browser will interpret HTML and related protocols to display content to the reader.

bursty traffic

A variable data traffic pattern.

bus-and-tag

> A 4.5 megabits-per-second mainframe channel developed by IBM in the 1960s.

bus topology

> A topology, based on a linear cable, whereby a data packet sent by one node to another is transmitted to all nodes.

C2 security

> A set of guidelines described in the Orange Book for commercial-level computer security. See *Orange Book*.

cable

> A transmission medium, such as twisted-pair and fiber-optic cables.

cable tester

> A network management device used by technicians to test cables for different characteristics.

call setup

> The procedure to make a call in a switched network to establish a connection between source and destination nodes.

capacity planning

> Active monitoring system for computer resources across multiple systems; includes system resources, such as CPU power, I/O transfer rate, memory size, disk storage, and network bandwidth.

carrier

> Service company providing third-party network connections, whether it be local-loop, long-distance, cable and/or wireless communications.

Category 3 UTP

> Lower-quality, data grade, unshielded, twisted-pair cable for data transmission up to 10 megabits per second.

Category 4 UTP

> Medium-quality, unshielded, twisted-pair cable for data transmission up to 16 megabits per second.

Category 5 UTP

> High-quality, unshielded, twisted-pair cable for data transmission up to 100 megabits per second over 100 meters.

C

CDDI

See *Copper Distributed Data Interface.*

cell

A 53-byte cell that is the basis for ATM switching.

Cell relay

See *Asynchronous Transfer Mode.*

central control

One central support group that serves to test for quality on a timely basis, decreases labor costs through the use of one location, simplifies problem determination, and implements and supports computing resources.

central processing unit

The part of the computer where data calculations and manipulations take place.

centralized backbone network

A backbone network based on one or more routers that are centralized in a common location.

CERT

See *Computer Emergency Response Team Coordination Center.*

Challenge Handshake Authentication Protocol (CHAP)

A protocol for secure dial-up access, using different encrypted passwords periodically.

channel

(1) A communication path. (2) Interface between a mainframe and peripheral devices.

Channel Interface Processor

A module from Cisco Systems to connect a router to a mainframe channel.

Channel Service Unit

A digital interface device to connect network equipment to digital lines (T1).

chassis-based hub

A concentrator based on a chassis where different types of modules can be inserted.

CIP

See *Channel Interface Processor.*

CIR

See *Committed Information Rate.*

circuit switching

A switching method whereby a connection is set up and maintained for the duration of the call. Once the connection is established, it behaves much like a dedicated connection.

CiscoWorks

A suite of network management applications from Cisco Systems.

Class A, B, and C

Different classes of IP addresses. In a Class A IP address, 8 bits are used for the network number, and 24 bits are used for the host number. A Class B address has 16-bit network and host numbers. In a Class C address, the network number is 24 bits, and the host number is 8 bits.

client

A system on the network that requests a service from a server.

client/server model

A computing model where the processing of applications is distributed across different systems on a network. The systems are often front-end clients and back-end servers.

Client/Server Production Acceptance

Originally called the Unix Production Acceptance (UPA), it comprises the guidelines and procedures developed to support and implement distributed, mission-critical business systems with mainframe disciplines and central control.

clist

A mainframe script that is often used for systems management.

coaxial cable

A type of transmission medium in which a copper conductor is surrounded by insulation and a shield.

collapsed backbone network

A centralized backbone network based on a single multiport router.

collision
> A term applied where two devices send data on the same transmission medium at the same time.

Committed Information Rate
> The largest number of bits per second that a telco guarantees to transmit through the Frame Relay network.

compression
> With respect to networks, a method of encoding data to reduce the bandwidth required for transmission.

CompuServe
> A large, online information service.

Computer Emergency Response Team Coordination Center
> An organization that coordinates and issues computer security alerts.

concentrator
> A device that forms the center of a star-wired network. Often refers to a multiport repeater.

congestion
> A high volume of data on the network.

connectionless
> A communications method by which the source node transmits data to the destination node without first setting up a logical connection.

connection-oriented
> A communications method by which a logical connection established between two devices before they exchange data is maintained during the transmission of data and then properly terminated.

connectivity
> The way in which different computers and other network devices are connected to each other.

console
> A terminal, or a dedicated window on the screen, where system messages are displayed.

constant bit rate

A quality-of-service item where the network provides a constant guaranteed bandwidth. Similar to the service provided by a dedicated line. Required by real-time applications such as voice and video.

contention

Term applies when two or more nodes attempt to access the network at the same time.

converge

Process whereby a set of routers acquires a common view of the network after a change in the network topology.

Copper Distributed Data Interface

FDDI using twisted-pair wire technology.

core backbone network

Part of the network hierarchy that interconnects the distribution and workgroup networks.

CPU

See *central processing unit*.

cross-connection

Use of a patch cable to establish a connection between two cable segments terminating at a distribution panel.

CSU

See *Channel Service Unit*.

cursor-screen

An ASCII text-based software application depicting simple fields in which a cursor helps guide the user through the program.

custom queuing

A method to ensure performance for time-sensitive data. It uses a bandwidth reservation scheme that guarantees a minimum-level bandwidth for specific applications.

cut-through switch

A fast switching method whereby the incoming packet is switched to the destination port as soon as the destination address is identified. The switch does not buffer the packet or perform error checking. See *network switch*.

C

D channel
> An ISDN channel for signaling to setup, maintain, and terminate network connections.

DAC
> See *Dual Attached Concentrator*.

DAS
> See *Dual Attached Station*.

data link layer
> Second layer of the OSI model that describes the data packets and the flow of data packets between two devices. It provides physical addressing, flow control, and error detection.

Data Link Switching
> A standard to connect SNA devices to a router-based IP network.

data packet
> A logical group of information sent across the network. It contains a header and data portion. Also referred to as a frame.

database
> A collection of related and organized information.

database management system
> A software system facilitating the creation and maintenance of a database and the execution of programs using the database.

DBMS
> See *database management system*.

DDR
> See *Dial-on-demand Routing*.

DECnet
> A set of communications protocols from Digital Equipment Corp.

dedicated analog line
> A nonswitched communications line that uses analog transmission such as a voice-grade leased line.

dedicated digital line
> A nonswitched communications line that uses digital transmission such as a T1 line.

Demand Priority Queuing

A deterministic access method for 100VG-AnyLAN.

Demilitarized Zone

A semisecure network between the internal enterprise network and the Internet.

departmental network

A network that connects the computers in a department or a part of the enterprise.

Desktop Management Interface

A DMTF standard to collect desktop systems information and manage desktop systems.

Desktop Management Task Force

An organization that coordinates the development of standards for desktop system management.

destination address

The address of a network device that receives a data packet.

deterministic protocol

An access method with a mechanism, such as token passing or polling, to ensure a node can access the network within a determined time. Contrasts with a contention-based access, such as CSMA/CD, where access to the network is more random.

DHCP

See *Dynamic Host Configuration Protocol*.

dial-back

A security method by which the user dials into an asynchronous gateway on the network and supplies a password. Then the gateway dials back to a predetermined number to establish a connection.

dial-in access

Network access via a switched telephone network.

Dial-on-demand routing

A method to establish dial-up connections between routers, on demand through ISDN, or analog telephone lines.

Digital Service Unit

A digital interface device to connect network equipment to digital lines (T1).

diskless workstation

A computer on a network that relies on a server for all of its disk storage and has no local disk drive.

Distance Vector Algorithm

A routing algorithm whereby routers send their routing tables to adjacent routers that contain the hop counts or distances to other routers and computers in the network.

distributed backbone network

A backbone network based on different routers that are distributed across different locations.

distributed network

A network in which processing and network functions are distributed across different network devices in different locations.

distribution network

Part of the network hierarchy that connects enterprise servers.

distribution panel

A component of a structured cabling system in which cable segments are terminated and interconnected.

DLSw

See *Data Link Switching*.

DLSw+

A proprietary version of DLSw from Cisco Systems. DLSw incorporates a number of enhancements to the original DLSw standard.

DMI

See *Desktop Management Interface*.

DMTF

See *Desktop Management Task Force*.

DMZ

See *Demilitarized Zone*.

DNS

See *Domain Name System*.

domain name

(1) The name assigned to a group of systems on a local network that share administrative files. The domain name is required for the network information service database to work properly. (2) A network naming convention used to define the hierarchy of a network and to assign nodes (and users) to that network.

Domain Name System

A hierarchical host name management system that spans the entire Internet. A network naming convention used to define the hierarchy of a network and to assign nodes (and users) to that network.

DOS

Disk Operating System is a single-user operating system for microcomputers.

download

To extract data from a central source and deliver it to another system, such as a desktop system, for local use.

DPA

See *Demand Priority Queuing*.

DSU

See *Digital Service Unit*.

dual-homing

Attaching a device to the network through two connections to provide redundancy.

Dual Attached Concentrator

An FDDI concentrator that connects to both rings of a dual ring FDDI network. It also provide connections to single attached devices such as desktop systems and servers.

Dual Attached Station

A device that connects to both rings of a dual ring FDDI network.

dumb terminal

A terminal without processing capability or disk drives. Sometimes referred to as a TTY terminal.

C

dynamic

> In the Information Technology world, any process that takes place in real time, automatically.

Dynamic Host Configuration Protocol

> Software that provides a method to dynamically allocate IP addresses, provide configuration parameters to desktop systems, and manage IP addresses.

dynamic routing

> Routing that adapts automatically to changes in the network topology. Routers use routing protocols to communicate information about network changes.

eavesdropping protection

> A method that prevents a device from viewing data that is transmitted on the network and is not addressed to the device.

EGP

> See *Exterior Gateway Protocol.*

EIA/TIA-568

> A commercial wiring standard from the Electronic Industries Association and Telecommunications Industries Association. EIA/TIA-568 guides the building of cabling systems for different types of networks, mainly the performance characteristics for twisted-pair and fiber-optic cables. See http://www.eia.org for more information.

EIA/TIA-569

> Defines guidelines for construction within and between buildings to support the cabling system. EIA/TIA-569 describes wiring closet layouts and space in wiring conduits.

EIA/TIA-606

> Guidelines for managing a building's network cable infrastructure. It specifies how to label and color-code cable components.

EIA/TIA-607

> Describes a building's electrical ground requirements.

EIGRP

> Enhanced Interior Gateway Routing Protocol. See *Interior Gateway Routing Protocol.*

electromagnetic interference

Electrical noise (electromagnetic radiation) that interferes with normal data signals. See *noise*.

electronic mail

A way to exchange messages across a network.

e-mail

See *electronic mail*.

e-mail gateway

A gateway that connects two or more electronic mail systems (especially dissimilar mail systems on two different networks) and transfers messages between them.

emulate

To imitate one system with another, primarily by hardware so the imitating system accepts the same data, executes the same computer programs, and achieves the same results as the imitated system.

EN

See *End Node*.

encapsulation

The process of embedding the header and data fields of one protocol in the data field of another protocol.

encapsulation bridge

A bridge that connects two networks of the same type across an intermediate network of a different type.

encryption

The alteration of data so it cannot be read by someone who is not authorized. It is typically based on an encryption algorithm and keys.

End Node

An end system for user applications in an APPN network.

enterprise network

A network that connects all the networks and computers in an organization, provides high levels of integration, and supports production systems.

EPROM

See *Erasable Programmable Read-Only Memory*.

Erasable Programmable Read-Only Memory

Read-only memory that is reprogrammable and does not lose its contents when the power is off.

error-free cut-through switch

A switch that operates in a fast cut-through mode but reverts to a store-and-forward mode when a specific data error threshold is exceeded. See *network switch*.

ESCON

Enterprise Systems CONnection is a 17-Mbps channel for an IBM mainframe.

Ethernet

A type of network and data link protocol that uses CSMA/CD and operates at 10 megabits per second. Often refers to the IEEE 802.3 standards.

Ethernet switch

See *network switch*.

explorer packet

A packet transmitted by a source node using source routing to discover the route to a destination node.

Exterior Gateway Protocol

A TCP/IP protocol that allows routing information to be exchanged between autonomous systems. Also refers to a specific, exterior gateway protocol.

external router

A router that is part of a security firewall. It connects an external network like the Internet to an intermediate network and filters packets.

Fast Ethernet

A network based on access methods similar to standard Ethernet, but operating at 100 megabits per second.

fast packet

A network that uses one of the fast packet switching technologies, such fast store-and-forward switches and routers, and cut-through switches.

FDDI

See *Fiber Distributed Data Interface.*

FDM

See *frequency-division multiplexing.*

FEP

See *front-end processor.*

Fiber Distributed Data Interface

A hardware and software specification for networks operating at 100 megabits per second over fiber-optic cables.

fiber optics

A type of cable that transmits light signals.

file

A sequence of bytes constituting a unit of text, data, or program. A file can be stored in the system memory or on an external medium, such as tape or disk.

file permissions

A set of permissions assigned to each file and directory that determines which users have access to read, write, and execute the contents.

file server

Server on a distributed network that stores or houses data.

File Transfer Protocol

A TCP/IP-based protocol for transferring files from one computer to another over a network.

Finger

A TCP/IP service that provides basic information about a user.

firewall

Security processes installed on a router and/or gateway between networks that allow each network packet to be monitored so unauthorized access can be managed.

firmware

Low-level software that directly controls hardware functions.

Flash EPROM

Read-only memory that can be erased and reprogrammed. Often used in remote devices to download software updates.

frame

See *data packet*.

Frame Relay

A high-speed technology for packet networks, based on variable-length packets. The majority of flow control and error control is left to higher-level protocols.

Frame Relay encapsulation

A standard to encapsulate SNA/SDLC data traffic in Frame Relay.

frequency-division multiplexing

A method whereby data from multiple inputs are combined and transmitted over a single link. Each input is allocated a different frequency.

front-end processor

A device that provides a network interface for another computer. Often refers to the IBM 3745.

FTP

See *File Transfer Protocol*.

full duplex

A method of transmitting data in both directions simultaneously.

full-stack

A method of configuring an SNA gateway whereby the entire SNA protocol stack resides on the desktop system emulating a 3270. See *split-stack*.

fully meshed backbone

A backbone network with a direct connection between every pair of routers at different locations.

gateway

The original Internet term for what is now called a router. In modern usage, the term "gateway" refers to a system that translates from some native format to another. Examples include gateways to translate between protocols.

Gbps

Gigabits per second. See *gigabits*.

gigabits

Two to the thirtieth power or 1,073,741,824 bits.

global

Having extended or generalized scope. For example, a global substitution of one word for another in a file affects all occurrences of the word. In networking, global refers to worldwide connectivity.

Gopher

Software to organize and retrieve data on the Internet.

graphical user interface

A graphical screen and a method of user interaction with the computer and its special applications, usually via a mouse or other selection device. The GUI usually includes such things as windows, an intuitive method of manipulating directories and files and icons.

GUI

See *graphical user interface*.

hardware

The mechanical and electrical components of a computer system. Another term for the collection of compute hardware is platform.

hardware platform

Refers to a processor and hardware architecture like i486 and RISC platforms.

HDLC

See *High-level Data Link Control*.

header

Part of a data packet that contains control information.

heterogeneous network

A network with different devices from different suppliers using different types of hardware, software, and protocols.

hierarchical backbone

A backbone network that comprises smaller networks in a well-defined structure.

High-level Data Link Control

A common data link control protocol for synchronous serial communications.

High Performance Routing

A dynamic routing method for APPN.

hop count

A routing metric based on the number of routers between sources and destination nodes.

horizontal access segment

A cable segment between a desktop system and an intermediate distribution panel in a wiring closet.

horizontal distribution segment

A cable segment between intermediate distribution panels in the wiring closets.

host identifier

Part of an IP address that identifies the host computer on a network. Also called host number. See *network identifier*.

host module

A module that is inserted into a modular concentrator the provide connections to desktop systems.

hot-standby routing protocol

A protocol that allows a LAN segment to connect to two routers in a redundant configuration.

hot-swappable component

The capability to remove and insert a module in a device without turning the power off.

HP-UX

A version of UNIX from Hewlett-Packard.

HPR

See *High Performance Routing*.

HTML

See *Hypertext Markup Language*.

HTTP

See *Hypertext Transfer Protocol.*

Hypertext

The way information is organized on the Web.

Hypertext Markup Language

Programming language used to provide content for the Web.

Hypertext Transfer Protocol

Used by servers to host Web content and answer to HTTP requests from browsers.

ICMP

See *Internet Control Message Protocol.*

IEEE

Institute of Electrical and Electronic Engineers publishes standards including standards for networks like the IEEE 802 standards.

IEEE 802

Standards that defines the physical and data link layers of networks.

IEEE 802.12

A standard that defines 100VG-AnyLAN.

IEEE 802.1d

A standard that defines network management and bridging.

IEEE 802.3

A standard that defines the access method and physical layer for CSMA/CD.

IEEE 802.5

A standard that defines the access method and physical layer, using token passing over twisted-pair cables.

IETF

See *Internet Engineering Task Force.*

IGP

See *Interior Gateway Protocol.*

C

industry standard
> Elements of a computer system hardware or software subsystem that have been standardized and adopted by the industry at large. Standardization occurs in two ways: through a rigorous procedure followed by the ANSI and ISO organizations or through wide acceptance by the industry.

infrastructure
> The functions that perform utility services, such as networking, data center, and system administration.

Input/Output
> Communications between the main computer and its peripheral devices like disks, printers, and devices on the network.

integrated hub
> A chassis-based hub with modules that integrate a variety of functions, like routing, switching, and remote access, in one device.

integrated network
> A network that connects all computers in the enterprise and provides access to all applications and data.

Integrated Services Digital Network
> A standard interface for a switched digital network.

interactive
> A process that requires the dynamic involvement of two or more users and/or program applications.

Interior Gateway Protocol
> A TCP/IP protocol to exchange routing information within an autonomous system.

Interior Gateway Routing Protocol
> A proprietary Interior Gateway Protocol from Cisco Systems. Designed to be an alternative to RIP in larger networks.

intermediate distribution panel
> A distribution panel, usually in a wiring closet, that interconnects cables to the desktop and main distribution panel.

intermediate network

A network that is part of a firewall between the internal enterprise network and an external network like the Internet. Also referred to as a demilitarized zone or DMZ.

intermediate system

A system that relays data packets between end systems on the network.

Intermediate Session Routing

A static routing method for APPN.

internal router

A router that is part of a firewall. It connects an internal network to an intermediate network and filters packets.

Internal Support Agreement

An understanding and agreement among the different IT groups. Its primary purpose is to clearly define support roles, responsibilities, and the set of expectations.

International Organization for Standardization

An international agency that reviews and approves independently designed products for use within specific industries. ISO is also responsible for developing standards for information exchange.

International Telecommunications Union

A United Nations organization responsible for a wide range of communications standards.

Internet

The largest internetwork in the world, consisting of large, national backbone nets (such as MILNET, NSFNET, and CREN) and a myriad of regional and local campus networks all over the world. The Internet uses the TCP/IP protocols.

Internet Control Message Protocol

Provides control functions and error reporting for TCP/IP.

Internet Engineering Task Force

The task force that is responsible for Internet engineering.

C

Internet Protocol

The cornerstone of the TCP/IP architecture. It operates at the network layer and provides addressing, which allows data packets to be routed.

Internet Service Provider

Companies that provide Point-of-Presence access to the Internet.

internetwork

Multiple networks that are connected, work together, and appear to be one network.

internetwork device

A device, like a router, that connects networks together.

Internetwork Packet Exchange

A network protocol used by NetWare from Novell.

InterNIC

The Internet Network Information Center administers domain names and IP addresses on the Internet.

interoperability

The ability of devices to operate together.

Interrupt Request

A signal to the CPU from another system component, such as a disk drive or network adapter. The CPU will interrupt its current activity, service the request, and return to what it was doing.

Intranet

The network space within a given enterprise, in which the common interface and supported technologies used on the Internet (mainly the World Wide Web) are utilized to share and process information within the company.

intrusion detection

A method to detect whether an unauthorized device is connected to the network.

I/O

See *Input/Output*.

IP

See *Internet Protocol*.

IP Address
> A 32-bit address used by the Internet Protocol to identify devices on the network.

IPX
> See *Internetwork Packet Exchange*.

IRQ
> See *Interrupt Request*.

ISA
> See *Internal Support Agreement*.

ISDN
> See *Integrated Services Digital Network*.

ISO
> International Organization for Standardization publishes standards including standards for networks like OSI.

ISP
> See *Internet Service Provider*.

ISR
> See *Intermediate Session Routing*.

ITU
> See *International Telecommunications Union*.

Java
> A network-based programming language that uses small pieces of software only when needed. See *applet*.

Kbps
> Kilobits per second. See *kilobit*.

keep-alive messages
> Short packets exchanged periodically between two networks nodes to ensure there is a functional channel for communications.

kilobit
> Two to the tenth power or 1024 bits.

LAN
> See *local area network*.

C

LAN emulation
> A standard for connection-oriented ATM networks to emulate connectionless Ethernet and Token Ring networks.

LAN switch
> See *network switch*.

LANE
> See *LAN emulation*.

leased line
> A communications line for private and permanent use. Also referred to as a private line.

Link State Algorithm
> A routing algorithm that allows a router to send updates about any changes to its links as they occur.

LLC
> See *Logical Link Control*.

LLC2
> A logical link control protocol that provides a connection-oriented service.

load balancing
> Distributing data traffic across multiple links so they appear as one. Used to improve performance and reliability.

local
> Having limited scope. Contrast with *global*.

local area network
> A group of computer systems in close proximity that can communicate with one another via some connecting hardware and software.

local loop
> A telephony term used to describe the service that delivers "last mile" or "local" access to a given customer.

local termination
> A method terminating SNA/SDLC keep-alive messages and acknowledgments at a router to reduce network traffic and avoid time-outs.

Logical Link Control

A protocol that specifies both the format of data packets in the data link layer and how they are exchanged.

logical network topology

A high-level description of the way different network functions, components, and data flows are related.

login

A process to gain access to a system. The user usually must enter a name and a password.

LU

Logical unit is a part of SNA whereby end-users and programs communicate with a node on the network.

LU6.2

A logical unit for peer-to-peer communications.

MAC

See *Media Access Control*.

MAC address

The physical address of a network device used in the data link layer. Also called physical address.

MAU

The Multistation Access Unit is a concentrator for a star-wired Token Ring network.

main distribution panel

A distribution panel, usually in the data center, that interconnects cables from the intermediate distribution panels.

mainframe

A large computer in the data center.

mainframe channel

A communications path on a mainframe for input/output operations.

Management Information Base

A database of network management variables that can be accessed via SNMP.

C

management module
> A module that is inserted into a modular concentrator to collect network information that is processed and sent to the central network management system.

Mbps
> Megabits per second. See *megabits*.

Mean Time Between Failure
> A measure of reliability, based on the number of failures over time.

media
> With respect to networks, the plural of medium, which is the physical mechanism used to transmit signals like fiber-optic and twisted-pair cables.

Media Access Control
> A sublayer of the data link layer that controls media access, such as CSMA and token passing.

megabits
> Two to the twentieth power or 1,048,576 bits.

megabytes
> Two to the twentieth power or 1,048,576 bytes.

meshed backbone
> A backbone network with some degree of direct connectivity between routers at different locations. See *partially meshed backbone* and *fully meshed backbone*.

MIB
> See *Management Information Base*.

micron
> A unit of measure that equals one one-thousandth of a millimeter.

migration strategy
> A plan to implement new and faster technologies while protecting investments in the installed base.

modem
> Acronym for modulator/demodulator. A device that enables the transfer of digital data through analog telephone lines.

modem pool
>Several modems managed one central server.

Mosaic
>A Web browser.

MPOA
>See *Multiprotocol over ATM*.

MTBF
>See *Mean Time Between Failure*.

multilayer switch
>A switch that combines layer-2 and layer-3 functions.

multimedia application
>An application that uses different types of information like data, image, voice, and video.

multiprotocol backbone network
>A backbone network that supports different protocols, such as TCP/IP and IPX.

Multiprotocol over ATM
>An emerging standard that allows different network-layer protocols to run on ATM.

MVS
>A mainframe operating system from IBM.

native protocol
>The primary protocol used by a specific software platform.

NCP
>See *Network Control Program*.

NDIS
>See *Network Driver Interface Specification*.

near-end crosstalk
>Interference between signals on different channels. A common problem near the end-to-UTP cables where the wires pairs are untwisted at the connector.

C

NetBIOS
> Network Basic Input/Output System is a protocol for microcomputers that operates at the upper layers of the OSI model.

NetView
> A network management platform from IBM.

NetWare
> A network operating system from Novell.

NetWare Link Services Protocol
> Link state protocol for NetWare. It replaces SAP and RIP for IPX.

network
> A collection of computers and other devices that are interconnected and can exchange data.

network adapter
> Hardware that allows a desktop system or other computers to physically access and communicate on the network. Sometimes called a network interface card.

network address
> Logical address of a network device used in the network layer.

network administration
> Tasks of the person who maintains a network, such as adding systems to a network or enabling sharing between systems.

network architecture
> A definition of the structure of the network and how different network components and functions work together.

network configuration management
> Monitoring and managing the configuration of the network, network devices, and other network components.

network control center
> A location with a network management system, tools, staff, and other resources to manage a distributed network.

Network Control Program (NCP)
> SNA software that runs on a front-end processor that performs communications processing for remote devices.

Network Driver Interface Specification

A standard driver interface from Microsoft for network adapters.

network identifier

The part of an IP address that identifies the network to which a host computer is connected. Also called network number. See *host identifier*.

network infrastructure

Refers to all aspects of the network, including the facilities, cabling system, network devices, and the network management processes and tools.

Network Interface Card

A card that allows a desktop system or server to physically access and communicate on the network. See *network adapter*.

network layer

Third layer of the OSI model that describes routing.

network management

Refers to all the aspects of planning, implementing, and operating the network to ensure it is reliable, available, and serviceable.

network management application

Specialized software to manage the network and different network devices.

network management domain

Part of a network with a common network management strategy.

network management platform

Software that integrates different network management applications.

network management strategy

Guidelines for making the transition through the various stages of development in the implementation of the tools, structure, and protocol that directly relate to the management of the network.

network management system

A network management platform and a collection of network management applications based on common standards.

network management tool

Any application or device used for managing the network; for example, SunNet Manager, cable testers, and protocol analyzers.

network map
> A graphical representation of the network.

network name
> A unique identifier assigned to network devices and other network components.

network node
> A node that provides routing in an APPN network.

network operating system
> Software that controls the utilization of various resources such as applications, files, printers, CD-ROMs, and modems, across the network.

network performance management
> Monitoring and managing the utilization and availability of network devices.

network service level
> A measure of network reliability, availability, and serviceability.

network simulator
> A tool that can model network performance and cost for various scenarios.

network switch
> A multiport device that connects LAN segments such as Ethernet and Token Ring segments. It switches a packet between segments, based on MAC addresses. Also called LAN switch. See cut-through switch, store-and-forward switch, and error-free cut-through switch.

network terminator
> A device between the user's ISDN terminal equipment and the subscriber loop that connects to the telco. It protects the telco's network from faulty terminal equipment.

network utilization
> The network capacity that is actually used to transmit data.

Network File System
> A TCP/IP application that provides distributed file services. Developed in the early 1980s by Sun Microsystems.

Newsgroups

Electronic bulletin boards used by many to share information, opinions and events, organized into special interest categories. Also called Usenet.

NEXT

Near-end crosstalk.

NFS

See *Network File System.*

NIC

See *Network Interface Card.*

NLSP

See *NetWare Link Services Protocol.*

NN

See *Network Node.*

node

A device connected to the network.

noise

Unwanted electrical energy that can have an adverse impact on the normal transfer of electrical signal.

nonroutable protocol

A protocol that does not have network layer information that can be accessed by a router to route a data packet.

Novell NetWare Address Registry

A product that administers IPX network addresses.

NOS

See *network operating system.*

NT1

See *network terminator.*

ODI

See *Open Data-link Interface.*

on line

Connected to a system and in operation.

C

Open Data-link Interface
A standard driver interface from Novell for network adapters.

Open Shortest Path First
A routing protocol that uses a link state algorithm.

open system
A system that incorporates components — regardless of manufacturer or model — that are based on published standards and that interoperate.

Open System Interconnection
Standards created by the ISO for computer communications.

OpenView
A network management platform from Hewlett-Packard.

operating system
A collection of programs that monitor the use of the system and supervise the other programs executed by it.

Optivity
A suite of network management applications from Bay Networks.

Orange Book
The U.S. government's guidelines for secure systems. It defines the requirements for four security levels of security: A is the high security level and D the lowest. Some levels are divided into subclasses. See *C2 security.*

OS/2
Operating System/2 is a single-user, multitasking operating system from IBM.

OS/400
The operating system for the AS/400 from IBM.

OSI
See *Open System Interconnection.*

OSI model
A seven-layer model for computer communications. It is described in the OSI standards created by the ISO.

OSPF

> See *Open Shortest Path First*.

OSPF area

> A logical area in a large OSPF network comprising a group of routers that exchange link status information.

packet

> See *data packet*.

packet filter

> A simple firewall based on packet filtering. It screens data packets according to certain criteria.

packet switching

> A method, based on data packets for sharing a network. Data is switched between devices on the network, based on information in the headers of the data packets. Packets from different sources can share the same physical link. Network bandwidth is allocated only during the transmission of a packet.

PAP

> See *Password Authentication Protocol*.

partially meshed backbone

> A backbone network in which there is not a direct connection between every pair of routers at each location.

password

> A unique string of characters that a user types in as an identification code.

Password Authentication Protocol

> A protocol for secure dial-up access, using a clear text password.

peer-to-peer

> A method of communications whereby a computer exchanges data directly with another computer on the network as equals, as opposed to master/slave.

performance monitoring

> A process or program that appraises and records status information about various network or system devices and other processes.

C

Perl

> Practical Extraction and Reporting Language is a UNIX-based programming language for text processing, system management, and scripts.

Permanent Virtual Circuit (PVC)

> A path between two network nodes that is permanently defined in a switched network. A call setup procedure is not required before the circuit can be used.

Personal Identification Number

> A personal code used to access a secured system.

physical address

> The physical or hardware address of a network device used in the data link layer. Also called MAC address.

physical layer

> First layer of the OSI network model that describes the characteristics of physical media used to transmit data.

physical network

> The interconnection of cables and network devices.

Physical Unit

> The component that manages the physical resources of a node on the SNA network.

PIN

> See *Personal Identification Number*.

ping

> A TCP/IP echo message used to test the reachability of a network node.

Point Of Presence

> A physical network hub that provides a single place (business or residence) access to a public or private network.

Point-to-Point Protocol

> A TCP/IP protocol to send IP over synchronous and asynchronous serial lines.

POP

> See *Point Of Presence.*

port

> (1) An interface on a device. (2) a location used by TCP/IP protocols to identify different connections to a computer.

POTS

> Plain Old Telephone Service. Inexpensive, analog telephone service commonly used for voice lines.

PPP

> See *Point-to-Point Protocol.*

presentation layer

> Layer 6 of the OSI reference model that controls how data is encoded while it is exchanged between two applications across the network.

PRI

> See *Primary Rate Interface.*

primary network

> Part of the wide area network hierarchy that provides high-speed connectivity to remote networks directly or indirectly through secondary networks. See *secondary network* and *tertiary network.*

Primary Rate Interface

> An ISDN service in the U.S. comprising twenty-three 64 kilobits-per-second B channels for information and one 64 kilobits-per-second D channel for signaling. Internationally, the service comprises 30 B channels and one D channel.

priority queuing

> A method of prioritizing data traffic according to various criteria such as protocol type and packet size.

private line

> A communications line for private and permanent use. Often referred to as a leased line.

production-quality network

> A network with high levels of reliability, availability, and serviceability to run production systems.

C

protocol

A formal description of messages to be exchanged and rules to be followed for two or more systems to exchange information.

protocol analyzer

A network management device used to analyze network data packets.

protocol stack

Layers of a protocol that work together.

PU

See *Physical Unit*.

punchdown block

A cabling device with small vertical connectors where wires are "punched down" to make cross-connections.

quality-of-service

A method to specify and measure the network resources required for different types of applications.

quartet coding

A coding method used by the DPA protocol to transmit data over four pairs of wires.

RAM

See *Random Access Memory*.

Random Access Memory

Fast memory that is used for the main memory in a computer.

RARP

See *Reverse Address Resolution Protocol*.

RAS

Reliability, availability, and serviceability. The fundamental disciplines for production-quality computing.

RBOC

See *Regional Bell Operating Companies*.

recover

To return to a stable condition after some error has occurred.

Regional Bell Operating Companies

> Those local providers of telephony services, formed when the breakup of Ma Bell (a.k.a. AT&T) was realized.

registered address

> An IP address assigned by the InterNIC that is guaranteed to be unique.

remote access

> The ability to access the network remotely independently of location.

remote control

> A method of accessing the network from a remote location where the remote desktop system controls another desktop system that is connected to the network. Only keystrokes and screens are transmitted between the desktop systems. See *remote node*.

remote execution

> TCP/IP services used to execute a program on a remote system.

remote node

> A method of accessing the network from a remote location where the remote desktop system dials-up a network-connected router and operates a real node on the network. See *remote control*.

remote subnet

> A subnet at a remote location that is connected to the backbone network.

repeater

> A device that amplifies electronic signals. It connects two networks at the physical layer to extend the size of the network.

Request for Comments

> Documentation for the Internet and related protocols.

Request for Information

> A formal way to present requirements to suppliers to get information.

Reverse Address Resolution Protocol

> A TCP/IP protocol that allows a node to determine its IP addresses, based on its physical MAC address.

RFC

> See *Request for Comments*.

C

RFI

See *Request for Information.*

RI

See *ring-in and ring-out.*

RIF

See *Routing Information Field.*

rightsizing

The process of determining the most effective platform on which a business system should execute; for example, central versus distributed, mainframe versus client/server.

ring-in and ring-out

Special ports on Token MAUs that provide connections to other MAUs.

ring topology

A topology where devices are connected to a cable in a ring.

RIP

See *Routing Information Protocol.*

RISC

Reduced Instruction Set Computing.

RJ-45

A standard 8-pin connector for UTP wiring.

rlogin

A service offered by UNIX that enables users of one machine to log into other UNIX systems (for which they are authorized) and interact as if their terminals were connected directly. Similar to Telnet.

RO

See ring-in and ring-out.

routable protocol

A protocol that has network layer information that can be accessed by a router to route a data packet.

router

A device that connects two or more physical networks and determines the best path for forwarding data packets. Routers operate at the network layer.

routing

The process of determining a pathway for data to be transferred from one node in a network to another.

Routing Information Field

A field in the packet header used by a source routing protocol to identify the path between the source and destination nodes.

Routing Information Protocol

A routing protocol that uses a distance vector algorithm.

routing metric

The method a router uses to compare one route to another. Metrics include hop count, cost, and bandwidth.

routing protocol

A protocol used by routers to exchange information about the network. See Routing Information Protocol, and Open Shortest Path First.

routing table

A table in a router that stores information about network routes.

RS-232C

A common physical layer interface for serial communications. Similar to the V.24 standard.

Runbook

The support requirements for a batch process on the mainframe.

SAP

See *Service Advertisement Protocol.*

SAS

See *Single Attached Station.*

SBA

See *Synchronous Bandwidth Allocation.*

SDLC

See *Synchronous Data Link Control.*

SDLC Conversion

A method of translating between SDLC and LLC2 so SNA devices can communicate across a router-based network.

C

SDLC Passthrough
>   A method that allows SDLC devices to communicate across a router-based network.

search engine
>   Data manipulation programs that enable the organization and retrieval of large amounts of information, either actively (searching) or through initiation.

secondary network
>   Part of the wide area network hierarchy that consolidates the connections from remote networks directly or through tertiary networks and connects them to the high-speed primary network. See *primary network* and *tertiary network.*

security policy
>   A document that identifies security objectives, sensitive information, potential risks, and required countermeasures.

segment
>   Often refers to a subnet. Also refers to a network connected to the backbone network. Also refers to part of a larger system, such as a cable segment of the cabling system. Also refers to dividing a network into smaller networks.

segmented backbone
>   A backbone network that comprises smaller networks and components.

Serial Line IP
>   A TCP/IP protocol to transmit IP over an asynchronous dial-up line.

serial port
>   An external computer port or a connection that is used for serial transmission of data.

serial transmission
>   A method in which bits that compose a character are transmitted sequentially, as contrasted with parallel or simultaneous transfer.

server
>   A system on the network that provides a service to a client.

Service Advertisement Protocol
> An IPX protocol from Novell that is used to advertise services across the network.

Service Level Agreement
> An agreement between the network users and the network operations. It describes the expected levels of network service.

session layer
> Layer 5 of the OSI reference model that controls the end-to-end dialog between two systems.

shielded twisted pair
> A type of cable that consists of one or more pairs of wires. The wires in each pair are twisted around each other. All pairs are surrounded by a braided shield.

shortest-path algorithm
> An algorithm used by OSPF to calculate the optimal network routes and to develop a network map.

signal-to-noise ratio
> A way to measure the noise that affects the data signal on a communications medium.

Simple Mail Transfer Protocol
> A TCP/IP protocol for electronic mail.

Simple Network Management Protocol
> The open network protocol of choice for TCP/IP-based network management systems.

Single Attached Station
> A device that has one connection to an FDDI ring.

SLA
> See *Service Level Agreement*.

SLIP
> See *Serial Line IP*.

SMS
> See *Systems Management Server*.

C

SMT

See *Station Management.*

SMTP

See *Simple Mail Transfer Protocol.*

SNA

See *Systems Network Architecture.*

SNA Gateway

A gateway that allow desktop systems to access mainframe applications.

SNMP

See *Simple Network Management Protocol.*

SNR

See *signal-to-noise ratio.*

source route bridge

A bridge that uses source routing protocols. Often used to interconnect Token Ring networks.

source routing

A protocol whereby the source node determines the route of a packet.

spanning-tree algorithm

An algorithm used to identify a spanning tree in a network. A spanning tree connects all nodes without loops.

SPARC

The 32-bit Scalable Processor ARChitecture from Sun. SPARC is based on a reduced instruction set computer (RISC) concept. The architecture was designed by Sun and its suppliers in an effort to significantly improve price and performance. SPARC is a registered trademark of SPARC International, Inc.

split-stack

A method of configuring an SNA gateway whereby the SNA protocol stack is split between the gateway and a desktop system emulating 3270. See *full-stack.*

STA

See *spanning-tree algorithm.*

stackable concentrator

A concentrator based on stackable components.

standalone

(1) A computer that does not require support from any other machine. It must have its own disk and may or may not be attached to an Ethernet network. It must have some type of medium, such as CD-ROM or tape drive, for software installation. Synonymous with single system. (2) A standalone diagnostic means the program can load from either local disk or Ethernet and runs in a non-UNIX environment.

star topology

A topology in which devices are connected to a single point.

static

Consistent. Term used in data communications to refer to those processes that take place only when prompted (nonautomatic) or at delayed intervals of time. See *dynamic*.

static routing

Routing based on tables that are maintained manually.

Station Management

The specification for FDDI ring management.

Statistical Time Division Multiplexer

A Time Division Multiplexer that dynamically allocates bandwidth, or time slots, to active inputs.

STDM

See *Statistical Time Division Multiplexer*.

store-and-forward switch

A switching method where the incoming packet is buffered temporarily before it is switched to its destination. See *network switch*.

STP

See *shielded twisted pair*.

structured cabling system

A cabling system based on well-defined subsystems and components that can be reconnected easily to satisfy different requirements and support different technologies.

C

structured network architecture
> An easy-to-modify network based on a well-defined structure and components.

subarea
> The part of an SNA network comprising the access method such as VTAM, or the collection of SNA devices under the control of an NCP.

subnet
> Often refers to a network connected to a backbone network. Also refers to a network segment. In TCP/IP, a network using the same subnet address.

subnet mask
> A 32-bit mask used to determine which IP address bits are used for the subnet address.

subnetting
> A way of dividing a network address space into smaller subnets.

SunNet Manager
> A network management tool developed at Sun Microsystems that actively monitors network events over the wide-area, campus-area, and local-area networks. It is essential to providing centralized control.

SunOS
> A version of UNIX from Sun Microsystems.

surge suppresser
> A device that guards other equipment against large surges in electrical voltage.

SVC
> See *Switched Virtual Circuit*.

switch
> A device used to establish a temporary communications path between two devices as required.

switched Ethernet
> See *network switch*.

Switched Major Node
> A PU/LU definition in VTAM for a switched connection in an SNA network.

switched network

A network in which the communications path between two devices is not permanent. A communications path is established as required by a switch.

Switched Virtual Circuit

A dynamic path between two nodes connected to a switch network. The virtual circuit is established as needed by using the call setup and then terminated.

synchronous

A method of communications with a timing relationship between devices. The sending and receiving devices synchronize their clocks.

Synchronous Bandwidth Allocation

A prioritization scheme that allows a fixed amount of bandwidth to be assigned to a network node or a group of nodes on an FDDI network.

Synchronous Data Link Control

A data link control protocol for synchronous serial communications in SNA networks.

system administration

The tasks of a person who performs maintenance to systems, servers, or desktop systems attached to a network. Also manages and supports the LAN with control of the building-level gateway down to the desktop.

system monitoring

Procedures by which IT monitors networked computing systems across multiple platforms and details system availability.

Systems Management Server

A Microsoft product that allows centralized management and monitoring of desktop systems.

Systems Network Architecture

A network architecture and set of communication protocols from IBM.

T1

A dedicated digital line that operates at 1.544 megabits per second.

Talk

An Internet online chat service.

C

TCP Wrapper

UNIX security software that controls access based on IP source address.

TCP/IP

See *Transmission Control Protocol/ Internet Protocol*.

TDM

See *Time Division Multiplexing*.

TE1

See *terminal equipment*.

TE2

See *terminal equipment*.

telco

Abbreviation for telephone company.

telephony

That which is related to the business and service of telephone technology.

Telnet

A terminal emulation protocol in TCP/IP.

terminal

A process running on a machine that originates with the physical device called a terminal, or as the software representation of such a physical device, like a window.

terminal adapter

An ISDN modem.

terminal emulation

An application that makes a computer appear to operate like a dumb terminal to another computer across the network.

terminal equipment

A device, such as computer, router, or telephone, connected to the ISDN line. One type of terminal equipment, called TE1, is ISDN ready. The other type, TE2, requires an ISDN terminal adapter to make it ISDN ready.

terminal server
> A device that enables terminals to connect to and access services over the network.

tertiary network
> Part of the wide area network hierarchy that provides relatively low speed connectivity between remote networks and higher-speed secondary and primary networks. See *primary network* and *secondary network*.

TFTP
> See *Trivial File Transfer Program*.

thick Ethernet
> A thick, stiff cable used for 10Base5.

thin Ethernet
> A thin, flexible cable used for 10Base2.

TIC
> See Token Ring Interface Coupler.

Time Division Multiplexing
> A method where data from multiple inputs are combined and transmitted over a single link. Each input is allocated a different time slot.

TN3270
> A TCP/IP terminal emulation application that allows a computer to operate like a 3270 terminal.

token
> A data packet that controls access to the network.

token passing
> An access method where access to the network is controlled by a token. A network device may transmit data when it acquires a free token.

Token Ring
> A token passing network similar to IEEE 802.5.

Token Ring Interface Coupler
> Connects IBM controllers and communications processors to a Token Ring network.

Token Ring switch

See network switch.

tool

A package of compact, well-designed programs designed to do a specific task well. Several tools can be linked to perform more complex tasks.

topology

The physical or logical layout of the network.

Traceroute

A debugging tool for TCP/IP protocols

translational bridge

A bridge that connects two or more networks of different types.

Transmission Control Protocol/Internet Protocol

A suite of network protocols to connect different types of computers.

transparent

Describes a device or function that works so smoothly and easily that it is invisible to the user.

transparent bridge

A bridge that connects two or more networks of the same type.

transport layer

Layer 4 of the OSI reference model that is responsible for reliable end-to-end communications between network nodes. It provides flow control and error control.

Trivial File Transfer Program

A simplified version of the TCP/IP-based FTP protocol for transferring files from one computer to another over a network. Often used to transfer configuration files.

Type-1 STP

A type of STP cable that is part of the IBM Cabling System and consists of two twisted pairs surround by a braided shield.

UL

See *Underwriters Laboratories*.

Underwriters Laboratories

An independent organization that provides product testing services.

UNI

See *User-to-Network interface.*

uninterruptible power supply

A power supply that has a backup unit to supply power if the primary unit fails.

Universal Record Locator

An address to access Web sites.

UNIX

A common, multiuser operating system to build open systems.

unregistered address

An IP address that is not guaranteed to be unique by the InterNIC. RFC 1597 recommends specific unregistered addresses for private use.

unshielded twisted pair

A type of cable that consists of one or more pairs of wires. The wires in each pair are twisted around each other.

UPS

See *uninterruptible power supply.*

URL

See *Universal Record Locator.*

Usenet

See *Newsgroups.*

user interface

Software that enables humans to interact with computers. Also see *graphical user interface* (GUI).

User-to-network Interface

The interface between user equipment, such as a router, and a Frame Relay or ATM network.

UTP

See *unshielded twisted pair.*

variable bit rate

A quality-of-service where the network provides variable bandwidth. Required by applications with bursty data traffic.

vertical distribution segment

A cable segment between the main distribution panel in the data center and an intermediate distribution panel in a wiring closet.

Vines

A network operating system from Banyan.

virtual circuit

A logical path between two network nodes through a switched network. Several virtual circuits may share the same physical link. Bandwidth is used by the virtual circuit when data is transmitted.

virtual LAN

A logical LAN comprising a workgroup that is independent of physical location and the network's physical layout.

Virtual Telecommunications Access Method

Software on the mainframe that centrally controls the SNA network.

virus

An undesirable program that reproduces and spreads to cause destruction.

VLAN

See *virtual LAN*.

VM

A mainframe operating system from IBM.

VMS

A multiuser operating system from Digital Equipment Corp.

voltage regulator

A device that guards other equipment against electrical fluctuations.

VTAM

See *Virtual Telecommunications Access Method*.

VT100

A common type of ASCII terminal.

WAN

See *wide area network.*

Web

See *World Wide Web.*

wide area network

A network consisting of many systems that provide connectivity over a large physical or geographical area, sometimes spanning the globe.

Windows

The graphical software platform from Microsoft. Windows 3.11 provides a graphical interface for DOS. Windows 95 is the enhanced replacement for Windows 3.11 on the desktop. Windows NT is a single-user, multitasking operating system. Windows NT is also a common server platform.

Winsock

A standard for Windows applications using TCP/IP.

wiring closet

An area designed for network cabling and equipment (distribution panels, concentrators, and routers) to connect networks.

workgroup

A group of people that work together on a common task.

workgroup concentrator

A concentrator with a small number of ports.

workgroup network

Part of the network hierarchy that connects desktops and workgroup servers.

World Wide Web

A common interface and supporting protocols within the world of the Internet that allow content providers and users to display data in the form of text, graphics, and sound, all combined to make the viewing navigation of information easy to use and pleasant to look at (and hear).

X Window System

A protocol for a graphical windowing system for UNIX systems.

C

X.121

A standard for addresses used in an X.25 packet network.

X.25

A standard to access a packet network.

X3T9.5

The ANSI committee that defined the standards for FDDI.

Index

BOOTP 103
Border Network Technologies 155
Boundary Gateway Protocol (BPG) 106
bridge
    basic definition 63, 65
bus 59
business unit IT 19

C

cable modem 177
cable tester 46
CACI Products 47
Category 3 UTP 134
Category 5 UTP 134
    standard 56
centralized software services 20
CERT (Computer Emergency Response Team) 147
Challenge Handshake Authentication Protocol 123
Challenge Handshake Authentication Protocol (CHAP) 150
change management 28
channel interface processor 95
channel-attached routers 95
CheckPoint Software Technologies 155
CIO 21
    in the new enterprise 17
Cisco
    APPN 119
    channel-attached routers 95
    DLSw+ 115
    Interior Gateway Routing Protocol 105
    network management applications 45
    remote access server 90
CiscoWorks 45, 48
Clarity Software 172
Class A 100
Class B 100
Client/Server Production Acceptance 9

Command Software 149
compression 125
CompuServe 36
Computer Associates 29
    CA-Unicenter 165, 169
configuration testing 28, 159
convergence 105
corporate applications 19
CSMA/CD 60, 63
    Fast Ethernet 133
Cubix 89

D

DDR 122, 123
DECnet 108
Demand Priority Queuing (DPA) 134
deployment 28, 160
Desktop Management Interface (DMI) 167
Desktop Management Task Force 167
DHCP 103, 108
    configuration management 165
dial-back security 150
dial-in security 150
DLSw 115
DNS 104
documentation 28, 159
domain names 183
DOS 14
    electronic mail 171
    in the new enterprise 10
    networking and 97
dynamic routing 104

E

E1 82
eavesdropping 148
EIA/TIA
    cable standards 54
EIA/TIA-568A
    twisted-pair and fiber-optic cable 54

EIA/TIA-569
    closet and conduit standards 54, 216
EIA/TIA-606
    label standards 55, 216
EIA/TIA-607
    ground requirement standards 55, 216
EIGRP
    load balancing 124
electronic mail
    defined 171
    in the new enterprise 11
encryption 148
Enhanced IGRP 105
enterprise services 20
EPROM 50, 121
equipment room 51
ESCON 95
Ethernet 59, 64, 113
    and distributed servers 92
    CSMA/CD 61
    fast 133
    full duplex 132
    hubs 62
    in the new enterprise 11
    LAN requirements 34
    security 148
    switching 129
Exterior Gateway Protocols (EGP) 106

F

Fast Ethernet 37
    LAN requirements 34
FDDI 37, 128
    and distributed servers 93
    and network design 70
    chassis hub 62
    LAN requirements 34
    network design and 69
    scaleability 135
    token passing 61
    topology 59

Finger 98, 174
Firefox 109
FireWall-1 155
firewalls
    application gateways 152
    defined 151
    logging 155
    packet filters 151
    Web servers and 190
Fluke 46
Frame Relay 81
    basic definition 87
    Committed Information Rate 87
    compression 125
    encapsulation 115
    leased lines verses 88
    PVC 88
    SVC 88
front-end processor 94
Frontier Technologies 98
FTP
    defined 173
    server 191
FTP Software 103

G

gateway
    multiple protocols 108
Gopher 173

H

Hewlett-Packard
    network management tools 46
HP Tornado 44
HP-UX
    in action 79
HTML 7
HTTP 189
hub
    chassis 62
    integrated 63
hub, integrated 63

Hummingbird Communications 98

I

IBM
    virus 168
IBM 3745 Communications Controller 94
IEEE 802.1d 66
IEEE 802.3
    CSMA/CD 61
    definition 37
    network design 69
IEEE 802.5
    definition 37
    network design 69
IGP 104
IGRP 105, 123
    load balancing 124
Information Technology
    new 2
    six steps 3
Ingress 45
Innosoft 172
Intel
    and desktop connectivity 96
    LANDDesk Management Suite 167
    LANProtect 149
    virus 168
Intermediate Session Routing (ISR) 119
Internal Support Agreement 5
Internet
    future 177
    security 185
Internet Engineering Task Force (IETF)
    140
Internet Service Providers 179
InterNIC 100, 185
Intranet 191
intranet 145
inventory management 28
IP addressing 185
IPX 47, 107, 108
    routers and 67

ISDN 81, 84, 181
    BRI 84
    dial-on-demand routing 122
    PRI 84

J

Java 192

L

LANE
    defined 139
LanRover 90
Legato Networker 166
LLC2 110
Lotus Notes
    help desk 168
    in action 79
LU 6.2 119

M

Macintosh
    electronic mail 171
mainframe
    differences in users 3
management
    configuration 165
    desktop 166
    help desk 168
    inventory 158
    organizing 161
    performance 164
    problem 164
    systems 165
marketing and sales
    in the new enterprise 19
McAfee Associates 149
McAffee
    virus 168
Microcom 89
Microsoft
    NDIS 98
    virus 168
Microsoft Internet Explorer 187

SunSoft PC Protocol Services 110
SuperProject 29
surge suppressor 52
switching 129
Sybase 45
Symantec 89

T

T1 81, 183
    Web server 188
Talk 98
TCP/IP 64
    and mainframe connectivity 94
    in the new enterprise 11
    routers and 67
    SLIP and PPP 82
TCP/IP routing 104
telnet
    defined 172
Terminal Access Controller Access Control System 150
TFTP 98
Tivoli 165
TN3270 110
Token Ring 64, 113
    and network design 70
    hubs 62
    LAN requirements 34
    mainframe connectivity 94
    scaleability 135
    security 148
    SNA networks 114
    token passing 61
    topology 59
Traceroute 98

U

U.S. Robotics
    remote access server 90

UNI
    3.0 139
    3.1 139
    4.0 139
    defined 139
Uniform Resource Locator 184
uninterruptable power supplies 52
UNIX 99
    electronic mail 171
    security 146
Unix 14
    differences in users 3
    in action 79
    in the new enterprise 10
    managing 165
unregistered address 101
Usenet 88
    defined 174

V

video conferencing 33
Vines 99
    managing 165
    security 146
virtual circuits
    permanent 86
    switched 86
virus protection 149
VLANs 131
VMS 99
voltage regulators 52
VTAM (Virtual Telecommunications Access Method) 110

W

WAN
    differences 81
Wandel & Goltermann
    network management tools 46
Web browser 175

Web server
    external 187
    internal 191
whois 184
Windows 14
    electronic mail 171
    in the new enterprise 10
    networking and 97
Windows 95 97
Windows NT 99
    management 166
    managing 165
    security 146
Winsock 2.0 98
wireless 178
wiring closets 51
World Wide Web 36, 88, 187
    defined 174
    WAN requirements 34
WRQ 98

X

X terminals 102
X Window System 98
X.121 86
X.25 85
    compression 125
Xylogics 90